THE LOGIC OF EXPLANATION
IN PSYCHOANALYSIS

THE LOGIC OF EXPLANATION
IN PSYCHOANALYSIS

Michael Sherwood

HARVARD MEDICAL SCHOOL
MASSACHUSETTS MENTAL HEALTH CENTER
BOSTON, MASSACHUSETTS

ACADEMIC PRESS   New York and London   1969

ACADEMIC PRESS, INC.
111 Fifth Avenue, New York, New York 10003

United Kingdom Edition published by
ACADEMIC PRESS, INC. (LONDON) LTD.
Berkeley Square House, London W.1

LIBRARY OF CONGRESS CATALOG CARD NUMBER: 68-28897

PRINTED IN THE UNITED STATES OF AMERICA

PREFACE

If psychoanalysis is no longer accepted without question as a theory of human behavior, it is at least partly because thoughtful philosophers of science value it enough to ask necessary questions concerning its characteristics as a theory and its status as a science. It is a chastening thought to many of us who wrestle a long day probing the unconscious thoughts and feelings of our patients to know that some philosophers claim, for instance, that feelings are not the causes of human behavior, or that the concept of "unconscious feelings" is meaningless. To me, at least, it has become clear that philosophy in general and philosophy of science, in particular, must eventually contribute in a large measure to our understanding of human behavior. Yet, while the need for an interdisciplinary approach is apparent, the exigencies of our system of medical education mitigate against it. There are few psychiatrists who read or can even understand fully much of the large and highly relevant philosophical literature on problems in psychiatry and psychoanalysis. Still, the attempt to come to terms with these issues must be made, and hence the need for this work seems clear.

There are in fact few detailed logical studies of psychiatric case histories; this is the first full-length study of a single case history written by a practicing psychiatrist from the standpoint of the philosophy of science. As such, this work unabashedly runs all the risks accruing whenever one tries to bridge two disciplines, and if it does not actually fall between the two stools of philosophy and psychiatry, it nevertheless most certainly rests uneasily upon them. It is written out of the conviction that psychoanalysis has a great deal to offer to a science of human behavior, but that its value can no longer be taken for granted—either as a method of therapy or as a general theory. It is, rather, an arguable collection of hypotheses; yet precisely because it *is* arguable, it must *be* argued, convincingly, systematically, and with an understanding not only of psychoanalysis itself but of those logical, conceptual issues arising from it about which so much philosophical discussion centers.

This book, then, is a contribution to that growing dialogue between philosophers of science and psychiatrists. Of necessity it ranges in scope from highly technical linguistic issues to problems concerning Freud's early theory of psychosexual development. Thus, the study's primary appeal will be, on the one hand, to those philosophers interested in logical problems in the behavioral sciences and, on the other, to those psychiatrists and psychoanalysts who are not content simply to worry about the very real difficulties of psychotherapy, but who also feel obliged to concern themselves with the scientific status of a psychodynamically oriented theory of human behavior. However, the importance and contemporary relevance of such an interdisciplinary approach will be apparent to a far wider audience. Therefore, an attempt has been made to present the material in a manner both appealing and comprehensible to readers who may lack the specialized knowledge required of either the philosopher or the psychiatrist. In so doing it is hoped that an even wider based dialogue can be established.

Because of its dual lineage, this work has had a rather long and peripatetic history. Certain portions were included in a thesis completed at Oxford University in 1965. In the next three years the work was continued at Harvard. Many scholars in both psychiatry and philosophy, on both sides of the Atlantic, have, therefore, exerted a personal influence on this study, and their many types of guidance and criticism are gratefully acknowledged. Of those whom I must single out and name, however, the first is Mr. Brian Farrell, the Wilde Reader in Mental Philosophy at Oxford. I had the privilege of working closely with Mr. Farrell over a period of three years, during which time I benefited immensely from his perceptive understanding of a number of issues arising in those areas in which philosophy and psychiatry intersect. Dr. P. M. Turquet of the Tavistock Institute of Human Relations in London was another critic whose kind efforts enabled me to spend much valuable time at that institution. The late Mr. James Strachey, the general editor of the standard edition of Freud's writings, was most helpful in supplying important information concerning certain of Freud's original manuscripts. Dr. George Talland of Harvard Medical School's Department of Psychiatry provided assistance of a more general nature in dealing with methodological problems in the behavioral sciences. His recent death cut short a remarkable career in experimental psychology just as its extraordinary promise was being widely recognized. His friendship will be sorely missed. Dr. David Ozonoff of the Massachusetts Institute of Technology has been another who played a vital critical role. Most important of all, perhaps, has been the steadfast encouragement and support of Dr. Dafydd Evans of the University of London.

As varied as the academic roots, so too were the financial aids. The Rhodes Trustees supported me for three years at Oxford. The U.S. Public Health Service, through Harvard Medical School, also contributed research funds. Most recently, a grant from the Borden Research Foundation has been received. Without the aid of these groups and institutions this research could not have been completed.

I have had the good fortune to work with a most intelligent and effective staff at Academic Press, whose ministrations on my behalf went far toward bringing this work to its fruition; to them and to Mr. Jeffrey Davies and Mr. George Schober, who aided in the manuscript's preparation, a special tribute.

Boston, Massachusetts   MICHAEL SHERWOOD
January, 1969

CONTENTS

Chapter 1/**PRELIMINARIES**

It has sometimes been claimed that philosophical inquiry has nothing to offer psychoanalysis, that a study such as this is ill-conceived and its program foredoomed to failure. I am convinced this view is wrong. It becomes ever more apparent that philosophy has a great deal to say on certain issues in psychoanalysis, and the fact that its influence up to the present has been negligible is certainly to the latter field's detriment. That psychoanalysis has had a disappointingly slow rate of development would, I think, be conceded by most analysts. One would be hard-pressed to find another scientific discipline in which current discussions of *live* issues rely so heavily on papers published 60 to 70 years ago. This book itself reflects this continuing concern with the documents of the past. In contrast, in other new fields of medical science it is common to speak of experiments only two or three years old as being "classical." In such fields, except for historical perspective, the usual bibliographies rarely reach back further than four or five years. It is perhaps not too exaggerated to state that the slow rate of progress in psychoanalysis is not so much because of a lack of analytic and clinical subtlety but an absence of philosophical clarity, a refusal to come to grips with the logical and methodological problems that must face any discipline purporting to be a science. In no other area, perhaps, is the concept of progress so ill-defined. The journals, as in other fields, are replete with new formulations and new hypotheses. Yet one is hard-pressed to decide the extent to which such new ideas represent real developments and are in fact superior to older theories. Where there is no clear canon of procedure, no criteria of evidence, no rules for systematic evaluation, then the very possibility of growth of theory becomes problematic.

In other ways, too, a comparison of psychoanalysis to other disciplines is disquieting. For instance, in such an arcane field as mathematical logic, the practical applications are largely unknown and not even necessarily pursued. For the logician can rest content knowing his theoretical foundations are secure and his contribution to man's body of knowledge assured.

Alternatively, in clinical medicine the well-substantiated effectiveness of such preparations as digitalis is enough to sustain the practitioner in its continued use even though its mechanism of action, its theoretical rationale, is unclear. In psychoanalysis, if one could be sure of its soundness as a theory of human behavior one could accept, perhaps even explain, its limited therapeutic efficacy. Alternatively, if the therapy were obviously effective one could accept the fuzziness of its theoretical formulations. Unfortunately, neither solace is presently available. We lack both the philosophical assurance of theoretical soundness and the more pragmatic workaday confidence that would come from consistently demonstrable clinical potency. It is in pursuit of the former that this study is directed.

The province of philosophical influence must, however, be carefully demarcated. It is quite proper that the analyst does not ask the philosopher or any other layman about the symptomatology, etiology, or therapy of, say, obsessional neuroses. Nevertheless, the insistence on clinical experience, and even on a personal psychoanalysis as prerequisites for any criticism at all is a simple and gross error; it rests upon the failure to distinguish theoretical from empirical problems. Provided he focuses on methodological and conceptual issues the philosopher is certainly within his proper field of investigation and may well have a valuable contribution to make. In line with this possibility this book will deal exclusively with certain aspects of psychoanalysis which fall within the province of the philosophy of science, and at some points this limitation will become apparent when we explicitly avoid other interesting and important problems in the field.

Surprisingly, although there is a legitimate role, and in fact a need for philosophical criticism, it is not at all clear that there is a corresponding interest on the part of many philosophers to take up the challenge. Some, for instance, claim that the discipline's problems are so many, and of such an elementary nature, that what is needed by psychoanalysts is simply a course in basic logic. Among medical men of other specialities there is also this same lack of interest in psychoanalysis, though for different reasons. In the latter case there is usually a conviction that the real future lies with neurophysiology, or even neurophysics. In contrast to these views is our contention that psychoanalysis has a great deal to offer to a science of human behavior, and that a study of this discipline can certainly be justified on grounds other than those of historical interest. Precisely because of this potential, however, it is incumbent upon those who would practice psychoanalysis to face forthrightly the methodological issues raised by philosophers of science.

It is necessary at the outset to clarify the use of the term "psychoanalysis." As early as 1896 Freud spoke of psychoanalytic method (1896a,

p. 151), and the word "psychoanalysis" gradually came to be used for several different things, so that by 1922 Freud wrote:

> Psycho-analysis is the name (1) of a procedure for the investigation of mental processes which are almost inaccessible in any other way, (2) of a method (based upon that investigation) for the treatment of neurotic disorders, and (3) of a collection of psychological information obtained along those lines, which is gradually being accumulated into a new scientific discipline (1922, p. 235).

This division has been maintained into the present and has even been extended. One psychoanalyst, for instance, divides Freud's third category, the collection of information, into two: a theoretical framework of concepts and hypotheses, and a body of psychological observations (Szasz, 1958). Within the general field today the term "psychoanalysis" is usually reserved to characterize those methods and theories considered to be derived from classical (i.e., orthodox Freudian) positions. This often includes the so-called neo-Freudian developments of ego psychology in America (Hartmann, Erikson, and others) and those of Melanie Klein in Britain. Apart from these one can distinguish other groups of varying importance, among which are the followers of Jung, Adler, Horney, Sullivan, Fromm, Rogers, Reich, and Rank. All of these latter groups tend to be distinguished, by Freudians and especially by the practitioners themselves, from classical psychoanalysis.

Side by side with this professional use of the term has developed another more general application among some lay people, particularly in the United States. On this use all psychiatrists tend to be called psychoanalysts and all psychiatric practice and theory, psychoanalytic. Whatever the historical reasons for this domination and however unjustified they may be, this second use of the term "psychoanalytic" is well established, but it must be emphasized that our use of the term will be the first, more technical one in which it refers exclusively to Freudian theory and practice, and its modern developments.

There are two separate clusters of philosophical issues concerning psychoanalysis, one somewhat empirical and the other logical. The first centers around problems of validation and can be summarized by the question: "Can psychoanalysis be refuted?" Included under this category is the enormous problem of "suggestion," the potential influence of the theoretically committed analyst upon the clinical phenomena observed. Admittedly, it seems that up to now no one has presented either a completely satisfactory defense against the charge of bias or, alternatively, a method of systematically separating "therapist-initiated" from "patient-initiated" material. This being granted however, it must nonetheless be emphasized that we shall not be concerned with either the evidence supporting psychoanalytic theory or the possibility that such theory has been constructed upon distorted data. Our concern is solely with a second group of issues, those connected with the logical features of psychoanalysis as a putative science, and specifically the logic of psychoanalytic explanations of human behavior.

How, then, to approach psychoanalytic explanations? Two methods seem possible, both unfortunately tending to be exclusive of each other: the examination of material relating to particular bits of behavior taken out of context from a number of cases, or else the examination of a single extended explanation of an individual patient's entire case history. Virtually every philosophical study in the past has opted for the breadth of coverage obtained by the first method, contenting itself with broad generalizations based upon the classical expository texts of Freud. The prime sources of examples have usually been *The Psychopathology of Everyday Life* (1901) and *The Interpretation of Dreams* (1899). The merits of such an approach cannot be denied. A wealth of different examples can certainly suggest the range of psychoanalytic explanations and their potential utility. But while such a procedure may achieve an admirable breadth of exposition, the suspicion remains that the whole enterprise is somewhat "free floating" and lacking in evidential support. It is surprising how even common language philosophers, the "clinicians" of philosophy, have tended to become grandly theoretical, ranging superficially over a very wide territory when studying psychoanalysis, instead of minutely examining actual cases. The end point of this method is seemingly reached in a book by a psychologist— F. V. Smith's *Explanation of Human Behaviour* (1951)—where in a long section on Freudian explanation there is virtually no mention of *any* case material at all, either in the form of anecdotal snippets or sections from the extended case histories.

We shall adopt the opposite approach of examining a single case history, a method based upon the conviction that the core of psychoanalytic procedure is the explanation of the "behavior" of particular individuals throughout extended periods of their lives. The concept of behavior as it is here used covers any phenomena for which a psychoanalyst might reasonably be expected to offer an explanation. This includes overt actions or movements on the one hand, and also all mental phenomena such as emotions, beliefs, and patterns of thought.[1] An important contention of our argument is that explanations of particular bits of behavior—dreams, jokes, slips of the tongue, etc.—are made only after long acquaintance with individual patients, and the value of any explanation of, say, a certain

---

[1] This use of the term "behavior" is common in both psychoanalysis and psychology (see, for instance, Ford & Urban, 1963, p. vii; Rapaport, 1960, p. 39).

dream must depend ultimately on the truth of the general account of that case history. Rarely, however, have the full explanations of actual case records been subjected to careful scrutiny. A sense of awe, or at least a feeling of incompetence, has often abetted this evasion on the part of philosophers. It is, perhaps, this absence of actual case material, as much as logical complexity, that has tended to frighten off psychoanalysts from the serious consideration of philosophical studies of their field.

The advantages of this method are, first, that we can use actual incidents from a life history and the actual words used by the psychoanalyst in explaining such incidents. We need not rely on caricatures of behavior, or upon skeleton outlines of what a "typical" psychoanalytic explanation *might* look like. Moreover, in using a case record we can examine psychoanalytic explanations as analysts actually formulate and present them for each other's benefit. They will be neither simplified for lay presentation, nor taken out of context for the sake of exposition of theory, as is the case with material in Freud's books mentioned above.

In examining a single case history there are obvious disadvantages which must also be recognized. Where many examples are used, however superficial, the influence of inappropriate or exceptional material is minimized; if only a single case is used its proper selection becomes a vital issue. Moreover, the danger of forming generalizations about the whole field on the basis of one example, no matter how apparently representative, is too obvious for comment. Any such conclusions must be eyed extremely critically. It might also be thought that this method ignores the possibility that the record might be distorted, owing to the influence of the analyst and the inevitable faultiness of the patient's memory. However, this possibility is irrelevant for our purposes, since we are only interested in the logical characteristics of the explanation. The actual truth of the explanation is here of no concern. It is therefore irrelevant whether the case has been accurately reported; it can be accepted for the sake of argument that the patient's history is presented correctly.

Our basic questions, then, are: Given that the behavior of a particular individual is such and such, what are the logical characteristics of the psychoanalytic explanation offered for that behavior? How does this psychoanalytic explanation compare with explanations in other scientific disciplines and with explanations in everyday experience? In order to deal adequately with these problems we shall first have to face two more general issues which are both interesting in their own right and essential preliminaries to the questions about psychoanalytic explanations. The first concerns the process of explanation itself, for only if we understand the logical characteristics of explanations in general can we adequately deal with the peculiarities of a particular variety such as those found in psychoanalysis. Following this, we must then deal with the still debated question of whether human behavior can ever be given truly scientific explanations of any sort at all, let alone of a psychoanalytic variety. The discussion of these general issues in Chapters 2 and 3 will thus provide a basis from which it will be possible to consider the complexities of a psychoanalytic explanation as it occurs in a single case history.

Chapter 2/SCIENTIFIC EXPLANATION: SOME PRELIMINARY OBSERVATIONS

It has often been thought, and sometimes even written, that the sole occupation and only aim of science is the *explanation* of objects and events, that all questions faced by the scientist are questions of explanation. Whether this supposition in fact holds true for science will be discussed later, but it is quite obviously not true with regard to everyday life; that is, at least in ordinary experience it is not the case that all our questions are requests for explanations. Perhaps the most illuminating way to bring out the characteristic features of explanations is first to focus briefly upon those *other* investigations where explanations are *not* sought. These might be considered under the rubric "gaps in knowledge."

It seems quite evident that in everyday experience innumerable occasions arise in which one is hampered by some lack of specific factual knowledge. Such gaps can be filled by information concerning past or future events or occurrences. Questions such as: "What will the weather be like tomorrow?" or "What happened in the Senate yesterday?" represent a common variety of inquiry. Other gaps in our knowledge might concern temporal or spatial placements. Thus, one might ask: "Where is the General Post Office?" or, "How far is it to the beach?" or, "What time did he arrive?" or, "In what year was the Magna Carta signed?" Of course the most typical gaps in knowledge are those concerned with past, present, or future states or properties of objects. Included in this group would be questions such as: "What was the corn production of the U. S. in 1962?" "What are the characteristics of furniture of the Louis Quinze period?" "What are the prerequisites for the advanced physics program?" "What is the average pattern of change in weight and height in the first year after birth of a normal infant?" "What will the average income per family be in 1975?"

In some cases, even when the phrase "Explain . . ." is used, the request is not in fact for an explanation but for factual information: "Explain how to start this motor scooter." In still other cases when the phrase "Explain . . ." is used, the demand is actually for justification, not explanation: "Explain your coming in at 4 A.M.!" "Explain why you bought a new car now when next year's models will be released in two weeks." Thus, not only are many everyday questions not demands for explanations, in some cases even when the demand is expressed in the form "Explain . . . ," the request is not in fact for an explanation at all, but for some factual information or for a justification.

From such random examples some important observations can be made. First, the varieties of questions and the types of factual knowledge solicited in other areas of everyday experience have their exact correlates when one turns to human behavior. A great number of our questions about other people and, indeed, about ourselves concern just such "gaps" in knowledge about conditions, states, or events. Representative inquiries attempt to discover what are, were, would or will be a person's desires, feelings, intentions, goals, dispositions, etc. These items are on all fours with the properties and states of other physical objects, at least in the sense that they are the object of empirical observation, inquiry, and investigation. That our knowledge of such behavioral facts is often less accurate and more fallible, that people are notoriously poor observers of such states in themselves—all this is platitude. The point remains that we continually are making judgments about these factors, that we do have methods, however fallible, of ascertaining them, and that a high degree of accuracy in such judgments is not at all uncommon. The problem of whether judgments about human desires, intentions, and the like can ever be completely confirmed is a separate issue not presently of concern. The important point is simply that there exist gaps in our knowledge of human behavior much like gaps in our knowledge in other areas, and these gaps can often be filled through factual, empirical investigation.

The second observation we can make from a consideration of the examples given is their close relationship to specifically scientific questions. Inquiries such as those above, common to everyday experience, shade imperceptibly into the problems faced in scientific investigations. In fact, while the original examples were chosen from common situations, each might with only slight modification be recast as a subject of formal research. Clearly, it would be a mistake to overemphasize this similarity and to disregard essential methodological and conceptual differences that would accompany such a transformation. Nevertheless, many of the problems under laboratory analysis or those in the social sciences are simply more detailed, more controlled, and more precise attempts to answer the same questions that arise in everyday experience. Consider questions such as the following:

1. What happens to our bones as we get older?
2. Is it going to rain tomorrow?
3. What did our grandparents do for entertainment, not having radio, movies, or television?

Each of these can easily be reformulated in a more scientific and exacting manner:

1a. What are the effects of aging on the structure and metabolism of bone?
2a. What will be the weather conditions in the next 24 hours?
3a. What are the changes in patterns and methods of leisure-time entertainment in middle-class homes from 1900 to 1960?

A great many scientific investigations of problems such as these are concerned with getting ever more careful observations, with describing ever more closely "the way it was, or is, or will be." Indeed, we can now be more precise by differentiating four distinct goals of scientific endeavors:

1. Gathering new information about events, states of affairs, etc.
2. Predicting events, states of affairs, etc.
3. Controlling, changing events, states of affairs, etc.
4. Understanding, explaining events, states of affairs, etc.

It is certainly arguable on the basis of both the history of science and the present state of technology that the first three goals may be successfully pursued without achieving the fourth goal of adequate explanation. The scientific questions outlined above, then, fall under the first category, where the demand is for new, factual information to fill a gap of knowledge.

Of course, circumstances can easily be conceived in which factual answers might function as an explanation, or part of one. We are not implying that such knowledge cannot *also* function in explanations. It is rather that it need not be and in practice often is not so used. Gaps in knowledge do not need explanations; they require only to be filled with facts and information, usually gathered from careful observation. The next question, then, is obvious. How is one to distinguish those situations, those inquiries in which the goal is an explanation from those in which it is not? What, precisely, are the characteristics of the context of explanation?

A. The Context of Explanation

In none of the cases so far mentioned are we in need of an explanation; there is nothing incongruous, demanding to be explained when one asks, say, what the weather shall be like, or what are the characteristics of Louis Quinze furniture. Likewise, it would be extremely odd to claim that in stating the U. S. 1962 corn production one had thereby explained anything. There is information missing, there is a lack of knowledge, there is ignorance; but there is *not* what we shall call an "incongruity" in our knowledge. In contrast, the demand for explanations arises in just those situations, those contexts, in which there is perceived a puzzle, an incongruity, a lack of understanding about the way that certain facts or observations fit together.

There are actually two varieties of situations that we can distinguish, at least theoretically, if not invariably in particular examples. First is the sort in which some phenomenon or piece of knowledge is *incompatible with* previous observations or previously accepted beliefs. In such cases it may be that one would have predicted something other than what is in fact observed. Thus, an incongruity is present for an individual, whether recognized or not, whenever two or more statements which that individual tends to believe are mutually inconsistent, either directly or through their logical corollaries. There is, on the other hand, a second type of situation in which the observation is not incompatible with, but simply *apart from* our body of belief and past experience. Here there is no question of reconciling conflicting observations, but only of attempting to fit apparently disparate phenomena into some organized and meaningful relation to one's other beliefs. We shall refer to both these sorts of situation as "incongruities," emphasizing the meaning "inability to fit together," whether because of inconsistency or simply because the relating facts are unknown. Thus incongruities arise from an inability either to relate or to reconcile accepted facts to each other. Out of such an incongruity emerges the need for an explanation which will convey understanding. Understanding itself might be considered as organized knowledge, knowledge placed within a framework, or the knowledge of the relationships between facts.

It will be advantageous at this point to clarify our concept of incongruity by examining three criticisms which might be raised. The most immediate criticism, almost a philosophical reflex whenever the word "context" is introduced, is that one is confusing psychological with logical features. That is, in emphasizing the situations, the contexts in which the demand for explanations arise, we are mistaking the psychology of persuasion and the psychological conditions of puzzlement with the logic of explanation. This is, indeed, a common pitfall. In fact it was precisely with this question in mind that the words "context" and "contextual" have been employed, rather than the more commonly used term "pragmatic,"[1] for

---

[1] For an example of this usage of "pragmatic," see Gallie (1964, p. 107, *et passim*).

the latter seems more obviously to imply a contrast with logical, as if the pragmatic aspects of a subject were somehow less essential to it and perhaps less interesting to analyze. It is just this implicit derogation which was meant to be avoided through the use of the term "context." Now, at the risk of being repetitious it is necessary to clarify this distinction between the psychology and the logic of explanation.

Our goal in this chapter is to abstract from the contexts in which the demand for explanations arise, certain logical features of explanation itself. The very real danger in such a procedure is that one will instead take up the psychological features of situations of puzzlement, since in the typical case an incongruity in knowledge is actually recognized by an individual and thereby leads in that individual to a sense of puzzlement. This need not always be the case, however, for an incongruity may go unrecognized, and conversely the psychological feeling of puzzlement can occur for other reasons than the recognition of an incongruity in knowledge. It is necessary to distinguish the following:

1. The psychological reasons for an individual's feeling a sense of bewilderment or puzzlement in a particular situation, of which reasons the recognition of a puzzle may or may not be one.
2. The psychological reasons for an individual's accepting an explanation of a puzzle, of which reasons the resolving of the puzzle may or may not be one.
3. The logical implications of a situation in which there exists a puzzle, an incongruity, or conflict of existing beliefs.

Statement 1 emphasizes that there can be many situations in which puzzlement is present where there is in fact no possibility of offering an explanation, since no actual incongruity is present. A person might, for example, be puzzled by the fact that purposive action is possible and ask: "Explain how something that does not yet, and indeed might never, exist (a future goal) can cause me to act in certain ways." We do not simply shrug our shoulders and say that such an explanation would be both impossible and unnecessary. Rather, we attempt to show the person the way in which his demand is logically confused; that is, we can explain and analyze his puzzlement, but not the supposed incongruity he originally wanted to have explained. In such a situation there is a psychological demand and need for an explanation but none is possible, since the requisite incongruity is not actually present.

Conversely, a conflict of beliefs may go unrecognized in a particular individual, in which case the demand for an explanation is never made: there is a "puzzle" but no puzzlement. Indeed, the human capacity to fail to recognize incongruity, or worse, to tolerate it placidly, is quite enormous; and there is little sign that it has decreased with passing generations.

Statement 2 above emphasizes that there may be a variety of factors influencing the acceptance of an explanation apart from or in addition to the logical considerations of whether or not it is adequate. Explanations may be accepted merely because of the authority which issues them, or because of the comfort and satisfaction which accompanies them. All of this is no doubt fascinating, but irrelevant to our task.

The conditions, then, for psychological puzzlement are independent of those for which an explanation is logically appropriate. Moreover, it is quite true that psychological factors must be extremely important in determining whether or not an explanation is accepted by an individual, and it would surely be a mistake to confuse the criteria of acceptance of an explanation with the logical standards for judging the explanation itself. Our concern, however, is with the subject of statement 3 above, and our point is a simple one: that an explanation logically requires that there be an incongruity, a conflict of fact or observation against which it is directed.

A second misconception might involve what we are here referring to as conflicting or incompatible observations. In fact, it must be emphasized that we do not seek explanations for perceptions per se, but for perceptions in a context, conceived of, described, characterized in some specific way— that is, for what we are hereby defining as "observations." Indeed, one cannot make sense of the concept of "incompatible phenomena." What other perception, for instance, would be incompatible, incongruous, with the perception of a green cow? Would it be a red cow, or a green cow becoming a red cow, or two green cows, or a five-legged green cow? The truth is that various perceived phenomena are never by themselves incompatible with each other; it is rather our conceptualizations or descriptions of such phenomena which may be either mutually incompatible or incompatible with other statements we hold to be true. This does not mean, of course, that we simply explain our statements or descriptions, rather than the observations themselves. When we ask, "Explain why water expands when it freezes," we do not intend to get, nor would we want to receive, an explanation of the expression "why water expands when it freezes." Instead, we desire an explanation of an observed phenomenon of nature. Thus, in both everyday experience and in our own discussion there is a certain implicit contextual understanding of what is meant by words such as "event," "phenomenon," and "occurrence." This contextual implication will be examined in detail and clarified in what follows, but any possible initial misconception on this point must be avoided.

To emphasize that the demand for explanation can logically arise only where there is an incongruity of knowledge is *not* to say that explanations themselves function by what might be called a "reduction to the familiar." This is a third possible misunderstanding which must be carefully avoided. Although almost never actually developed in any detail, this idea is stated in terms such as the following:

> I believe that examination will show that the essence of an explanation consists in reducing a situation to elements with which we are so familiar that we accept them as a matter of course, so that our curiosity rests (Bridgman, 1927, p. 37).

First of all this position, at least as quoted above, is guilty of the very same error that was first discussed—the mistaking of psychological factors for logical ones. To analyze explanations in terms of familiarity is simply the other side of analyzing the origins of explanations in terms of *feelings* of puzzlement. In both cases the mistake is obvious. But quite apart from this vital criticism is another, equally damaging. The view rests on a mistaken assumption: What is most familiar must be least puzzling; what is least familiar, most puzzling. It is true, as we have pointed out, that the need for explanation arises out of a puzzle, an incongruity in our knowledge. And it is likewise agreed that an explanation attempts to remove such incongruity. This is the core of truth involved in the quoted position. But it is not at all true that familiar objects or occurrences are never puzzling. Lightning, the turning color of the leaves in autumn, the resemblance of offspring to their parents, the falling of apples—upon reflection such things may nonetheless be profoundly puzzling for all their familiarity. Familiarity, then, is not a sufficient guarantee that no incongruity is present.

Second, it is surely wrong to hold that a scientific explanation reduces strange phenomena to simple and familiar terms. The scientific explanation of lightning involves terminology like accumulated charge, ions, electrical resistance, and electromotive force—hardly familiar language. And whatever else Newton did, he certainly did not simplify our knowledge of falling apples. Often just the opposite is the case. One may be puzzled over the most familiar incidents, such as a balloon's bursting when placed near a fire; and one may not be satisfied until receiving an explanation in terms of the kinetic theory of gases. Familiarity, then, is not a necessary mark of an adequate explanation. The emphasis on resolving of incongruities, therefore, must not be taken as equivalent to a reduction to the familiar, for the removal of incongruity by an adequate explanation will most often involve a new, higher level, theoretical organization of the familiar observations.

While it is true, therefore, that there may be puzzlement without any logical puzzle being present, and while it is likewise true that an incongruity may exist without its being recognized and engendering bewilderment, nevertheless in the typical situation the incongruity is recognized and the psychological feeling of puzzlement gives rise to a demand for an explanation. This situation will be taken to be the central one for our purposes of analysis, but it is quite obvious that other situations occur in which an explanation is sought or delivered without there being any actual puzzlement. Thus, a teacher might ask a student to explain a certain phenomenon while obviously aware of the true explanation himself. Likewise a lecturer may offer unsolicited explanations to his audience. In such cases the puzzle or incongruity is presented to the student or audience, or assumed "for the sake of argument" by the teacher or lecturer. But all such cases are derivative usages clearly related to the root situation of one individual recognizing a conflict in facts or beliefs and demanding an explanation, either from himself or from another.

Obviously, in resolving an incongruity an explanation often will relate or describe facts, convey new information. Nevertheless, the function of these new facts in an explanatory context is different from their function in those situations where there is only a gap in knowledge. An example will make this clear. The following is a list of descriptive, factual statements concerning the physiological sensitivity and structure of the normal human retina:

1. The major light-sensitive pigment extractable from human rod cells is rhodopsin.
2. Rhodopsin shows an electromagnetic absorption maximum at a wavelength of 502 mμ.
3. The major light-sensitive pigment extractable from human cone cells is iodopsin.
4. Iodopsin has an absorption maximum of 562 mμ.
5. The cone cells are distributed in decreasing concentration from the center of the visual field, the fovea centralis, to the periphery of the retina.
6. The rod cells are distributed in increasing concentration from the center to the periphery, and are absent from the fovea centralis itself.

By themselves these factual descriptions of the composition and distribution of rods and cones do not make up an explanation; yet it can easily be seen that such facts could become parts of proper explanations in certain contexts. For instance,

Q1: Explain why color vision is substantially limited to the center of the visual field.
A1: Color vision is a function of the cones and their distribution accounts for the limitation of it to the center of the visual field.

Q2: Explain why in the dark-adapted state the eye is most sensitive to light of approximately 502 mμ.

A2: Dark-adapted (scotopic) vision is a function almost exclusively of the rods, and rhodopsin, the main rod pigment, has its absorption maximum at 502 mμ.

In these examples the descriptive statements of fact have *become* an explanation when placed into a certain context. The body of facts and descriptions already are known and can be used selectively in given situations, together with new relational information, such as that color vision is a function of cones. Thus, the difference between explanations and factual descriptions is not to be found in the informational *content* of the explanation but in its *role* within a given context. An explanation uses facts and descriptions, but its purpose is not simply to convey this information, to fill a gap in knowledge, but rather to employ it to solve a puzzle, to put the facts into an understandable relationship.

Let us now look at a second example of explanation, imaginary, but adapted from various sources:

> Certain Australian aborigines live in fairly small totemic groups. These groups often follow an exact migration route that is repeated each year. The routes are usually circuitous with many reversals of direction. There seems to be no particular goal or plan that structures them, such as following the movements of wild game, or searching for ripening fruits, or harvesting crops. Yet the route is an exact one, repeated carefully each year. Now the question arises: How can one explain the particular migratory route of, say, the tortoise group? A full geographical description of the route is available but, as has been stated, it seems random. Yet this randomness is incompatible with the other observation that the migration course is repeated each year, implying a certain importance and plan to the exact route. Hence the demand for an explanation.
>
> In fact it was finally established that the apparently random course corresponded to the path taken by the totem spirit, in this case the tortoise, in the tribe's myth of creation. Thus, in following that route the tribe was reliving the mythic migration of their totem spirit, and symbolically reenacting the tribe's own creation during the passage of each year.

Such an explanation is, like the previous example, nothing more than a factual description, although it is now given in different terms. The geographical description, however, was not explanatory, and this demonstrates an important point. In the vision and in the anthropology examples one can note two different ways in which statements of fact can become explanations. In the vision case a collection of facts, a description of properties, can be marshaled directly as part of an explanation if the proper questions in the proper contexts are raised. No new information is given, except in the sense that new relationships between facts are asserted. Thus, the responder selects certain information, the light absorption of rhodopsin and the sensitivity maximum of scotopic vision and asserts a certain relationship between these facts.

In the anthropology example, however, the ordinary geographical description is not at all explanatory. It is precisely this description in terms of the lakes, deserts, and mountains along the route which is so puzzling. The request for an explanation in this case is really the request for a new description, a new way of looking at the migratory route that will make sense of it, that will fit it into our other knowledge of the tribe, such as the fact that the same route is repeated annually. The demand for explanation is a demand for a new description, perhaps one from a higher conceptual level or simply, as in the example, from a different viewpoint. The explanation given says: Consider this route not geographically, but as the tribal reenactment of the mythical journey of their totemic spirit through the world. If true, this new description is indeed explanatory; it makes the facts understandable, it resolves a particular incongruity.

Thus in both the vision and the anthropology examples the explanation offered contains a factual description. But what differentiates the explanation from other collections of facts or descriptions is that it has a point. Explanations have a purpose, a direction that the same statements as descriptions lack; they function within a context that has certain specific logical characteristics. Of course to give a new description, say, in terms of a totemic spirit's migration, is to convey new factual information. But the purpose is not simply to add to our knowledge; it is to make our present knowledge understandable.

The fact that explanations are "context-dependent" and originate in situations which include a particular sort of puzzle or incongruity implies that complete resolution of that puzzle should be possible. Because the goal is a limited one, the explanation desired is also limited and, hence, attainable, at least in theory. There is, however, a possible confusion concerning this assertion, for "completeness" is often mistakenly taken to mean that the stage is reached where an explanation-demanding question can no longer be asked. Thus, it is sometimes said that an explanation that leads directly to another question is no explanation at all. But this is quite wrong. It is logically possible, given that X explains Y, to ask: What is the explanation of X? But whether or not we can answer this second question need cast no doubt upon our ability to answer the first question: What is the explanation of Y? The fact that we cannot explain everything is no evidence for the claim that we cannot explain anything. To say that nothing can explain anything unless it itself is explained is to demand that we ask every question at once, that we explain everything before we explain anything; and this would be absurd. Nor is it a valid objection to point out that there can be no limit to the number of situations which can be puzzling or to the depth of bewilderment they may engender. For this, while psychologically true, is philosophically irrelevant. To think otherwise is to commit the mistake pointed out earlier of confusing the logical fact of the origin of explanations in a puzzle with the psychological fact that such puzzles often are recognized and therefore connected with feelings of bewilderment and puzzlement. Our interest, it must be repeated, is with the logic of explanation and the types of puzzles, of incongruities toward which explanations are directed. The varieties of psychological puzzlement and the methods of alleviating such feelings, while interesting, form no part of the present investigation.

The argument so far has stressed the point that a conflict or incongruity of a certain sort is the central logical feature of those situations in which an explanation is to be given. The context of explanation, however, has other logical features as well—characteristics which can be represented as various "presumptions" inherent in any explanatory situation. The first of these can be called the "presumption of interest," by which we mean that the context of explanation must always convey, explicitly or implicitly, a particular point of view. The explanatory context presupposes a terminology, a frame of reference within which an explanation is to be given. These terms constitute a part of the description of the subject in question. One's interests in a situation set the terms in which it is described, and thus in which an explanation must be cast, but this is not to say that the description is thereby subjective or random. All description is selective, from a point of view, but it is by no means arbitrary because of that.

There are in fact two distinct levels of selectivity operating. First, one's interests pick out a particular set of features from an indefinite number possible. Once this frame of reference is established a second order of variability is possible, dependent upon the level of knowledge already available. It will not do to say that a particular description will necessarily encompass those from other viewpoints. Various descriptions may be only partially overlapping or even mutually exclusive. The entomologist's interest and hence description of a butterfly will be quite different from that of the artist. Likewise, the biology student's will differ from that of his teacher, but in a different way, in the degree of expertise rather than area of interest.

In distinguishing and emphasizing the presumption of interest our point is simply that explanations always function within a particular context, and that this context cannot be excluded from any logical examination of that explanation. In short, explanations are always explanations in terms of something; and these terms are set by the interests and purposes of the person demanding the explanation. Thus, for instance, one might be confronted with a large wooden square painted red, and the following question could be asked.

　Q1: Explain why (how is it that) that square is red.

According to one's interests in the particular situation, two entirely different sorts of answers might be expected as in the following.

　　A1: The square's surface is coated with a compound, the molecules of
　　　　which absorb from the white light impinging upon it all those
　　　　wavelengths of the visible spectrum except . . .
　　A2: It is painted red to warn people that . . .

The field of interest or "universe of discourse" will therefore vary according to the purposes and interests of the questioner. Indeed in the same situation two or more frameworks may be implied, and explanations desired in each.

　Given the particular framework of interest, the logical possibility for demanding any explanation, we have argued, depends upon the presence of some particular incongruity in the questioner's mind, and this is the second presumption inherent in an explanatory context. Yet just as there is this presumption of an incongruity, against which an explanation is directed, so there is also a presumption of knowledge. That is to say, the responder accepts a certain foundation of knowledge to be present in the questioner, a certain minimum upon which the explanation to be given shall rest. In order for something to be explained there must be something else which is *not* explained, but accepted, some other facts or beliefs to which the subject can be related. Unless there is a body of accepted knowledge, no new fact can give rise to incongruity, since nothing is already accepted to conflict with it. Where nothing is known or believed there may be much ignorance but no real puzzle, no incongruity, and hence no possibility for explanation. This is not to say that these presuppositions themselves cannot also be questioned. It is only to assert that one cannot logically question everything at once, and *a fortiori* one cannot logically explain everything at once. The presumed knowledge is not questioned in the particular situation. But the reason for its not being questioned is not necessarily that such knowledge is already fully explained. Certain facts may simply be accepted without question in order that other facts or occurrences can be explained.

　Consider the following example. Two people, A, a layman, and B, a geology student, are examining some specimens of rock known by them to have been collected on Salisbury Plain. Noticing a whitish rock of irregular shape, A asks B the following.

A1: How do you explain these chalk deposits?

Then, B might respond in the following way.

B1: Well, the whole area used to be under the sea in Cretaceous times.

Then, A might say, "Oh, I understand, I see now" and be satisfied with B's explanation. Should this occur one could be quite sure that A1 reflects a puzzle over the origin of the chalk. The question might be paraphrased: "What is chalk doing in an inland area such as Salisbury Plain?" "How do you explain its presence there?" The reason that A1 is a request for an explanation is that it implies both a definite incongruity and certain pieces of knowledge or beliefs in A's mind. The only reason finding chalk on Salisbury Plain is an incongruity for A is that he knows or believes that chalk is formed under the sea. Moreover, even in asking for the explanation A shows a certain further knowledge by recognizing that the whitish rock is in fact chalk. Thus, if A had the textbook knowledge that chalk forms under the sea, but did not perceive the rock as a specimen of chalk, then he would not have asked question A1. Likewise, if he recognized the rock as being chalk, but had no particular beliefs about where it was normally to be found or how it was formed, then again he would not have asked A1. In either of these latter cases no incongruity would have presented itself to A, and therefore there would be nothing to explain. The problem is to reconcile the finding of chalk inland with A's presumed knowledge of how chalk is formed. This is accomplished by B1, which states that the chalk originated under a sea which once covered that area.

All explanations are therefore in one sense incomplete, in that a certain basis of knowledge is presupposed and left unmentioned. Explanations are selective, aiming to fill in our knowledge with an understanding of the relation between what is already known and accepted and what is being questioned. Thus, a full explanation must be considered to include the knowledge already presumed to be accepted by the inquirer.

Wherever the presumed knowledge varies, the type of explanation necessary may also vary, in three separate ways. First, as we have already seen, a difference in the presumed knowledge may lead to a difference in one's interests in any given situation, and hence to a difference in the sort of explanations one desires. Second, the presumed knowledge will often determine what particular phenomena or observations one finds incongruous. Thus, in the example discussed above, a layman, knowing only that chalk originates from the mineral deposits of the exoskeletons of minute sea organisms, might well find incongruous its occurrence in an inland plateau region. A geologist, however, with a great deal more knowledge about Salisbury Plain, would probably realize that the area was once under the sea, yet would want an explanation of the actual tectonic shifts which eventuated in the elevation of that specific area of sea floor. Finally, and most obviously, a difference in the presumed knowledge of the questioner will alter the precision, complexity and sophistication of any explanation given him. For instance, the amount of physical and chemical details of the origin of chalk which would be included in an explanation would depend upon the knowledge one presumed the questioner to have. In the first two cases, entirely different explanations will be given, depending upon the presumed knowledge and interests of the questioner. In the third case it is clear that there are not a number of different explanations possible, but that the less detailed statements are a "sketch" for or an approximation to the complete account.

Our emphasis on the contextual, situational origin of explanations has so far brought out three logical characteristics, which we have labeled as the presumptions of interest, incongruity, and knowledge. A fourth logical property of the context of explanation can be appreciated by considering the reasons for which explanations can go astray or be unsuccessful; for they can go wrong in other ways beside their being false. Truth is only one criterion of the successful explanation. Another, equally important, is appropriateness. By this we mean, roughly, that the explanation must address itself (1) to the specified incongruity, (2) in the proper frame of reference, and (3) at the proper level of complexity. Otherwise the explanation is rejected: "No, that's not what I meant at all." "Of course, I understood *that*, what puzzled me was rather. . . ." In such a situation the question of truth or falsity is beside the point. It is just that the response has failed to address itself to the proper puzzle, or has not been given at the proper level of complexity; the proposed explanation, in short, is simply inappropriate.

Of course, even if an explanation is appropriate in the sense outlined above, it may still go wrong in two other, more obvious ways. It may simply fail to draw the relationships necessary to remove the puzzle; the incongruity remains. Or finally, it may contain false statements. Thus, an explanation may be

1. Inappropriate, because it does not address itself:
   a. to the proper frame of reference,
   b. to the proper puzzle within that frame of reference, or
   c. at the proper level of complexity (assuming the proper level of knowledge held by the questioner).
2. Inadequate, because it does not draw the relationships necessary to remove the incongruity.
3. Inaccurate, because it contains one or more false propositions.

The fact that explanations can go wrong in at least three different ways is a valuable observation. The latter two points, concerning adequacy and accuracy, will be developed in Chapter 7. For our present purposes, however, it is the first way, the possibility of inappropriateness, which is important. The point is not simply that the inquirer who requests an explanation *can* in fact make his own judgment of an explanation's appropriateness; it is rather that, logically, he *must* be able to do so in order that his request be legitimate. That is to say, there is implicit in the context of explanatory inquiry the presumption of criteria of appropriateness. The questioner is presumed to be aware of the sort of information that would be appropriate in the sense discussed above. Of course, this need not be a consciously formulated knowledge. All that is necessary is that when a potential explanation is offered the inquirer be able to accept or reject it on the grounds of its being appropriate to the field of interest, the particular puzzle involved, and his own body of knowledge.

This is not to imply that the questioner has the last word, that he is the sole judge of whether or not an explanation is appropriate. Obviously, an appropriate explanation may be mistakenly rejected by the questioner for all sorts of reasons, ranging from the simple misunderstanding of just what he was asking in his question, to unconscious fears about the knowledge the explanation imparts. Our point is simply that the criteria of appropriateness must be present in the questioner, that with proper inquiry they can be made explicit; but we do not insist that he be infallible in his application of these criteria in a particular situation.

Whenever criteria of appropriateness are not present in the questioner, then the logical conventions of explanation have been violated; one of the presumptions necessary for the context of explanation is in fact missing. In such a situation where there is no clear-cut understanding of the particular incongruity on the part of the inquirer, then his request for an explanation is invalid. If one does not know what would make a good explanation then one cannot know what would be a bad one, and this would mean that no explanation at all could be given. It is the absence of just such criteria of appropriateness, however poorly formulated, that accounts for at least a part of the frustration encountered in attempting to give explanations to children or to people whose knowledge of a field is virtually nil. In these cases there is often bewilderment and ignorance, but the crystallization of such feelings into the awareness of a particular incongruity in knowledge is absent; hence, the logical prerequisites for an explanation remain unfulfilled.

In this section we have emphasized that explanations are always context-dependent—given in a particular situation to particular individuals in whom there is a particular incongruity between various accepted facts.

Without this incongruity the demand for an explanation cannot even be made; moreover, the presumed existence of such an incongruity implies several further logical features of these contexts in which explanations are sought. These additional properties were discussed as the presumptions of interest, knowledge, and criteria of appropriateness. Taken together these four presumptions represent the logical implications of the contextual origin of explanations. In order for explanation to be logically possible, these presumptions must be held, implicitly or explicitly, by the questioner. If they prove to be contradictory or confused in any respect then the demand for an explanation is invalid and must be rejected. Thus, the frame of reference presumed by the questioner may have no applicability, or the type of puzzle may be inappropriate for the subject matter, or the questioner may have no clear idea of just what is incongruent and what sort of information therefore is desired. Conversely, these four presumptions must be grasped by the responder, if he is to answer the request properly. If they are not understood by him, the explanation he gives will most likely be rejected by the questioner as being inappropriate, regardless of its truth and adequacy.

B. A Classification of Explanations

It has been emphasized in the previous section that all explanations are aimed at resolving an incongruity in knowledge; and one might define such incongruities as a lack of understanding about how certain facts, events, etc., are related to each other, or fit into the rest of one's body of accepted belief. Explanations, then, are communications of understanding, a presentation of the relationship between the subject matter and other knowledge. Thus explanation seeks to organize knowledge by placing information within an interrelated framework. The type of explanatory framework used, the type of relations pointed out, will depend upon the way in which the subject matter is found to be ill-fitting or incongruent. If we can isolate the varieties of incongruity, therefore, a useful classification of explanation should emerge, one which will find good application when we examine in detail a psychoanalytic case history.

The following classificatory system has several limitations. First, of course, it is by no means exhaustive; there is an indefinite number of ways in which things may be genuinely incongruous for different people at various times. Yet it often appears that when an explanation is demanded a particular sort of puzzle accounts for a large part of the trouble, and these major types are not nearly so numerous as one might at first suspect.

Second, these categories are not meant to be mutually exclusive; often it is quite probable that more than one sort of incongruity is involved simultaneously. And even if only one puzzle is in fact apparent at a particular time, it will be quite obvious that other puzzles, in other circumstances, might have easily arisen over the same subject. On the other hand, it is not implied that all the varieties discussed can arise with regard to any and all subject matters; that is, these categories are not universally applicable. Finally, after having emphasized the importance of context we will be forced to sketch it only incompletely, in the interest of giving a larger number of examples. Unavoidably, then, the examples run the risk of ambiguity, as to just what sort of explanation is actually being demanded. Nevertheless, it is hoped that the single interpretation given will be at least one plausible possibility, if not the only one.

Aside from the considerations just mentioned the classification will be limited in a much more general way by the over-all purposes of this study. Our goal is not a thorough documentation of all the varieties of explanation that can occur, but only the study of explanations of human behavior. To this end it is essential that one becomes clear as to the complexity of just this area of explanation alone, and an important step in this process is to appreciate the various types of incongruity, the variety of questions concerning human behavior that can arise. The classification of explanations presented below is therefore to be regarded as simply an introduction into our more limited field of interest. It is primarily of value insofar as the varieties of incongruity distinguished will be found to have their counterparts in explanations of human behavior. The adequacy of the explanations given in the following examples is unimportant. Certain of them are obviously mere sketches, and perhaps all could be improved. But this would be irrelevant to our purpose, for the whole point of developing such a classification is simply to suggest the various types of incongruity that can require explanation. What is essential is to grasp the fact that all explanations are given in response to particular incongruities of very different kinds, and that the explanations themselves may therefore be of quite varied types.

In this discussion an effort has been made to standardize the examples in certain ways, both for ease of presentation and to point out certain features. Thus, they are given in the form of questions and answers, although the simple interrogative form is not employed. This has been done to emphasize that in the typical situation there is an implicit or explicit incongruity which is recognized by one party, the questioner, and for which an explanation is sought. Those questions which usually do require explanations are often expressed with such idioms as: "How do you explain . . . ?", "Why is it that . . . ?", "What is the explanation of . . . ?", and "How do you account for . . . ?". In order to simplify the examples and to emphasize that all are requests for explanations, these various phrases have been paraphrased by the grammatical form: "Explain . . . ." However, as we have seen, this by no means implies that all statements *normally* expressed in this form are in fact requests for explanations.

One of the first rough divisions that can be made among the various types of explanations is according to whether (1) the incongruity concerns the subject matter by itself, or (2) its possible relations to other objects, events, etc. One can subdivide the first group into two large categories, which we may call, rather artificially, incongruities of origin and of genesis. At the same time it must be acknowledged both that there are internal differences among examples in each and that the two categories themselves represent the ends of a broad and continuous spectrum.

1. Explanations in Terms of Origin

The first category we shall delineate includes those explanations in which the incongruity concerns what can broadly be called an "origin," "original cause," "originating event," "originating condition," or "source." Examples of such explanations and the puzzles giving rise to them include the following.

Q1: Explain how the fire started in the hotel.
A1: One tenant fell asleep and left a cigarette burning on a stuffed chair.

Q2: Explain why it is that she walks with a limp.
A2: There was a hip injury at birth that was never corrected until too late.

Q3: Explain the presence of bacteria cultures on these culture plates that were supposedly kept under sterile conditions.
A3: The vapor lock was not functioning, so that room air was present in the sterile locker.

Q4: Explain the outbreak of marijuana smoking among the sixth form students.
A4: The most admired student began smoking it while overseas and brought back a quantity to sell his friends.

Q5: Explain the high nickel content of this rock.
A5: It is a fragment of a meteorite.

From these examples it is evident that explanations in terms of origin can be given for many types of subject matter besides specific objects—including events, conditions or properties, and factual observations. One can distinguish several different types of explanation within this category. In

Q1 and Q2 the puzzle is not over the complete mechanism, or the "natural history" of an occurrence or a condition. It is a question of the originating event. There is presumed an understanding, in Q1, of how fires once started can spread; the puzzle requiring explanation is over what in this specific case was the originating event. Likewise in Q2 there is most probably no concern for the detailed orthopedic and neurological account of exactly how the limping motion occurs, but rather over why the person limps at all, what was the originating injury.

In Q3 and Q4 there is an incongruity between some observed occurrence and what one assumes normally to be the case in the relevant situations. How do bacteria grow in a "sterile" locker? What accounts for an outbreak of marijuana smoking in a boys' school? In each case the explanation is provided by giving an "originating condition" that was present. Such a condition might be a physical factor, the presence of normal room air as a contaminating source, or a social factor, the influence of a single highly regarded student's example.

Yet another type of explanation in terms of origin is illustrated in A5. Here the incongruity arises not from the nature of the observation itself, say of rocks with high nickel content, but from the apparent incompatibility with the location. How is it that a few rocks of such high nickel content should be located in an area without appreciable nickel deposits? The explanation is given by pointing out the origin or source of the subject in question. Once the origin is known the observation follows as a matter of course.

It can be appreciated from even such a short look at various examples that, while some general relationship does seem to hold between them, there are numerous variations and borderline cases. There is in fact a spectrum of explanations given in response to incongruities concerning some subject matter by itself. At one extreme lie those described above as explanations in terms of origin. Of course, there is nothing unique about the first event or condition in a series; the point is simply that in a particular explanatory context one's attention may well be directed toward the end of the spectrum. In a number of cases, however, one's interest in the originating event or condition may not be clearly separate from one's interest in the intervening states, and therefore the type of explanation described above shades over into the second catgory, which we label explanation in terms of genesis.

2. Explanations in Terms of Genesis

The explanations in this category are concerned with antecedent or future states of the subject in question, and more particularly, with the connection between such states and the subject's present condition. The word "genesis" was chosen in spite of several obvious limitations because it is sufficiently general to be at least somewhat appropriate to all the various types to be described. However, it is well to recognize the term's faults at the outset. This label is apt to be misleading in any of several possible ways. First, we are applying it to a whole range of explanations of subjects outside the class of living organisms. In this usage it will make sense to speak, for instance, of the genesis of particular events or observed facts and occurrences. Moreover, the term will be used to refer both to the past and the future. In certain of the following examples it will be evident that the phrase "causal explanation" could be used. However, the term "cause" has been assiduously avoided for several reasons. First, the word "cause" has a multitude of usages some of which cut across the present classification and obscure those distinctions being pointed out. Moreover, it would be most helpful at this stage to remain as neutral as possible with regard to various philosophical analyses of causation. For these reasons, then, we shall avoid the term "cause" until a later chapter when it can command our full attention.

The central puzzle about genesis involves a question of change—change in state or condition or location. The following examples represent some of the types included.

Q1: Explain why the farms in the north of the country are so much smaller than those in the south.

A1: Farm size will always be only as large as the capacity of the farmer to work it. In the south a richer soil free of rocks requires less labor for equivalent yields than the farmland in the north. Second, the farmers have formed many cooperatives in the south, and because a division of labor is possible the average farm size of the partners can be larger than if each worked singly, as is the case in the north. Finally, the greater wealth of southern farmers, especially when grouped into cooperatives, has allowed for a much greater investment in fertilizers and mechanized equipment.

Q2: Explain the effect of hypothyroidism in the pathogenesis of cretinism.

A2: Thyroxin is necessary for the proper growth and maturation of the skeletal, nervous, and gonadal systems. It acts in a synergistic manner with pituitary growth hormone, either by increasing the pituitary output or facilitating the uptake and/or responsiveness of the various target organs. In adult or infantile hypothyroidism there will also be the deposition of a mucoprotein in the skin giving it a yellow color and thick, scaly, coarse texture. The characteristic signs of cretinism are mental retardation, retarded skeletal development (especially maturation, closing of epiphyses, etc.), infantile gonadal development, yellow scaly skin, and dry, coarse hair—all features explainable by a lack of thyroxin.

Q3: Explain the disappearance of the money from my desk.

A3: Apparently, your wife needed it to go shopping and forgot to mention her taking it.

Q4: Explain the presence of Peruvian sweet potatoes under cultivation on many Polynesian islands, reported as early as the 1700's by the first explorers of the region.

A4: Since they could not have floated over without rotting, they must have been brought, either by birds, which is barely conceivable, or by the inhabitants who populated the islands by immigration on rafts from South America.

In all these examples the incongruity is over a change or difference from one state or condition or location to another. The basic question can always be phrased: "How do you account for . . . ?" or "What is the connection between . . . ?" or "How did . . . come about?" In Q1 the subject matter is some observed property or difference in properties, but the connections sought may also be between certain present conditions, such as hypothyroidism, and a future condition, cretinism. Thus, Q2 is an example of what can be referred to as "future genesis," the tracing out of connections between present and future states. Of course, the genesis need not be a pathogenesis or even unusual. The relation of normal thyroid function to normal bone growth and maturation can likewise require a detailed explanation showing the connections between changes in the function of the one and the properties of the other. Events, too, such as the disappearance of money in Q3 may require an explanation in terms of genesis. Finally, the changes may be only changes in location rather than state, as in Q4. Here, giving the origin of the potatoes, far from explaining their presence in Polynesia, is precisely what raises the incongruity. How could potatoes of known Peruvian origin get to Polynesia? Once again, the explanation resolves this puzzle by stating how the present situation, the present location, comes about.

3. Explanations in Terms of Function

The first two varieties of explanation so far discussed have focused upon incongruities arising about particular subject matters by themselves, about the origin or genesis of properties, events, factual observations, etc.

Often, however, the incongruity arises not over the subject matter by itself or taken as a whole, not over its past history or future development, but rather with that subject's relationship to other objects. The explanations concerned with such incongruities are extremely varied; for our present purposes, however, we shall divide them into two rough categories: explanations of function and explanations of significance.

The first subgroup of function explanations emphasizes the relationships holding between the various parts of the subject matter itself, not the relationship of that subject to other objects.

Q1: Explain how this electric can opener works.

A1: You turn switch A on, set lever B on top of the can. This is magnetized and will lift the cut top off. Then the can is engaged with the gear wheels. These are strong steel and when rotated will cut tin or other soft metals. Once properly engaged the can will be held tight. Then press start button, S, and the can is rotated against the spinning gear wheel and the top comes off. The motor stops after 360° of rotation, the can drops, and the top remains held to the magnet.

In such an example the question could be paraphrased: "Explain how each of the parts of the can opener functions." Such cases are common and seem to present no difficulties.

A second variety of these explanations deals with the function of the subject in relation to other objects, in contrast to the function of the parts of the subject itself.

Q2: Explain how the powdered glass mixed into highway paint functions to reduce traffic accidents.

A2: The powdered glass is suspended evenly in the paint and held by it to the road surface. The glass surface tends to repel the paint and therefore remains for the most part uncoated. This allows it to act as a reflector surface, and millions of glass particles make the lines clearly visible at night in the headlights.

Such an example is typical of a large group. The incongruity in such cases concerns how the subject matter is related to some other object or state of affairs; that is: How does the powdered glass serve to, help to, reduce accidents?[2] It is not a question of the origin or genesis of, say, the powdered glass, but how it functions to help to bring about a specific end.

---

[2] By using the more normal idioms "serve to" or "help to" in these paraphrases, the schematic nature of our use of "function to" is brought out. Nevertheless, our examples while being artificial in this way, still appear to capture the essential meaning of the more usual wordings.

It is important to note that in Q2 the question is *not* "What is the function of . . . ?" but "How is such and such a function achieved?" To ask the former question is not in fact to demand an explanation at all, but only to request some additional information. It is only the answer to the second question, where a relationship between the subject and its presumed goal is elucidated, which can be called an explanation. The distinction, however, is not quite so straightforward as it seems, particularly with regard to human behavior. Consider the following example.

Q3: Explain why John is pounding nails into that tire.
A3: He is earning money.

Question 3 could be paraphrased: "What is the function (purpose, goal) of John's pounding nails into that tire?" Answer 3 might well be considered unsatisfactory as an explanation because in asking Q3, we are probably also meaning to ask *how* the goal is to be achieved through such a peculiar activity. Thus, although the question may appear to ask only for factual information, it may in addition often be implicitly the request for an explanation. In such a case, we might answer as follows.

A3a: John has been offered a good wage to demonstrate that brand of tire for various sales groups, and he is rehearsing his presentation.

Thus, the questions both of what a subject's function is and how that function is achieved may, in certain circumstances, both be considered proper requests for explanations; yet the difference between these questions must be kept clearly in mind.

A variety of rather different types have thus been isolated and placed under the category of explanations in terms of function. It now remains to discuss the second category mentioned earlier, explanations of significance, where the complexities are even greater than with explanations of function.

4. Explanations in Terms of Significance

The fourth category of explanations presents the most mixed bag of all. The term "significance," like each of the labels used previously, is apt to be misleading and represents only one among several possible choices. Indeed, whether the thread running through the various examples to be discussed is enough to warrant their being placed together at all is perhaps debatable. But whatever connection there may be, it should emerge from the following examples.

Of course the most obvious variety consists of explanations of the meaning of words or phrases.

Q1: Explain the word "arcane."

A1: "Arcane" means secret, mysterious, withheld from view, especially because of remoteness.

Here the question is interpreted as: "Explain the meaning of . . ." and the answer given is a straightforward definition. From this extreme there runs a gamut of explanatory types all obviously related, yet of increasing complexity.

Q2: Explain the law of eminent domain.

A2: The law of eminent domain is a prerogative, a right, reserved by or granted to the government in many societies. It allows for the lawful appropriation of private property whenever such holdings are found necessary for government use, with a fair compensation given to the private owner.

Answer 2 seems to be a fairly adequate explanation of eminent domain. Normally, this would be called an explanation of meaning, as with A1, although this would be taken in a broad sense. The bare synonymous expression "superior dominion" (of the state over private property) would be only a small part of what is here referred to as meaning.

In the following example the definition of words plays virtually no part at all; yet it is clearly related to explanations of meaning in the sense of the previous two examples.

Q3: Explain the maxim: "You can lead a horse to water, but you can't make him drink."

A3: The maxim's central meaning is that there are limits to the powers of persuasion and coercion when it comes to altering a human being's behavior. One's methods can accomplish only so much; the rest remains the choice of the individual to do or to accept.

Answer 3 is only a sketch of an explanation of such a maxim. But it suggests the sort of material one would expect if one asked Q3. It seems that such examples are on a middle ground between "meaning" in the sense of Q1 and Q2 and what one might call "significance." It is certainly not the meaning of the words themselves which is desired in Q3. The various usages of the maxim would be helpful and might be a part of the explanation, but one might be aware of the situations in which a maxim is used and still not know the meaning. Such is commonly the case when one uses a foreign language that is grasped only imperfectly. Moreover, it is conceivable that certain maxims no longer are used in any situations at all; they are obsolete. The uses of the maxim, then, cannot comprise the whole of the explanation. Yet one would hesitate to say that the maxim signified anything *apart from* its meaning. But for all the ambiguity or uncertainty over what to call this sort of explanation, the proper response to Q3 is not at all mysterious; one knows just what sort of explanation is required.

Further along the range of explanations within this category are those where the term "meaning," if used at all, has a connotation entirely separate from the previous examples.

Q4: Explain my dream of two black snakes coiled around each other lying in the cradle of my child.

A4: The snakes represent the "black" aspect of sexuality, the painful outcome of having a child that becomes the center of your wife's attention and affection. The snakes lying in the cradle emphasize the relations to your child and symbolize your repressed hostility toward him.

Here in Q4 it is no longer a question of actual meaning but of symbolic meaning or significance. Question 4 could be expressed: "Explain my dream" or "What is the meaning of my dream?" or "What does my dream symbolize?" or "What is the significance of my dream?" or "What does my dream stand for?" All of these locutions could in most situations be used interchangeably. The explanation given is obviously quite different from that concerning the meaning of a word or a maxim. Nevertheless, the connection of A4 with those earlier varieties of explanation seems apparent. That is, there is some kind of similarity between asking for the meaning of a word, Q1; or the meaning of a law, Q2; or the meaning of a maxim, Q3; or the meaning of a dream, Q4. Just precisely what is the connection, as we shall see, is very difficult to ascertain.

Finally, a last set of examples of still a different sort of explanation in terms of significance.

Q5: Explain the significance of finding Peruvian sweet potatoes under cultivation in Polynesia.

A5: Since these potatoes rot quickly in sea water the original specimens could not have floated westward from South America and still remained viable. Their transport by sea birds is likewise improbable. The only alternative is that they were brought along with immigrants who migrated by rafts from South America to Polynesia. The finding of these potatoes, then, is highly significant as evidence for the settlement of Polynesia by migrants from the East.

In this example the word "meaning" might also be used, but in still a different sense than in any of the previous cases. The question here could be paraphrased: "What are the anthropological implications of . . . ?" or "What is the meaning in anthropological terms of . . . ?" In contrast to

Q4, the phrases "symbolize" or "stand for" would now be completely inappropriate.

In all these examples the problem is to discover what if any connections relate certain items together; in each case there seems to be a peculiar sort of puzzle or incongruity. The difficulty is how to describe that puzzle and draw out its logical implications. Let us consider the range of cases as running from Q1, "Explain the meaning of a word," to Q4, "Explain the meaning of a dream," to Q5, "Explain the meaning of a particular scientific observation." In each case the basic incongruity could be considered to concern a logical relationship between the subject matter and something else. That is, X means Y, Q1; X symbolizes (signifies) Z, Q4; X implies W, Q5. All three relations are, roughly speaking, "logical" ones; the explanation desired in each case is one that will place the subject matter into some sort of "logical" relation. One can now see at least some justification for employing the term "significance," since it is closely related to each of these types of relationships and at the same time has the desired "logical" connotation. But there is no necessity to agree on such a label; the important point is to see that such explanations are in fact related insofar as the incongruity they attempt to dispel arises over a relationship of a broadly logical kind between the subject matter and other objects.

Explanations in terms of origin or genesis aim to place the subject into relation with its own antecedent or future states, or events in its own past or future history. Explanations in terms of function aim to place the subject into relation with other objects in a functioning system, or else into a means relation to some further state of affairs or events. Explanations in terms of significance, like functional ones, reach beyond the subject matter itself. Yet in contrast to them, explanations of significance do not concern a relation of function or of means to an end but rather any of several varieties of logical relations—of meaning, of symbolization, or of implication. That is, explanations of significance attempt to relate their subject to words or concepts, in the case of meaning; or by analogy (instead of physically or functionally) to other objects, in the case of symbolization; or to factual statements, in the case of implication.

5. Explanations in Terms of Expectation

There is a fifth important variety of incongruity that requires explanations. It is in certain respects a broader type than any of the others; yet in other ways, as we shall see, it is less comprehensive. Consider the following two examples.

> Q1: Explain the water pipe's bursting last night (a winter night with the temperature well below freezing).

A1: Because the underground main valve was not shut off, a full head of water filled the main pipe running along the outside wall of the house to the first floor. As the temperature fell the water cooled to its freezing point where a molecular rearrangement formed a stable, solid mass. The solid crystalline structure of water requires approximately 10% more volume for equivalent masses than in liquid state. Hence, as the water froze its volume expanded. Being held by the pressure of the central reservoir and the closed taps within the house there was no space within the pipe for expansion and it burst at the right-angle joint, its weakest point.

Q2: Explain the water pipe's bursting last night (a mild summer night, no other burst pipes in the neighborhood).

A2: Those pipes are over sixty years old and have sprung leaks several times before. Yesterday the new reservoir was going to be brought into the community water supply system, raising the mean house pressure by about 4 pounds per square inch. This puts the pressure at a higher level than the city has had for many years, so you should have expected that a leak or a burst might well occur.

Now these two cases are quite different from each other. In the Q1 situation there is most probably no sense of surprise in the incident's occurrence. A houseowner typically does expect freezes to produce frozen water lines and, often, burst pipes unless various precautions are taken. The demand for explanation is likely to be only the rueful desire to understand the exact physical steps by which the incident occurred. In our classification the explanation A1 would be a genetic type, answering the question: "How exactly did this event come about?"

With Q2 the situation is different. Given the absence of certain factors often associated with other similar incidents, freezing weather, etc., Q2 most probably expresses surprise and puzzlement on the part of the house-owner as to the unexpected nature of the event. The qustion might be rephrased: "How could one have expected or predicted the occurrence? What considerations might (or should) have made one expect it?" The question reflects a general sort of surprise, which is the effect of recogniz-ing the incongruity between what one had expected and what in fact occurred. Of course, one might easily go on to ask for the precise genetic explanation of the event; yet, as it stands, A2 is not such an explanation but rather what we shall call an explanation in terms of expectation or prediction.

In other cases there need be no particular outcome or event that is expected, in contrast to Q2 where the expectation was that the pipe would not burst. Yet the type of explanation is quite similar.

Q3: Explain why the probability of there being blue-eyed children among the offspring of one blue-eyed and one brown-eyed parent may be either .50 or zero.

A3: Eye color is determined by a single pair of genes, one from each parent. The gene for brown eyes is dominant, that for blue eyes recessive. Therefore, a blue-eyed parent must be homozygous (bb) for blue eyes; that is, both genes must be for blue eyes, since otherwise the trait could not appear. The brown-eyed parent, however, might be homozygous for brown (BB) or heterozygous (Bb); either case would still yield the trait. Now, their offspring will all be Bb, if the brown-eyed parent is homozygous, and there will be zero probability of finding a blue-eyed child. If the brown-eyed parent is heterozygous, then half the offspring will be bb and half Bb. Therefore in this case the probability of getting blue-eyed children would be .50.

Q4: Explain why it is impossible to connect five different points on a plane surface with each other, without any lines crossing.

A4: This famous problem cannot yet be proved; there is no explanation available.

In these examples the question is: "How could I have predicted this observation? How might I have expected this?" There is in Q3, presumably, no particular expectation as to what the probability of blue-eyed children is in this case; thus the answers, .50 or zero, do not conflict with some other expectation, as was the case in Q2. Instead, the incongruity arises over how this result *fits into,* is related to some theoretical framework. Specifically, how does this result follow from our knowledge of genetics? In contrast, A4 states precisely that such a relationship of the observation to other mathematical theorems is missing. The explanation is unknown; that is, we cannot yet show how this finding fits into, is derivable from, is predicted by our mathematics.

It is obvious that we are here touching the issue of the relationship between explanation and prediction, but it is not the present concern to propose answers to the questions of whether or not there can be any explanation without prediction, or any prediction without explanation; these problems will be discussed in Chapter 7. The issue at hand is solely a descriptive one, to examine the varieties of explanation commonly found in everyday experience; and whatever one decides about the logical relationship between prediction and explanation in *general,* it nevertheless remains true that at least in certain circumstances the request "Explain . . ." is equivalent to the question "How could one have expected . . . ?"; i.e., it is a request for information upon which a prediction could have been based. It is this variety of incongruity that is now under consideration, and several points can be made about these explanations.

The information needed to resolve incongruities of this kind can involve any of the other types of explanation. That is, understanding of the origin, genesis, function, or significance of a particular event or fact can all tend to make that event more predictable, more expected, less surprising. This feature is what was referred to earlier by saying that the category is a more general one than the others. In contrast to those other varieties there is no particular sort of information with regard to origin, genesis, function or significance, which matches up with the particular puzzle over expectation.

It is this fact which accounts for the observation that there is sometimes only a rather vague division between explanations in terms of prediction and those of some other sort. Thus, Q3 and Q4 involve a type of incongruity that one could hardly confuse with any of the other varieties. Even if one were to paraphrase Q3 as: "How does it come about that the probability of blue-eyed children is either .50 or zero?", it still seems clear that the sense intended is very different from what we have meant by genesis, by an emphasis on change. With Q2, however, this difference is not so evident. Indeed, this was the reason for presenting Q1, a genetic explanation context, alongside Q2. Part of this difficulty is inevitable: One creates borderlines and hence borderline cases by the very act of classification. But two further specific sources of this difficulty can be distinguished. First, the point made previously that the sort of information required to resolve the incongruity over expectation may include that taken from any of the other types of explanation. Second, a general puzzle over an event's unexpectedness, once resolved, may easily be elaborated into the expression of an incongruity demanding an explanation of a more specific variety. Thus, having been told that the new reservoir came into service the day before, I should have expected that the old pipes might burst. But I may then go on to ask how exactly the pipes did burst, how did it come about that the new reservoir's additional pressure should have led to the bursting. In this way a new incongruity demanding a genetic explanation arises from the original explanation in terms of expectation.

Lest the generality of this factor of prediction tends to let it be mistaken for the fundamental component of all explanations, certain limitations must be pointed out. First, a minor point. When explanations in terms of expectation are given, the information conveyed may not by itself be predictive. Only together with the knowledge already accepted by the questioner could the explanatory material provide the complete logical basis for a prediction. But more important, the concept of prediction is meaningful only with regard to certain subject matters, notably events and, in a related sense, facts. That is, a typical prediction is essentially a description of an event asserted to occur at some spatio-temporal location, or an observation asserted to hold true under certain conditions. Where the concepts of temporality or spatiality are out of place, as with laws expressed in timeless terms, then it will not be meaningful to speak of prediction. Likewise, it would seem odd to speak of predicting the meaning of a theory, except in the minor sense of predicting the meaning of the words based on one's knowledge of the language. Yet we have already seen that it is a common and proper request to explain a law or a theory. The application of the term explanation, then, is wider than that of prediction. We can properly ask for explanations in situations where a request for prediction would be meaningless. Nevertheless in dealing with certain subjects the request for an explanation is often best interpreted as a request for information that will resolve a puzzle over the unexpectedness or unpredictable nature of the subject. The category of explanation in terms of expectation, then, forms a definite variety in our classification scheme.

Throughout this chapter's discussion examples of explanations of individual human behavior were for the most part avoided in order to underline the fairly wide applicability of the classification schema. The next task would be to see to what extent the puzzles and types of explanations so far discussed have their counterparts within psychoanalytic explanations of human behavior. But before we can examine psychoanalytic explanations, we must face the important general objection that scientific explanations of human behavior, of any kind whatever, are unattainable for various theoretical reasons. This is the problem we discuss in the following chapter.

Chapter 3/**THEORETICAL OBJECTIONS TO A SCIENCE OF HUMAN BEHAVIOR**

The present study focuses upon psychoanalytic explanations of human behavior and upon a comparison of these with explanations in other scientific disciplines. Yet it is important to realize that the very *possibility* of such a science of human behavior, the possibility of developing any sort of scientific explanations of behavior, has been seriously and repeatedly challenged. There are, in fact, two distinct issues being raised in this challenge. The first could be called "the thesis of the separate domain," the view that human behavior is composed of "actions" and must be explained by reference to "reasons, motives," etc. The point of this position is not that explanations of behavior are impossible, but that this "social" aspect of behavior renders all such explanations logically different from those in the physical sciences. This is not an objection to a science of human behavior as such, but only to a particular analysis of the properties such a science must exhibit. In Chapter 5 we shall discuss this objection in detail.

A second, more basic question is whether a science of human behavior, constructed on any model at all, is logically possible. Clearly this latter question must be taken up prior to the former; the present chapter, therefore, will be devoted exclusively to it. If the general *a priori* objections to the scientific explanation of behavior can be met, then we will be able to go on to examine the further issues of just what are the logical features of specifically psychoanalytic explanations, and to what extent they can justly be considered "scientific."

To begin the discussion a single source will be used as our basic text, a paper by J. D. Mabbott.[1]

> Science reveals no compulsions and establishes no necessities. All that is observed is regular conjunction. Scientific laws are only probable, and the measurements on which they rest are only approximate. No scientist would

---

[1] These arguments are for the most part standard ones, and Mabbott makes no attempt to state them in a comprehensive manner. It is, rather, just because they are formulated so concisely that we have chosen his paper to open our discussion.

now claim that, given sufficient evidence, he could in principle predict with exactness and certainty the behaviour of any physical object. . . .

But there are further special reasons which make even the cautious type of prediction characteristic of modern science inapplicable to human conduct. There are three features of scientific method which are essential for any approximation to accurate prediction. The first is measurement. . . . But many of the psychological factors involved in the empirical study of human conduct are not measurable. States such as pain or grief, motives such as hope and fear, . . . —none of these can be given numerical values.

The other two features of scientific method which render it inapplicable in its full rigor to human conduct are analysis and generalization. By "analysis" I mean the assumption that, for any specific piece of explanation, some features of the object are irrelevant (chemical constitution when gravity is being studied, mass when spectroscopic behaviour is under examination). The irrelevant features are assumed to make no difference to the operation of the features the special enquiry concerns. There are good grounds for holding that the elements of a human personality are not related in this way. . . . The human personality defies such dissection.

The third essential feature of scientific prediction is generalization, the assumption that the behaviour of some members of a species is good evidence for the behaviour of others. But human personalities are unique. . . . (1956, pp. 290–291).

It is apparent from this quotation that the argument relies upon two separate sets of factors. First, are the characteristics that one takes to be the logical prerequisites of science or the scientific method as such. Thus, for Mabbott there are at least three necessary features of scientific method: measurement, analysis, and generalization. But apart from the particular conception of science involved there is a second aspect to be considered: those features that one takes to characterize human behavior, such as the uniqueness which is one of the factors mentioned in the quotation above. Clearly, whether one believes that a science of human behavior is or is not possible on *a priori* grounds will depend upon an evaluation of these two distinct components: one's conception of scientific method, and the features that one takes to characterize human behavior. In order to evaluate Mabbott's and other related arguments these two aspects of the problem will be dealt with in order.

A. Limitations Based upon Supposed Demands of Scientific Method

1. Measurement, Quantification, and Comparison

Mabbott sees the possibility of measurement as one of the features necessary to a scientific discipline which is lacking from behavioral studies, or at least studies of important varieties of human behavior. His argument uses the word "measurement," but what seems in fact to be at issue is the problem of quantification. As a first step it will be necessary to distinguish carefully between these two concepts.

"Measurable" is definitely the broader idea. In certain cases it simply means "perceptible," as when one speaks of a particular act producing no measurable effect. In a great many other situations the implication is that something is both capable of being *perceived* and of being *compared* to various other objects or standards. Such comparison can take an indefinite number of forms depending not only upon the subject matter itself but also upon the particular interests of the person carrying out the comparison.

Measurement is a complex matter, varying in method and degree of precision.[2] At the lowest level of comparison there is a simple categorization of the phenomena, with no attempt to relate the individual divisions to each other. At the next stage a rank ordering of categories is established, which may be extremely complex and sophisticated: the seven levels of beatitude, or the 33 degrees of Masonic initiation. Third, one can construct an interval scale, a ranking in which the intervals between divisions are assumed to be equal—centigrade temperature, for example. Finally, where the equality of ratios between two measures is assumed, we reach the full-fledged numerical scale. The difference between these last two forms of measurement or comparison can be brought out by considering the difference between 10°C and 20°C, and 10°K and 20°K. Only in the latter pair does it make sense to say that the second member is twice as hot as the first member.

It would be wrong to suppose that these various forms of measurement necessarily and in all cases form an ascending order of scientific respectability, of progress, and of usefulness, albeit in certain fields such as physics this would appear to be the case. Apparently contrasting examples from sociological or historical studies spring to mind. Consider the following questions:

1. Compare the role of the father in Samoan families with that in nineteenth-century middle-class American families.
2. Compare and contrast the social consequences of the French Revolution with those of the revolution of 1848.

Examples of a more strictly scientific nature can also be found:

3. Compare the xylem–phloem system of higher plants with the skeletal, circulatory, and excretory systems of mammals.

---

[2] For a classic discussion of the types of measurement that we outline, see Stevens (1951).

Such questions pose problems quite amenable to rigorous, rational investigation; yet strictly quantitative measurement of the paired subjects in each case seems meaningless. This is not to deny that certain *aspects* of each question might be studied quantitatively: for instance, the number of executions during both revolutions, or the speeds of transport in the two circulation systems. What we are suggesting, then, is that the possibility of rational judgments and comparisons is quite compatible with the practical or even theoretical impossibility of quantification.

It is interesting to note that certain psychoanalysts have adopted this same defense of their methods. Thus, David Rapaport writes:

> Psychoanalysis—like all other sciences—orders, equates, compares, and distinguishes observables, and these procedures, once made precise, reveal themselves as mathematical operations. . . .
> Since mathematization may be either metric or non-metric, quantification is only one form of it. . . . It would certainly be premature to judge that quantification is the kind of mathematization which is appropriate to psychoanalytic theory (1960, pp. 90–91).

Rapaport's distinction between quantification and mathematization parallels our own between quantifiability and measurability. Now, although Mabbott uses the term "measurement," it is quite clear that he has in mind what we have called quantification:

> States such as pain or grief, motives such as hope and fear . . .—none of these can be given numerical values (1956, p. 290).

In fact, this assertion has been denied by various researchers.[3] However, many of the arguments presented on this question of the quantifiability of human feelings have suffered from a failure to distinguish empirical issues from logical ones. That is, certain operationally defined parameters are shown to be quantifiable, and this is taken to be evidence that various aspects of human behavior are thus quantifiable. But the standard objection is always that the experimental parameters chosen for quantifying, say, pain or pleasure do not in fact measure or refer to what is normally considered to constitute these two feelings. The problem of whether a particular operational definition is useful is quite separate from the question of how such definitions compare with commonsense meanings, or even the more basic question whether *any* single meaning, operational or otherwise, can

---

[3] There is a vast literature on the quantification of feelings. A good example is the work of J. D. Hardy and his associates on pain sensations, one of the feelings mentioned by Mabbott. For an account of some of this work and, particularly, the development of the "dol" as a unit of pain sensation, see Hardy, Wolff, Goodell (1952).

be given to a term like "pain." A discussion of these issues, however, would take us too far afield. We shall therefore ignore the question of whether and in what ways human feelings are quantifiable, and instead ask: Why should the possibility of quantification be considered a necessary and/or sufficient condition for a scientific discipline?

On the face of it, it seems unlikely that quantification should be taken as a *sine qua non* of a scientific discipline. The history of science offers several examples of fields in which the appearance of mathematical formulations has been a late development, occurring only after a relatively long and fruitful period of observation and inquiry. Consider the development of the cell theory in the nineteenth century.[4] Once good achromatic lens systems were developed, by about 1827, microscopists quickly began making important contributions. In 1831, Robert Brown discovered the nucleus. Then Schlieden in 1838 discovered the nucleolus and suggested that the cell was the basic unit of all plant life. A year later Schwann extended the theory to animal life and clarified the principle that all organisms are made up of individual, independent cells. In the development of this theory quantification played a minor role. Yet the Schlieden-Schwann theory was no less scientific simply for its lack of mathematical formulation. It was, moreover, completely open to testing and modification on the basis of further microscopic observation.

If we were to choose quantification as a defining characteristic of any scientific discipline, then areas such as nineteenth century cytology would have to be placed beyond the pale. The problem would then be to create some new borderland into which such fields could be placed. The alternative procedure would be to give up the contention that quantification is a necessary feature of scientific disciplines.

The appeal to the history of science leaves open the issue of whether the mathematical formulation of all observations and laws is or ought to be the *goal,* the final end state of any science, but this latter question is independent of the one we are discussing at present. It is, however, connected with another objection that could be raised at this point. It might be said that a particular field need not actually make use of quantification at an early period in its growth, but that quantification of its variables must be possible as an eventual development. Thus, the possibility of quantification and not its actual presence would then be the necessary characteristic. There are, however, several difficulties with this contention. It seems quite conceivable that whether or not quantification of findings

---

[4] A good review of the subject is in Erik Nordenskiöld's *The History of Biology* (1920–1924).

in a particular field eventually occurs may be a contingency to be settled only by future developments within the discipline. That is, quantification may be a contingent, not a necessary, possibility or impossibility. If this were so, one would be in the awkward position of having groups of men recording observations, collecting data, publishing papers—all waiting on pins and needles to find out if they will become "scientists." Moreover there seems embedded in this position the rather dogmatic and unsupported belief that all of nature must be quantifiable or, alternatively, that only those areas that are quantifiable, are capable of scientific study. But surely whatever characterizes scientific method is not some feature common to all the various types of phenomena it studies, but particular ways of approaching and dealing with whatever subject it chooses. Science is characterized by its method of approach, not its subject matter.

Perhaps the only safe conclusion one can draw is that without quantification the expression of laws in numerical terms is impossible. But this is no more than a tautology; it becomes a limiting condition for any scientific discipline only if it is incorporated into the definition of "science," and we have pointed out several arguments against making such a move. Indeed one major aim of our study will be to suggest the possibility of an analysis of scientific explanation based upon much wider ground than that of a reduction to quantitative laws. In the behavioral sciences particularly, there seems no reason to doubt that the ordering and comparing of phenomena is possible.[5] Mabbott and other writers on the behavioral sciences would certainly agree. But if this is so, then the possibility of developing scientific explanations of human behavior founded upon such comparisons is preserved. Hence the objection to the absence of quantification loses its point, and this is true even without contesting the critics' assertion that feelings, beliefs, and the like are not quantifiable, as has in fact been done by many defenders of the behavioral sciences. This latter issue, while vital for the understanding of the differences and similarities of subject matter between the behavioral and physical sciences, no longer weighs upon the question of the theoretical possibility of their being such sciences at all. For once one grasps the distinction between comparability and quantifiability, between comparing as a varied, general procedure and assigning numerical values, it becomes clear that in the relevant sense behavioral phenomena are quite comparable and hence amenable, at least insofar as this particular feature is concerned, to scientific study.

---

[5] For ease of discussion the phrases "behavioral sciences" and "behavioral scientist" will often be used, rather than some clumsy circumlocution. It must be borne in mind, of course, that the question under discussion is precisely whether there can *be* such a *science* or such *scientists* in some rigorous sense of these terms.

2. Analysis and the Isolation of Factors

The second characteristic considered by Mabbott necessary to any scientific discipline which appears to be lacking in behavioral studies is designated "analysis."

> By 'analysis' I mean the assumption that, for any specific piece of explanation, some features of the object are irrelevant. . . . The irrelevant features are assumed to make no difference to the operation of the features the special enquiry concerns (1956, p. 291).

The term "analysis" as it is usually used may suggest an unusual, sophisticated, and technical sort of description. It might be, however, that Mabbott has, as at least a part of his meaning, the inevitable selectivity that precedes any description at all, in everyday language or in science. Like explanations, all descriptions are descriptions "from the point of view of . . . ," or "with reference to . . . ," or "in terms of. . . ." The particular description chosen depends, as we have discussed in the previous chapter, upon the prior knowledge and interests of the observer, and these factors determine the viewpoint, the frame of reference within which a particular selection of features are composed into a unified description. But if selection of a viewpoint or frame of reference must precede description, then an "unselected description," a "complete" description, is logically impossible. Thus, the incompleteness of descriptions is in fact a necessary and not a contingent characteristic; it reflects the selectivity of our language, not the complexity of our subject matter. It is, however, misleading of Mabbott to claim that in scientific inquiry "some features of the object are [assumed to be] irrelevant." Insofar as we choose a certain frame of reference we must of necessity *not* choose an indefinite number of other viewpoints, but this is *not* to imply that these other viewpoints are irrelevant. More importantly, however, this selective or "analytic" function is a necessary precondition for any sort of description at all, scientific or unscientific, of physical objects or human emotions. Whatever logical conclusions follow from this fact of selectivity, they must be equally applicable to any science, physical or behavioral.

The objector might at this juncture retort that if what we have said is true, then all description in any empirical science is distorted. At this stage several points can be made. First, from the assertion that selection is a precondition of all description, it follows logically that there can be no single, complete description. But this is a logical point about language and is quite different from the empirical assertion that every description is distorted. Yet it is this latter claim which the objector makes. Second, one need not be defensive about this logical necessity of selection. We can be more positive and ask how else would our objector have it. If all our usual descriptions are distorted, then either one has some other access to reality (e.g., an intuitive one) against which one can compare the description, or else the word "distorted" has lost its meaning, for want of a contrast. Now it is not our purpose to discuss the possibility of an intuitive faculty, but only to draw attention to the need for some such faculty if the objection is taken in its wider interpretation that all description in any empirical science is distorted.

Since Mabbott does not argue for an intuitive faculty, it seems he must have some additional and more specific meaning in mind for his term "analysis." His examples make clear just what this meaning is. In the physical sciences there are independent features, such as mass and spectroscopic properties. In studying one of these factors certain others can safely be ignored as "irrelevant." In the field of human behavior, however, such selective disregard seems impossible, since human traits are interconnected. The characteristics of the human personality interact with each other and interpenetrate to such an extent that the "isolation" of separate factors is impossible. As an illustration of his point, Mabbott uses the example, perhaps only slightly exaggerated, of an employer's form to be given to referees for new personnel, which asks that the applicant be described under some 29 headings:

> . . . intelligence, imagination, orderliness of mind, industry, conscientiousness, reliability, social tact, savoir faire, sense of humour, etc. . . . What would the man's intelligence be without his imagination? . . . The human personality defies such dissection (1956, p. 291).

The core of Mabbott's objection now becomes clear. Analysis refers to the isolation of separate factors, the dissecting out of discrete variables. And the operative word, as Mabbott makes explicit, is "dissection." Analysis of behavioral phenomena, it is said, necessarily must *distort* its subject matter by cutting it up into parts, or indeed, by cutting *out* only a few parts for study and throwing the rest away.

There is a kernel of truth in this argument; the factors of human behavior are all "relevant" to each other, and none can safely be ignored in any thorough analysis. But Mabbott is quite wrong to believe that a science of behavior could only proceed by dissecting out a factor like intelligence and ignoring its obvious interdependence upon other aspects of the personality. Stated in such bald terms it quickly becomes apparent that this analogy with dissection simply will not do. Quentin Gibson, in a good discussion of this point, states:

> When we consider the parts of a picture separately, there is something which is left out—the pattern they form—the way the parts are related to one another in the whole. But if we consider the features of a situation separately there is nothing comparable left out at all (1960, p. 11).

The features of a situation have no arrangement mirroring the parts or the pattern of the subject matter. To emphasize a particular characteristic is not necessarily to deny that all such features are interrelated; nor is it necessarily to distort those interrelationships. Any comparison of description to dissection is very misleading. An accurate description of a complex subject would emphasize especially the interrelations between various features. Such interaction, far from being lost, is precisely what careful description would be sure to pick up. Even the lowly pair of apples has properties not inherent in the individual apples. And if one insists, it can be conceded that "the whole is therefore greater than the sum of its parts," in the sense of having properties not found in those parts. Yet the whole group is not any the less describable for all that, and the interrelation between the two apples would form an important part of any description of them.

There is a second bad analogy, not explicit in Mabbott's argument, which sometimes appears in other similar discussions. Description in scientific terms, it is said, involves abstracting general features, while what is necessary is some intuitive grasp, from the inside, of the phenomena. But there is certainly a false dichotomy here between the "insides" and "outsides" of events. We describe inner states as well as outward experiences. Such descriptions may be inadequate and liable to particular forms of distortion, but this is different from saying they are impossible to achieve at all. Of course, *knowing* what happened and *experiencing* what happened are different things, and we should be in a sorry state if they were not. It might even be argued (although it is not in this study) that experiencing an event is a necessary condition for knowledge of it. Yet whatever the truth of this claim, it nevertheless remains the case that knowing and experiencing are separate states or episodes, and the inside–outside model collapses this true distinction and creates a false dichotomy between two supposed *ways of knowing:* an "empathetic," experiential method and an analytic, descriptive one. This error is similar, therefore, to that perpetuated by the analogy of description with dissection.

Even if we were to allow this rigid distinction between analytic and empathetic knowledge, we would still be faced with difficulties. It is certainly admirable that psychiatrists understand and empathize with their patients; it may even be essential for adequate therapy. Nevertheless, observations made through the exercise of empathy are not necessarily correct, nor even necessarily more accurate than those arising from more usual scientific observation. In fact, a good deal of evidence suggests that just the reverse may be true. Moreover, empathetic understanding of a psychotic, for example, no matter how deep may not be sufficient for explaining his behavior. The point is that we can and must avoid considering the *source* of explanatory hypotheses when evaluating the hypotheses themselves. To fail to do so is to commit oneself to the genetic fallacy, the error of evaluating scientific hypotheses on the basis of their origins rather than by some standard canon of evidence. Whether based upon long and intimate acquaintance or upon a battery of standardized tests, judgments concerning an individual's behavior must still be tested in the same way; and no source, empathy or anything else, can guarantee truth or assure error. Nor does some degree of distortion in our observations necessarily preclude our using them for scientific purposes. Bad data have often led to brilliant insight, and not just in psychoanalysis.

It seems therefore that the second objection to the possibility of a science of human behavior, like the first, is misguided. Insofar as the term "analysis" emphasizes the necessity of selection and the impossibility of ever giving total descriptions, the point is simply a logical one concerning language and relevant to all discourse, scientific or otherwise. If the objection is based upon the necessary distortion such selectivity introduces, then it has no significance since no contrasting method of reaching an "undistorted" reality is offered. Finally, if the distortion is based on the complexity and interrelatedness of human traits, then the fault lies with a poor analogy of description with dissection. For whatever interaction between factors exists, careful description may be quite capable of rendering it in all its richness and complexity.

3. Experimentation

A third possible objection to a science of human behavior, not mentioned by Mabbott, concerns experimentation. It has often been argued that one essential feature of the scientific method is experimentation, the controlled manipulation of variables under conditions where systematic observation is possible. Where intervention is haphazard, without a distinct separation of independent and dependent variables, then no conclusions as to the mechanism of action can be drawn. Likewise, where no manipulation at all is possible the formation and testing of hypotheses seems again to fail. In fact, both of these objections, haphazard manipulation and the lack of manipulation, have been at different times charged against the behavioral sciences. In either case the conclusion follows that since controlled manipulation is impossible, a truly scientific discipline is therefore unattainable.

As with the previous two arguments, we shall find in this case that an important point is brought out. Nevertheless, the radical conclusion—that a science of human behavior is impossible—does not in fact follow. There are two separate reasons for this, which we will discuss in turn: first, the manipulation of variables is neither a necessary nor a sufficient criterion for judging a discipline to be scientific. And second, manipulation is in fact possible in the behavioral sciences.

It is quite obvious that the emphasis on manipulation derives primarily from a model based on the physical sciences. The ideal is that of an automated laboratory operating under controlled conditions carrying out standardized procedures. Once this model becomes apparent it can be seen to be inapplicable to certain disciplines that one would definitely label scientific. Experimentation, in the sense of controlled manipulation of variables, plays little role in, say, astronomy or ecology. No one would claim that these fields are not yielding practical knowledge and more or less confirmed theories; yet, except in isolated instances, experimental manipulations have been virtually absent.

It is important to note that we are not denying that "experiments" of a scientific sort can be carried out; we are arguing only against experimentation defined as manipulation of variables. Lest it be thought that we are merely legislating a new and idiosyncratic usage, we can consult a dictionary. The Shorter Oxford English Dictionary gives the major definition of experiment as "an action or operation undertaken in order to discover something unknown, to test a hypothesis, or establish or illuminate some known truth." Our point is that such actions may be nothing more than the proper sort of observation.

We can find a good example of this if we turn to the classic experiment testing Einstein's General Theory of Relativity. Einstein's theory was definitively set forth in 1916. In 1918, A. S. Eddington wrote an account of the theory and described two important predictions which were derived from it. The first concerned the deflection of light as it passes near a large gravitational force.

> [The amount of deflection calculated on Newtonian principles] is only half the deflection indicated by Einstein's theory; and the experimental amount of the deflection should thus provide a crucial test (1920, p. 56).

The second prediction concerned the shift toward the red of spectral lines of light from certain stars.

> If the displacement of the solar lines were confirmed, it would be the first *experimental* evidence that relativity holds for quantum phenomena (1920, p. 58).[6]

In May, 1919, during a solar eclipse the first prediction was tested. The published report states: "The results of the observations . . . confirm Einstein's generalized relativity theory (Dyson, Eddington, & Davidson,

---

[6] Eddington's italics.

1920). And there are several additional phrases like "testing the effect" and "test of the law." In December, 1919, Eddington added a new preface to a second edition of his *Report,* outlining the experimental results obtained earlier that year, which had not yet been published. In that preface he writes:

> . . . what part of the theory can now be considered to rest on a definitely experimental basis. I think it may now be stated that Einstein's law of gravitation is definitely established by observation in the following form . . . (1920, preface to 2nd ed., p. ix).

There is no doubt, then, that the scientists involved in this work believed, and with good reason, that they were carrying out an experiment. Yet there certainly was no manipulation of variables. The conclusion seems to be that manipulation of the relevant variables is not a necessary condition for a scientific discipline, since several fields get along for the most part without it.

If these disciplines are in fact scientific one can rightfully ask what are the features which make them so, if experimental manipulation of variables is not a necessary criterion. This question is obviously far too large for its proper treatment in this study. Out of the previous discussion, however, we can see a factor that may well be *one* of the necessary features of any scientific discipline. It was mentioned earlier that in the physical sciences we are usually able to control and manipulate the variables under conditions in which systematic observation is possible. The criticism of the behavioral sciences that we have been examining emphasizes the *manipulation* as being the essential feature. Instead, a much stronger case can be made for the systematic observation being the distinguishing characteristic.

The phrase "systematic observation" is here used simply as a tag to cover what is in fact a rather complex theoretical point about scientific method. It will be remembered that in Chapter 2 four logical presumptions of the explanatory context were discussed. Using these concepts it now seems possible to distinguish between various sorts of "looking" or "observing" on the basis of the presence or absence of certain of these presuppositions. We shall differentiate four possible paradigm situations.

a. A young boy walking along a woodland path sees a squirrel jump out and climb a tree.

b. A naturalist walking along a woodland path is counting the number of squirrels he sees.

c. A biologist walking along a woodland path counts the number of squirrels to decide whether it is true that gray squirrels have almost entirely replaced red squirrels in the neighborhood.

d. A biologist walking along a woodland path watches the behavior of red and gray squirrels in an effort to determine why the gray variety have been so much more successful in competing with the red squirrels for their particular ecological niche in this area.

In case a let us assume there is no conscious "structuring" of perception; the boy *ex hypothesi* has no particular interests or beliefs concerning any squirrels he may see. Thus, in case a none of the presumptions of explanation are present. In case b the naturalist has a particular interest in mind, counting squirrels; to that extent at least the presumption of interest is in operation. The naturalist is an observer in some important sense, while the young boy is not; that is, he approaches his situation from a particular point of view, with a particular purpose or interest—the counting of squirrels—in mind.

Case c one would describe without hesitation as an instance of scientific observation. It is not simply observation with an interest or purpose in mind, for the naturalist, too, had a purpose. The biologist of case c, in addition to the presumption of interest, holds a presumption of knowledge, that is, some beliefs, hypotheses, presumed to be true. The biologist *brings to* the situation this knowledge and places it "in jeopardy," as it were, exposing it to the possibility of confirmation or refutation through new observation. The naturalist in situation b has a purpose, an interest in his observation, and, indeed, may know a great deal about squirrels, but he lacks a presumption of knowledge, and hence the risking of belief is lacking. It seems that one essential prerequisite for doing science must be this presumption, this committing of knowledge in the observational situation.[7] The biologist in case c makes such a commitment and might therefore be said to be conducting an experiment. But when precisely does the shift from observation to experimentation take place? Not when manipulation of variables occurs, but rather when beliefs are put to risk, when the presumption of knowledge is made.

In comparing case c and case d we see that not all scientific observation is aimed at discovering explanations. In case c the biologist brings to his observations a testable hypothesis; yet he is not concerned with elucidating an explanation. It is only in case d that we find a full-fledged explanatory inquiry. Here, in addition to the presumptions of interest and knowledge that the scientist of case c had, there is the presumption of a specific

---

[7] Obviously, if one considers science as a separate and sharply defined entity, then in our view science could never begin at all, since it would at every point presuppose some prior presumption of knowledge. The truth is, of course, that science grew slowly and only gradually separated its methods and point of view from those inherent in the everyday existence of common men. It is only insofar as this development and separation has occurred that one can meaningfully speak of a presumption of knowledge as a characteristic feature.

incongruity—namely, the problem of why the gray squirrels have replaced the red squirrels. The four cases, then, form a spectrum from "looking" to "observation" to "experimentation" or "scientific, systematic observation" up to case d, the scientific pursuit of explanation. Yet the difference between these cases was never a function of active manipulation, but of presumptions held by the observer. These four examples must not, of course, be taken to suggest that four clear-cut categories can in fact be distinguished. The fallacy of accepting such a division has been well criticized (see, for example, Farrell, 1961b). Indeed, our use of the word "spectrum" implies just the opposite, that there can be no sharp division between scientific and nonscientific observation. We are simply attempting to bring out one particular aspect, one possible way of ordering this spectrum.

If we are correct about this particular feature of the scientific method then two further points become understandable. It was argued that experimentation in the sense of "manipulation" is not a necessary condition for a scientific discipline, but in fact it seems it is not even a sufficient condition either. That is, there are or have been nonscientific fields with practitioners who did perform manipulations in an effort to discover various sorts of facts; alchemy is an obvious example. Boiling fluids in cauldrons, freezing materials, mixing potions, performing rituals, reciting incantations—all such procedures are or could be incorporated into experimental manipulations. Yet the outcome in this case was rarely a scientific finding. Indeed, one has grave doubts about placing Paracelsus within the history of chemistry in the way that Lavoisier fits in.[8] Nor is it simply the primitiveness of thought, which would be on our part a demonstration of a very unhistorical parochialism. Democritus and certain other Greek natural philosophers seem to find a niche much more easily. It is rather that an attitude is missing, that the alchemical approach is unscientific in ways quite apart from any considerations of accuracy.

The idea of a commitment of knowledge seems to provide at least a partial answer, for it is precisely this which seems to be lacking. The alchemist and other practitioners of the same sort do not bring to their observations any commitments. One is usually unable to find any beliefs that are in jeopardy, any presumptions of knowledge capable of confirmation or refutation in the particular situation. And this peculiar sort of

---

[8] Professor Thorndike writes: "Not merely as a physician was he ready to try anything, but in his philosophy he drew no sharp dividing line between heavens and earth, natural and supernatural, or animate and inanimate. . . . In short, for Paracelsus there is no such thing as natural law and consequently no such thing as natural science. Even the force of the stars may be sidetracked, thwarted or qualified by the interference of a demon. Even the most hopeless disease may yield to a timely incantation or magic rite. Everywhere there is mystery, animism, invisible forces" (1941, p. 628).

safety, of insulation, this type of incorrigibility is ultimately the most damning. For it is the lack of such commitment which prevents our accepting these disciplines as being scientific.

The presence of a presumption of knowledge on the part of researchers can likewise account for the possibility of real experimentation even in the absence of manipulation of variables. It seems such is the case in studies of human behavior. While the elaborate and controlled methods characteristic of the physics laboratory usually are, for several reasons, impossible or impractical in behavioral studies, it is just not true that no experimentation takes place. What is implied by "experiment" is observation in situations where some commitment of knowledge is made, in which hypotheses or beliefs are in some way placed in jeopardy, made relevant to and potentially falsifiable by the outcome of that situation. Whether or not one can create such experimental situations will depend upon the field of study.

In human behavior it is usually not possible to manipulate people and events to test results. Nevertheless this by no means prevents the formulation of hypotheses relevant to interpersonal situations that one knows *do* arise. Although we cannot often *create* the event, if we are ingenious enough, wait long enough, or simply look in the proper corners of society the relevant situation may present itself. And when it does, provided the presumption of knowledge is made, then that situation can be an experimental one and the outcome evidence for or against the beliefs in question. This is precisely how historical, social, and behavioral researches are most often carried out. Clinical medicine is another example of a field in which manipulation is the exception, not the rule. Here we find the doctor relying on what are sometimes called "nature's experiments," the diseased and malformed patients who eventually get to clinic or hospital. But the point about such patients is that they are not really *nature's* experiments at all, but the doctor's. Nature has merely presented him with a certain situation. It becomes an experiment only because of what the doctor brings into that situation, and how he structures and observes it.

Finally, a last comment on this question of the possibility of experimentation in the behavioral sciences. The discussion so far has attempted to clarify just what is and what is not an essential feature of experiments in a scientific discipline. We have argued that it was not the presence of manipulation but of beliefs, hypotheses capable of falsification, that was essential. Furthermore, we claimed that such a commitment of knowledge can in fact often be made in observing human activities. If our argument is correct, then even if there were no manipulation this would not mean that a science of human behavior would be impossible. In fact, however, a great deal of manipulation and controlled testing does occur even in the behavioral sciences. One can think of three different types of experiments of this kind. First, those cases in which people are involuntarily held in situations where such control and manipulation are possible. Concentration camps, prisoner of war camps, prisons, the armed services—these come immediately to mind as environments where laboratory controls could be and have been approximated. That there are ethical objections to such techniques being used generally in the behavioral sciences is of course true, but irrelevant. The fact that data are collected by illegal or immoral means has no bearing upon its potential scientific utility. Second, an ever-growing accumulation of observations has come from experimental psychology studies performed on volunteers. These studies employ controlled situations and intricate testing devices and materials. Finally, there is the multitude of studies of animal behavior, both in natural and in laboratory settings. Of course with all three of these types of experimental situations the issue can properly be raised of the relevance of any findings to human behavior under more normal, uncontrolled conditions. However, whether the rat running a maze has any relationship to human beings under stress is a problem not to be answered by fiat but by investigation. Such a question is an empirical, not a theoretical one and outside the scope of this study.

B. Limitations Based upon Supposed Peculiarities of Human Behavior

We have discussed three features often claimed to be necessary for there to be even the possibility of a scientific discipline. These prerequisites have been examined from two viewpoints: to what extent they are in fact defining features of scientific method, and to what extent they can be fulfilled in studies of human behavior. On the basis of that discussion we denied the assertion that a science of human behavior is impossible, at least for lack of those features. There is, however, a second group of arguments against a behavioral science that also demands attention. These objections are based not upon various alleged prerequisites of the scientific method but upon the existence of certain peculiarities of the subject matter itself. It has been argued that these characteristics of all or most human behavior are such as to pose an effective limit to the development of a scientific discipline in this area. We must now discuss these objections in detail.

1. Uniqueness

The classic observation often made about human behavior is that it is *unique* in some important sense. This claim forms Mabbott's third objection to the possibility of a science of human behavior:

> The third essential feature of scientific prediction is generalization, the assumption that the behaviour of some members of a species is good evidence for the behaviour of others. But human personalities are unique (1956, p. 291).

This objection is, however, quite unenlightening until one gets clear in just what sense "uniqueness" is being used. The problem then becomes very complex, since one finds disconcerting shifts in meaning among philosophers and social scientists who posit or deny uniqueness. To point out just one ambiguity, there is on the one hand the contention that all human beings are unique, that the human personality as a whole is unique. Eloquent statements of this position can be found in the philosophical literature.[9] On the other hand is the idea that particular human actions, individual bits of human behavior, are unique. Naturally, these two positions are not mutually exclusive but very closely related. Still, it is well to keep clear about their separate claims, particularly in view of the fact that it is at least logically possible to affirm the one, yet deny the other. That is, one might say that it is not particular acts which are unique, in the relevant sense, but only the whole set of such acts which go to make up a life history. Alternatively, one might argue that although particular acts are in some sense unique, nevertheless individuals as a whole are not unique and can therefore be the subject of generalizations.

Further complexities of this concept of "uniqueness" can be brought out by quoting from a recent discussion of the relation of science to psychoanalysis by an analyst:

> . . . the adaptive abilities of humans vary tremendously, as do the stresses to which any individual is exposed. The word individual is the significant one. Perhaps, for individual, 'unique' should be substituted. Each person is unique, in the sense of endowment, interpersonal contacts, experiences, and the specific time at which they occur (McLaughlin, 1963, p. 459).

Unfortunately, as is so often the case, the author does not elaborate his point but takes the truth of his statement to be immediately obvious and undisputed. Several distinctions, however, are here lumped together and must be disentangled. First, the references to "endowment" and "experiences" suggest a distinction similar to that mentioned above between the uniqueness of individuals as a whole and the uniqueness of their particular experiences and activities. Second, and more importantly, the uniqueness of "specific time" is noted. Here there seems to be lurking the idea of quantitative, spatio-temporal uniqueness, in addition to some sort of qualitative individuality. These various possible interpretations must be

---

[9] The writings of Bergson suggest themselves as immediate sources of examples.

explored in order to clarify our own understanding and weighting of the "unique" aspect of human behavior.

The first possible meaning of unique that we shall deal with is "quantitatively or numerically unique." It has been argued that the individual actions upon which the behavioral scientist focuses are unique in a way that chemical or physical interactions are not. The physicist, it is said, studies whole classes of events, types of phenomena; but human behavior is often, if not always, composed of unique events. Now just what could be implied by the term "unique" in such arguments? First, it might be suggested that unique means "numerically unique." That is, the phenomena of human behavior are such that each event is numerically, quantitatively distinct from every other. Now this is undoubtedly true but devoid of methodological implication. For it is certainly the case that *all* conceivable objects and events are unique in this sense. How could it be otherwise? It is impossible that two objects could have exactly the same spatial and temporal coordinates and yet remain distinct. Hence if there really *are* two objects they must really *be* numerically distinct or unique. Whatever generalization physical science accomplishes, it must begin like any behavioral study from the observation of unique occurrences. This meaning of unique, then, while true, is unenlightening and offers no grounds for the claim that the subject matter of behavioral studies is separate from that of the physical sciences. Apparently, then, some other meaning of unique must be involved.

A second possible interpretation of the claim that human behavior is unique is the view that it is in some sense indescribable. There are at least two reasons that can be adduced for this indescribability. First is the point previously discussed in regard to the possibility of "analysis" in the behavioral sciences. The argument runs thus: "Selection of features is equivalent to abstracting discrete and independent characteristics. In human behavior, however, there are no such independent variables, but an interpenetration, an interaction between properties that makes abstraction impossible. But if abstraction is impossible, then so is scientific description." The alternative is in some way to grasp the subject in its "unique individuality" as a "unique totality." The faulty analogy of description to dissection has already been discussed in some detail and need not be repeated here. It will suffice to repeat the original conclusion: the interdependence and complexity of a phenomenon's features are quite compatible, logically, with their study and description. All description presupposes the selection of a frame of reference, a viewpoint, dependent upon one's interests and prior knowledge; but this is a logical point and poses no special limitation in those areas such as human behavior where the phenomena are particularly complex.

The alternative reason for holding that human behavior is indescribable does not rely on the interpenetration and interdependence of the features of behavior but on the belief that there are no "features" at all in the required sense. To say that human behavior is unique on this account is to assert that it is indescribable, not because the characteristics are complicated and interdependent, but because each event is in some *absolute* sense unique, apart from any other event. The point is not simply that every event is a *particular* event, that is, numerically, quantitatively distinct. Nor is the point that human behavior presents particularly complex and interdependent events. It is rather that individual behavioral events do not belong to any class at all; no general features, and hence no generalizations, are found. Not only are human behavioral phenomena not simply *particular* instances; in an important sense they are not *instances* at all, but are unclassifiable in the root meaning of that term. There is a qualitative uniqueness, a much more radical novelty than mere quantitative uniqueness, that precludes scientific generalization. And this, perhaps, is the real point of the assertion that human behavior is unique. For the possibility of generalization depends on there being repeating or repeatable phenomena, and features or characteristics having a general occurrence. Without repetition there is no possibility of even *forming* generalizations, let alone confirming them. But, so this argument would claim, the phenomena of human behavior never repeat themselves. Hence there is no possibility of developing a science of human behavior.

This interpretation of the term "unique" makes a much more extreme claim than did the first two. Those two on examination appeared to be true of human behavior but harmless to our position. That is, human behavior *is* numerically, temporal-spatially unique, and human traits *are* interdependent; but neither of these facts rules out a science of behavior. This third sort of uniqueness, however, if true would certainly form an obstacle to such a science. But it can be criticized on several grounds.

The idea of qualitative uniqueness as opposed to merely quantitative difference seems on the face of it a very dubious concept. One must ask: "What would 'absolute and total novelty' be like?" "How could it be descovered?" Let us first consider the possibility that one *perceives* such novelty. The immediate objection is that everything that is seen, heard, smelled, felt, etc., has some relationship to other perceptions of the same modality, if only the relation of difference, or not being red, or shrill, or sulfurous, or rough, etc. "Absolute novelty," then, could not be a perceptible characteristic, a property or feature of behavioral phenomena at all, since no perceptions are "absolutely novel." We must agree with Hume on this point.[10] There may well exist shades of blue to which I have never been exposed; yet this certainly does not imply that such a shade would be

---

[10] Hume's example occurs in Section II, "Of the Origin of Ideas," of *An Inquiry Concerning Human Understanding.*

absolutely novel to me, that it would not fit into a definite relation to other shades of blue of past experience.

Alternatively, one might say that "absolute novelty" is *not* perceived; rather, one would *know* that something is absolutely novel. The problem, however, is that one must "know" this fact *by virtue of* some detectable features, unless one opts for a direct intuition of novelty. Yet whatever features we perceive, not being the novelty itself, they are presumably general features. Hence the subject matter in question, having such general features, still could not be absolutely novel. Thus, the objection to a science of human behavior based upon the characteristic of absolute novelty loses its force, since it could not refer either to a directly perceived feature or to a feature known indirectly from what is perceived.

The meanings of unique we have discussed so far seem seriously deficient. If we mean "numerically distinct," then every object and every event is unique. On the other hand, to assert "absolute uniqueness" seems meaningless. But we can, I think, find a meaningful usage for the concept. Uniqueness, in our view, is a relative, not an absolute property. Our usage is such that in different contexts it can be asserted or denied about the same subject. Patrick Gardiner in discussing this issue offers the following definition:

> . . . to say that something is unique is to describe some feature or features belonging to it (perceived or "intuited") and not belonging to other things (1952, p. 43).

We can take this statement as a basis for elaborating our own usage of the term. First, the point is presumably not that the object has a feature shared with no other thing at all, but only that it has features not shared by certain other objects also under consideration. That is, to say "X_1 is unique" is to assert that X_1 has at least a single property, P_1, not shared by other objects, X_2, X_3 . . ., which along with X_1 are under comparison, and which may all share various other properties P_2, P_3. . . . Implicit is the view that uniqueness is not simply "being different from" but "being *relevantly* different," different in certain important respects now under consideration from other rather similar objects or events that one might otherwise classify together in a single group.

The ascription of uniqueness is therefore possible only where there are previously adopted criteria whereby similarity or dissimilarity can be noted. In every case there must first be an implicit decision made as to what shall count as similar, and in what respects objects are to be considered as similar or dissimilar to each other. There is, then, a presumption of standards, of criteria for judging uniqueness; moreover, these standards can be made explicit, and can also be altered according to the situation.

Gardiner rightly observes that "the extent to which we regard something as unique, or as an instance of a type, is a function of our interest" (1952, p. 45). Indeed, it is a function of our interests or purposes *and* of our level of knowledge. Thus, what has sometimes been mistaken for a peculiarity of subject matter is in fact a reflection of a difference in purpose and approach.

Uniqueness, then, is a "second-order" property, not "first-order" like "red," "shrill," etc. It is not another property of the same logical level as P_1 and P_2. We do not perceive uniqueness the way we perceive red. Rather, we assign or withhold the label "unique" on the basis of our observing and comparing the properties P_1, P_2 . . . that various objects have.

We can now see clearly how the concept of "absolute uniqueness" involves an inconsistency. Uniqueness always refers to standards; X is unique in respect of certain criteria. Yet "absolute uniqueness" would mean "unique apart from any standards at all." Moreover, uniqueness is assigned or withheld on the basis of observing the various features of the object at hand. Yet absolute uniqueness would have to be asserted without reference to any properties at all, since by definition there could be no general features if the object were to be absolutely unique. The fact is that, far from implying indescribability, the ascription of uniqueness *presupposes* that careful description and comparison has occurred.

We can summarize our conclusions on this issue of uniqueness by using one of the old chestnuts of many discussions in this area: the French Revolution. For X to say that the French Revolution was a unique event is *not* to say that:

a. It was numerically unique or distinct.
   All events, not just those in history or human behavior, have this in common.
b. It was indescribable, incapable of being described by reference to general features.
   In fact the application of the term "unique" is as descriptive as any other term might be, and presupposes the observing of features and comparison of the event to other possibly similar cases.
c. It was qualitatively, absolutely unique and hence incapable of repetition.
   Absolute uniqueness, total novelty, is an empty concept. As far as being qualitatively different in at least certain respects, this, too, is probably true of all events. In any case, the question of repetition is always open, since one is always free to choose the criteria of identity and similarity of events. That is, it is always necessary to *decide* just how many features must be similar for a second

event to count as a repetition of the first, and such a ruling will depend upon one's interests and purposes.

These three possible usages were examined in detail above. Instead, we maintain that for X to say that the French Revolution was a unique event is, in part at least,

 a. to say that it differs in important, detectable respects from other events termed "revolutions."
 b. to reveal that X is interested in explaining this event in its peculiarity; that is, X wants to explain those specific features that distinguish this event from others like it.

The historian, like the psychoanalyst, is most often interested in explaining his subject matter *in all its particularity,* in accounting for all those features which make it distinct from other objects or events of a similar nature. Thus, when he applies the label of "uniqueness," it by no means rules out, on an *a priori* basis, the possibility of developing a scientific, systematic explanation of the event in question. Whether such an explanation is in fact or can logically be achieved is another matter entirely, and one that remains independent of the ascription of uniqueness.

This seems a reasonable interpretation of the concept of uniqueness, but it is diametrically opposed to the view that uniqueness is some indescribable, intuitable quality. The only problem is that having adopted such a usage for the term "unique," the concept no longer remains a distinguishing feature of behavioral phenomena as opposed to those in the physical sciences. The collapse of a bridge may be just as unique for the physicist as is a general's blowing the bridge up for the historian. Thus, as with the idea of numerical distinction, uniqueness is seen to be a property applicable to various sorts of subject matter and not at all the exclusive hallmark of human behavior. What is more important, however, is the fact that such uniqueness as may be present in behavioral phenomena in no way precludes there being scientific explanations. Uniqueness, as we understand it, offers no obstacle at all to the *theoretical possibility* of there being a science of human behavior, or of history.

2. Absence of Generalizations

In Mabbott's argument the third point is the falsity of what he calls the principle of "generalization," that is

> . . . the assumption that the behaviour of some members of a species is good evidence for the behaviour of others. But human personalities are unique (1956, p. 291).

The above statement fails to distinguish two distinct objections: the impossibility of forming empirical generalizations and the uniqueness of the human personality. Although the reason *for* the impossibility of generalization is stated to be the uniqueness of the personality, this need not be the only reason possible. Moreover, as we have seen, the concept of uniqueness, as we are using it, does not have the consequence that generalizations about human behavior are logically impossible. We argued precisely the opposite point, that to ascribe uniqueness to some object or event presupposed that the observation of various general properties had occurred.

Nevertheless, having reached this conclusion about uniqueness one is not thereby allowed to ignore the criticism of the absence of generalizations. For now the argument is rather different. In the previous section we interpreted Mabbott as arguing: because human behavior is unique, therefore no generalizations, and hence no science of behavior is possible. It could be countered, however, that we have so far missed, and indeed reversed, the real argument of Mabbott's thesis: The essential point is that no generalizations are possible about human behavior, and in this sense we could say that human behavior is unique.

I do not want to discuss the question of whether it would offend linguistic propriety to use the term "unique" in this way, for the important issue is the presence or absence of generalizations. Before we can answer this question, however, we must get clear on just what is meant by an empirical generalization. One important difficulty centers on the distinction between conditional and unconditional generalizations. The view has sometimes been adopted, especially in the recent past, that any scientific generalizations must be unconditional—that is, universal both in time and in space.[11] The model analysis of such generalizations would seem to be:

G1: AB is (always) the case.[12]

But, so the argument runs, such generalizations could never be found applicable to human behavior, since human nature changes through time, through different periods of history. Therefore, at the very least, conditions restricting the temporal applicability would have to be introduced.

Now insofar as "human nature" is used as an approximate equivalent of "habitual or usual behavior" it seems obviously true that "human nature" does indeed tend to change through time. Of course there is often

---

[11] In Chapter 7 we shall discuss one such theory in detail.

[12] In this and the following schemas the "AB" is to be read as "such and such." Thus, it would be correct in each schema to substitute, for instance, "if A, then B" for "AB." Such an alteration would not affect our argument.

some additional meaning given to this ill-defined concept. But rather than explore this point we can concede it and alter our model. Thus, we can frame a second schema for a behavioral generalization, taking account of its being applicable only during certain periods of time.

G2: At times $T_1 \ldots T_n$, AB is the case.

We shall interpret this temporal condition as encompassing two common forms.

1. Historical time: "In the seventeenth century. . . ."
2. Personal time: "At ages two to four the child. . . ."

For our purposes this distinction can be ignored.

Not only is it true that human nature varies through historical periods, but it also varies at the same time under changes of physical, social, or psychological conditions. A generalization might even hold true only under certain spatial conditions; that is, it would be true only in specific locations. Thus let us add a further modification to account for this, emphasizing that our generalization is applicable solely under certain more or less specifiable conditions.

G3: At times $T_1 \ldots T_n$, under conditions $C_1 \ldots C_k$, AB is the case.

We have now added modifications to take into account the possibly limited applicability with regard to temporal change and situational, including spatial, conditions. But still a third limitation is quite conceivable. It is possible that "laws" of human behavior in the sense of empirical generalizations might in fact be applicable only to certain individuals. By this we do not mean that a generalization of the form G3 is in fact only applicable to certain persons because at times $T_1 \ldots T_n$ the conditions $C_1 \ldots C_k$ are found only in certain persons. This could be called a case of the "factual limitation of instantiation." Its extreme form would be a generalization of form G3 with but a single instance, a single situation in which it could be applied. Rather, what we now have in mind is the possibility of developing generalizations about small groups of people or even individuals which by their form are applicable only to those subjects;[13] that is, a generalization of the form

G4: At times $T_1 \ldots T_n$, under conditions $C_1 \ldots C_k$, for individuals $P_1 \ldots P_j$, AB is the case.

---

[13] A similar distinction has been developed by Gordon Allport in *Personality* (1937), where it is referred to in terms of nomothetic vs. idiographic laws.

Such generalizations might even be applicable only to single individuals, that is, P_1 alone. It is conceivable that by dint of keen observation we could discover generalizations of the form G4 which are true of John Jones but no one else. This would be a case of the "formal limitation of instantiation," where the application to a single individual is not an empirical contingency, but incorporated into the generalization itself.

Finally, a modification is necessary to take into consideration the probabilistic nature of many, if not all, generalizations. This particular change has been one of the outstanding developments of twentieth century science. Not only in the biological sciences and medicine but also in the physical sciences more and more generalizations now take the form of statements of probabilities concerning the outcome of series of events. Indeed, it has been suggested that perhaps all generalizations in physics will turn out to be statistical, rather than absolute or "deterministic." In any case, unless one holds that the generalizations of quantum mechanics will eventually be superseded by such deterministic generalizations, there will remain at least some that must be stated probabilistically.[14] We shall therefore have to add a probabilistic condition to our previous schemas. Of course this modification, like each of the earlier three, might be adopted independently of the others. The conditions need not have been adopted in the order in which we have discussed them; that is, one might add this probability condition to any of the earlier schemas. For instance, example G1 with a probability condition added becomes

G5: AB is the case in $p\%$ of cases.

It seems possible that for human behavior whatever generalizations might be discovered would have all four of the modifications discussed; that is, any generalizations, and certainly those in the initial period of the development of the behavioral sciences, would most probably have limitations of time, antecedent conditions including location, individuals to whom applicable, and probability of outcome.

G6: At times $T_1 \ldots T_n$, under conditions $C_1 \ldots C_k$, for individuals $P_1 \ldots P_j$, AB is the case in $p\%$ of cases.

We can take G6 as a schema for the weakest, most limited variety of generalization.

Now having outlined the various sorts of generalization, one further problem remains. We must distinguish between different meanings of the term "universal" as used in the phrase "universal generalization." First is

---

[14] See Braithwaite (1953), especially Chapter 5, for a discussion of this point and its implications.

the usage of "universal" as equivalent to "unconditional." In this sense only generalizations of the G1 form would be universal. Second is the usage of "universal" as equivalent to "nonprobabilistic." In this sense schemas G1, G2, G3, and G4 could all be considered universal. Here it would not be the absence of any conditions at all, but only of probabilistic limitations that would be significant. Obviously, generalizations of a form similar to G6 are not "universal" in either of these two senses. Yet in a third sense, simply as "nonparticular, not referring to a single event or single series of events," then any generalizations, even of form G6, will by definition be universal. Of course, it seems clear that this third usage is not the most usual interpretation. What is important, however, is that we can see a natural resemblance between G6 generalizations and those totally unconditional ones of the form G1.

Let us now return to Mabbott's objection that no generalizations exist in the area of human behavior. Certainly it seems evident that there must be numerous true G6 generalizations (that is, generalizations of the weakest form possible), and Mabbott would undoubtedly concede this; thus he must have in mind generalizations of a more inclusive and stronger form. His brief statement of the objection, however, does not allow us to answer this question definitely, but let us assume that he believes that there are no true unconditional generalizations about human behavior.

In fact, many psychologists and psychoanalysts would disagree with Mabbott on this point. A number of theoreticians have claimed that such unconditional generalizations were discoverable, and moreover, that their particular methods had actually succeeded in uncovering at least some of them. It will be useful to examine briefly two examples of such "laws of human behavior" to see whether they refute Mabbott's contention.

Our first example is from the psychoanalyst David Rapaport. He set out the "Projective Hypothesis" that:

> All behavior manifestations of the human being, including the least and the most significant, are revealing and expressive of his personality, by which we mean that individual principle of which he is the carrier (1942, pp. 213–214).

More recently the author reformulated this "hypothesis" as the "postulate" that:

> All behavior is integral to, and characteristic of, the behaving personality (1960, p. 43).

The problem is that if this statement is taken to be an empirical generalization about human behavior, it is most probably false, at least in its straightforward interpretation. A great deal of behavior consists of attitudes and actions quite "uncharacteristic" of the individual, quite "out of character." Much of daily activity is not at all "integral" and "characteristic" but impulsive and uncharacteristic; yet one would certainly not refuse to call it behavior. Of course one could *define* behavior in such a limiting fashion that the above postulate is tautologously true. The problem is that one would then be left with great chunks of human activity that could not be called behavior. Alternatively (and this is the more likely option for a psychoanalyst), one could interpret this principle to mean that since all behavior emanates from the individual, it must therefore in some way, however difficult to discover, be the effect of certain basic motivations or factors active in that individual; so that to the extent one understands that piece of behavior, one also understands those factors. Of course, here too, we approach tautology and are confronted with a "law of human behavior" that is empirically empty.

Thus the first conclusion one is tempted to draw is that the law "all behavior is integral to, and characteristic of, the behaving personality" is either a tautology or false. Clearly, this is not a very promising conclusion about a supposedly basic law of the science of human behavior, and Mabbott remains unrefuted. In fact, however, this so-called empirical hypothesis is not descriptive at all, but normative as can be seen from this statement:

> What [this postulate] asserts is not that each behavior is a microcosm which reflects the macrocosm of the personality, but rather that an explanation of behavior, in order to have any claim to completeness, must specify its place within the functional and structural framework of the total personality and, therefore, must include statements about the *degree* and *kind* of involvement, in the behavior in question, of all the relevant conceptualized aspects of personality (Rapaport, 1960, p. 43).[15]

Without going into the explication of this quotation it is nevertheless apparent that this postulate is used as a regulative principle and is not descriptive at all. The rule sets a particular standard for judging explanations; it states what such explanations must specify "in order to have any claim to completeness." Our question: "Is this generalization true or false?" is no longer appropriate. The "Projective Hypothesis" is apparently not meant to be an assertion at all, either empirical or tautological, but a procedural rule, a criterion for evaluating explanations. Unfortunately the author does not seem to realize this distinction. Instead, at one and the same time he offers empirical evidence for the truth of his law, states it as a definition, and uses it as a regulative principle. His alternation between the words "hypothesis" and "postulate" explicitly mirrors this confusion.

---

[15] Rapaport's italics.

Lest we concede to Mabbott's objection too quickly, let us look at another supposed universal generalization about human behavior. Our second example comes from Carl Rogers' work. In outlining his theory of personality and behavior Rogers lists several basic generalizations. Moreover, he explicitly recognizes the difference in logical status between empirical assertions and assumed rules of procedure. Rogers admits that:

> Some of these propositions must be regarded as assumptions, while the majority may be regarded as hypotheses subject to proof or disproof (1951, p. 482).

The problem is that having made such an announcement, there is no further attempt, when he actually states his propositions, to distinguish between these two varieties. For instance:

> The organism has one basic tendency and striving—to actualize, maintain, and enhance the experiencing organism (1951, p. 487).

The text discussion makes clear that this unconditional generalization is intended to be the result of extended clinical observation. Yet it is not at all evident that such a generalization expressed in these terms is testable. For instance, what sort of activity is an "actualizing" one for an actually living organism? On the other hand, if it were tightened up to be amenable to observation it might well prove to be false.

In presenting these two examples, one from orthodox psychoanalytic and one from psychiatric literature, the aim is neither to evaluate each statement properly nor to ridicule both. Rather it has been to highlight a particular problem, often virtually unrecognized and unexamined, that occurs in many theoretical discussions of proposed psychological generalizations.

The problem is this. When Mabbott denies that there are universal generalizations true of human behavior, it is clear that he must have in mind empirical hypotheses. However, when we turn to supposed examples of such generalizations, they turn out to be either so vaguely formulated as to be untestable, or else not really empirical hypotheses at all, but normative rules or definitions. We are now touching upon the issue of the difference between statements used as empirical generalizations and those employed in various "logical" roles, as definitions or methodological rules of procedure. This issue is an important one, and it is just as well to say a few words about it before we go on, since we can thereby clarify Mabbott's criticism, and we can, moreover, bring out the reasons why both Rapaport's and Rogers' attempts to answer such a criticism seem unsuccessful.

It is not implied in this discussion that the ancient and honorable analytic–synthetic and logical–empirical distinctions hold true in anything like their original senses. Several valuable recent studies have brought out the importance of the particular context in which statements are used and the various possible functions to which they can be put. It has been argued by W. V. Quine (1961) that all statements are revisable in principle, that a rational man need hold no proposition totally immune from correction or change. Hilary Putnam (1962), although taking issue with Quine, has pointed out how laws in the physical sciences have a life history, beginning as empirical generalizations and becoming, gradually and often without conscious decision, statements no longer directly amenable to observation. In an excellent discussion, N. R. Hanson (1958, Ch. 5) has demonstrated that even at the very same time in an experimental physics situation a statement like $F = m(d^2s/dt^2)$ can function in several different ways. Hanson lists four uses in which $F = m(d^2s/dt^2)$ could be said to be true:

1. True by definition ("classical" analytic statement).
2. True because it is psychologically inconceivable that it be false; the mind cannot picture circumstances in which this relation would not hold.
3. Empirically true, yet not falsifiable, in the usual sense, since it is embedded in theory to such an extent that one would often choose to modify the theory to allow for otherwise inconsistent findings, rather than throw out the law.
4. Empirically true, because it is simply a generalization based on evidence and as liable to disproof on the basis of further evidence as any other generalization ("classical" synthetic statement).

In addition, Hanson notes the possibility of not considering $F = m(d^2s/dt^2)$ as a statement at all, and hence neither true nor false, neither analytic nor synthetic. Various functions for the formula are possible here, too, but for our purposes these could all be considered as aspects of its use as a methodological convention or procedural rule for ordering and interpreting various experimental data and theoretical statements.

Even from such a brief sketch we can, I think, grasp Hanson's essential point that scientific statements are used, often simultaneously, in a variety of ways. In our own argument of the previous chapter we have tried to bring out a similar point—that explanatory statements fulfill a variety of roles which are context-dependent. Now Mabbott's criticism that we are here discussing is concerned with one of these roles. When it is said that there are no laws of human behavior what is meant would seem to be unconditional empirical generalizations. This is not to say that any proposed statements must function solely in this way, for we have now seen that there can be several simultaneous uses. But what is necessary is that such a statement have an empirical, experiential basis. It would certainly be improper to answer Mabbott's criticism by pointing to definitional formulations or methodological generalizations about procedure.

The shortcomings of Rapaport's and Rogers' purported laws of human behavior now become quite clear. The distinctions carefully outlined by Hanson have been completely ignored. We do not mean by this to insist on a rigid empirical–logical dichotomy, but there is all the difference in the world between refusing to adopt, for various well-considered reasons, some previously accepted distinction, and failing to recognize that distinction at all. Unfortunately, it is this latter situation which has characterized a good deal of psychiatric and psychoanalytic writing.[16] For example, Rapaport's "Projective Hypothesis" turns out not to be an empirical hypothesis at all, but either a definition or a procedural rule for judging explanations. Rogers' law, on the other hand, while supposedly empirically founded, turns out to be so loosely stated as to be incapable of experiential confirmation or refutation.

It is, however, not only the failure of examples such as these which lends weight to Mabbott's contention that there can be no laws of human behavior. The very nature of the subject matter intuitively suggests that laws in any way as simple as those of, say, physics will never be found. In fact, the idea that what is needed is a Galileo of the behavioral sciences is probably quite wrong. It does not seem that the lack of either genius or prolonged observation is what has so far prevented the discovery of such laws, but their absence from the subject matter. And this possibility is of course not inconceivable. The assumption that general laws exist may be a fruitful heuristic device to encourage research, but we have no logical reasons to believe that some benevolent deity has in fact arranged that all matter, and all subject matters, do actually operate according to laws.[17]

On the other hand, there are several considerations that weigh against the claim that no generalizations at all can be found in human behavior. First, ordinary language is filled with supposedly true beliefs and maxims. If one were to take seriously the view that no generalizations of even a modified variety exist, it would be difficult to account for the often strikingly accurate and subtle observations that comprise the shared body of common-sense knowledge available to members of a society. Many such observations are trivial, some perhaps too vague for precise formulation, still others not in fact true—yet, surely, it seems that at least *some* of the commonsense generalizations about human behavior could well be true. Certainly in ordinary discourse we often *assume* both the possibility of forming generalizations and the truth of certain maxims already possessed.

---

[16] I have elsewhere discussed this problem in somewhat greater detail as it arises in regard to another example of psychoanalytic writing, namely, a theory of group behavior (see Sherwood, 1964).

[17] I am ignoring the Kantian rejoinder that whether or not laws do in fact operate, it is a necessary fact that we perceive things *as* operating according to laws (see p. 67).

Perhaps the most telling objection to the claim that no generalizations whatever are applicable to human nature is that one can scarcely conceive of a universe of phenomena of which this could be true. That is, the imagination fairly boggles at attempting to picture a domain of objects and events about which no generalizations at all could truly be made. Certainly it would still be the case that phenomena would be perceived in terms of general features, just because this is the way our minds function. Our arguments on this point were discussed earlier, with reference to the concept of "absolute novelty." It is true, however, that the necessity of perceiving in terms of general features does not imply that generalizations *must* in fact occur.

As an experiment we could attempt to give a logical formulation for such a domain. There might be the following.

$1, \ldots n$ different objects, each of which might possess one or more of:
$1, \ldots f$ features or properties. And there would be:
$1, \ldots r$ relations holding between the objects.

Now, for there to be no true generalizations possible, certain conditions would have to hold; namely, those conditions which would rule out the truth of even a G6 type (the weakest) generalization.

G6: At times $T_1 \ldots T_n$, under conditions $C_1 \ldots C_k$, for individual objects $P_1 \ldots P_j$, AB is the case in $p\%$ of cases.

The question is: Could one formulate a logically consistent set of conditions that would necessarily preclude the possibility of there being any true G6 generalizations? One problem is that the statements of the general conditions that we desire would in fact be generalizations of the very type which we wanted to prove impossible; it would, apparently, take a set of generalizations to demonstrate logically that generalizations could not exist.

But if logical proof seems to be self-contradictory, another alternative remains. We might simply discover in an empirical fashion that no generalizations could be true. To reach this conclusion we should have to know:

1. The truth conditions of all true propositions asserted about the domain.
2. That none of these true propositions are generalizations.
3. That there could exist no other propositions that would be true of the domain.

Once again as before, when we emphasize the conditions that must be fulfilled in order that our claim that no generalizations are possible be substantiated, we realize the complexity, and perhaps inconsistency, of the task.

It seems, therefore, that Mabbott's final objection cannot hold up as an established principle, however seriously we accept it as a practical warning. In short, we must conclude that generalizations in human behavior will be less easy to find, less broad in scope, and less certain as a basis for prediction. This being so, any science of human behavior will be more difficult to develop, more circumspect in its applications, and more dubious in its conclusions. All this, however, is platitude. That the road will be a hard one was known at the beginning. We can however be confident that the goal is at least possible, that there are no insurmountable theoretical obstacles which could stop us before we begin.

Chapter 4/CASE STUDY: A PSYCHOANALYTIC
EXPLANATION OF AN INDIVIDUAL'S BEHAVIOR

A. SELECTION OF CASE MATERIAL

One might suppose that in a field such as psychoanalysis, where clinical observation has been systematically conducted and reported upon for over 60 years, the source material available for a logical study would be very extensive. But this preliminary assumption would be quite mistaken. The fact is that the potentially useful material is extraordinarily limited, and by this we have in mind extended reports of individual histories together with reports, or if possible actual records, of the analytic sessions. The reasons for this unfortunate situation are both historical and technological.

Psychoanalysis, to a greater extent than most other disciplines, was the creation of a single man working for the most part outside established medical circles. Even after a small group of followers grew up around Freud in the first decade of this century, the movement found little acceptance from either lay or professional groups, and recognition came only slowly. But this lack of acceptance, as is so often the case, created its own counter force in the zeal with which the doctrines of psychoanalysis were promulgated. Needless to say, the originality of both the methods and the theories, together with the strong and individual personalities of the early investigators, were important additional factors. For these and other reasons detailed observation and collection of data from single histories seemed often to be sacrificed for the presentation of broad generalizations more or less supported by clinical impressions based upon many cases. Instead of the simple massing of observations, perhaps under the pressure of proving the field's importance, the early investigators often concentrated on the elaboration of broad theories of human behavior and highly suggestive, but controversial, sociological commentaries. In April 1908, at the very first general meeting of psychoanalysts, this wide-ranging and synoptic viewpoint was much in evidence, as can be seen from the titles of the papers presented. Included in the nine were: Jones' "Rationalization in Everyday Life," Riklin's "Some Problems of Myth Interpretation," Adler's "Sadism in Life and in Neurosis," and Ferenczi's "Psychoanalysis and Pedagogy." There sometimes seemed to be a quite unnecessary apologetic tone in the detailed discussion of single cases, as if it had been forgotten that the fundamental confirmatory evidence for psychoanalytic theory was rooted in precise observation of just such individual patients. Psychoanalysis may be an example of a field that, at least initially, overreached itself. The basic problems of establishing procedures for the observation of phenomena and validation of hypotheses, so essential for the orderly growth of any discipline, were only partially recognized and never adequately dealt with.

Of course there was also a technological reason for the lack of adequate records. Given that the therapeutic dyad of analyst and patient was not to be altered by the addition of an observer, plus the fact that analysts found note-taking during sessions both disturbing and obstructive, the only alternative would be to use recording devices.[1] Adequate systems, first using wire recorders, were not adopted for this use until the late 1930's by Carl Rogers and his co-workers. The first verbatim record of a complete course of psychotherapy was the famous case of Herbert Bryan, published in 1942.[2] Thus, for over 40 years prior to this time outside commentators on the field had no access to published records of the actual transactions that took place in therapy and hence could never evaluate the influence and possible distortion introduced by the theoretical commitment of the analyst. The situation is almost unique; in perhaps no other field has so great a body of theory been built upon such a small public record of raw data, and it is interesting to note in this regard that the first verbatim records of complete psychotherapy courses have been published by Rogerian or client-centered psychotherapists, who are rather outside the orthodox Freudian tradition.

We are not implying that complete recording of cases would be the final answer. It is rightly objected that sound or even audio–visual recordings can never capture all of the complex and to varying degrees nonverbal communication that occurs within the therapeutic session (for a modern discussion and defense of this position, see Pickford, 1954, pp. 1–5). Nevertheless, it remains a fact that where cases are written up after each session or, worse, after the whole analysis is terminated, there arises the unanswerable problem of evaluating the analyst's influence.

Since the verbatim records published are so few, and for the most part limited to a single, rather heterodox branch of psychiatry, they do not

---

[1] The possibility of note-taking is discussed and rejected by Freud (1912). Freud makes the same point in the Lorenz case itself (1909b, p. 159).

[2] This case appears in Carl Rogers' *Counseling and Psycho-Therapy* (1942, pp. 261–437).

appear to be useful for our purposes.[3] The next alternative is to examine other case histories that are not recorded verbatim. These records make up the vast majority of published clinical material. Virtually without exception they are presented in the form of narrative accounts of an individual's history and therapeutic progress, together with psychoanalytic interpretations and explanations interspersed. In such records the dangers of distortion have been compounded. First, there is the analyst's influence upon the patient's own statements, which remains a completely unassessable factor since verbatim records are not available. Second, there is the selective nature of the analyst's recollections of the case and the possibility of his reconstructing earlier material in the light of later observations. Thus, the psychoanalyst's theoretical commitment can influence both the patient's utterances themselves and the manner in which they are organized, written up, and interpreted. Finally, almost all psychoanalytic case histories, in contrast to those standard for physical medicine, do not differentiate between exposition of the case—including chief complaint, present illness, and personal history—and diagnosis, etiology, pathogenesis, and prognosis. While there may be valid reasons, practical and theoretical, for this lumping together of exposition with explanation, nevertheless it remains a further source of distortion that must be recognized.[4]

If the possibility of distortion and bias is so serious, it might be thought that our insistence on using an actual case history is misguided. The problem, however, is that in the absence of usable verbatim records no real alternative exists. Short anecdotal snippets taken from many clinical observations would all be subject to the same errors. They are even more likely to be biased, selected as they are out of context to demonstrate particular points of theory. But more positive justification exists, for psychoanalysts have traditionally insisted that the core of their theories and their confirmation rest upon the long and intensive observation of individuals under analytic conditions. Moreover, case records have always been the basic material through which the theories have been taught to new practitioners.[5] In examining whole case histories, however distorted they might

---

[3] The only non-Rogerian case I know of is a nine-session record given by Lewis Wolberg in *The Technique of Psychotherapy* (1967). But in this case, for various reasons, no real attempt is made to explore the unconscious and infantile elements of the problem, and instead a moderately directive course of psychotherapy is given.

[4] Heinz Hartmann has discussed this problem from an analyst's point of view (1964, pp. 297–317).

[5] Corroboration for this point can be found in the training prospectuses of various psychoanalytic institutes; for instance, a major part of the program outlined in a recent prospectus of the British Psycho-analytical Society and Institute of Psychoanalysis (1963–1964) consists of supervised case work. Interestingly, the curriculum also contains an intensive study of Freud's case histories, including the one examined in this book.

be, we are examining the fundamental data providing the medium by which analysts communicate with and instruct each other.

The problem now becomes one of selection according to some set of criteria. It will be worthwhile to list each of the criteria we have applied and to comment upon them briefly.

1. The case should be of a Freudian or neo-Freudian variety. Whatever its ultimate theoretical or practical value may turn out to be, the Freudian viewpoint has undoubtedly been historically the most influential psychoanalytic school. If we are limited to the close examination of but a single case, then it behooves us to remain within a tradition that is perhaps the central one in the field. This restriction rules out from consideration material from Jungian, Adlerian, existentialist, and culturalist viewpoints. The use of such material would raise a host of new problems concerning parallels and divergencies between the various schools and their alternative explanations of the behavior in question. While such comparative studies would be extremely valuable, and essential if one were facing the issue of confirming or disproving the various theories, our present purposes can best be served by remaining within the classical Freudian tradition with its theory that seems both central to and representative of the whole of psychoanalysis. We do not mean in this way to impute any greater degree of truth to Freudian doctrine. Our decision is taken simply for the sake of keeping close to our major task, for our concern is with the logical features embodied in any adequate psychoanalytic explanation, not whether particular explanations are in fact true.

2. The case should involve a commonly seen disturbance, and one whose diagnosis is comparatively straightforward. Wherever a particular disorder is easily recognized and often encountered one can expect that it has enjoyed rather intensive study and that the explanation of that disorder might be rather more fully documented than in other, more rare or complex conditions where even the diagnosis seems problematical.

3. The case should have been written up for a generally didactic purpose, that of presenting a typical disorder and a typical analysis of that disorder. Frequently, the extended case histories, particularly more recent ones, are not didactic but aim at the introduction of new theoretical constructs or original interpretations. Hence the tone is often argumentative and the presentation slanted to highlight a particular feature or the utility of some new concept.

4. The case should be published and generally available. It would be pointless to deal with material that an analyst either did not feel enough conviction about to publish, or which for professional reasons could not be made public.

5. The case should be generally accepted by analysts as an adequate specimen of psychoanalytic technique and as a more or less accurate explanation of an individual's behavior along standard psychoanalytic principles. If possible, it should be one that has been so influential as to have engendered commentaries and elaborations by other analysts.

Given that a case in the Freudian tradition is desired, the choice of one of Freud's six published cases seems appropriate, for they are even today unusually esteemed. Ernest Jones says:

> . . . these six essays of Freud's far excel, both in presentation and in original content, anything any other analyst has attempted. They are in the first rank of the classics of psychoanalytical literature (1955, p. 255).

In accordance with the above criteria we have chosen the "Case of an Obsessional Neurosis," first published by Freud in 1909 (1909b). This is the "rat man" case, the only one of the six published cases which records a complete and successful analysis actually carried out by Freud.[6] Obsessional neuroses form one of the few clear-cut neurotic syndromes and one which has long been recognized as a discrete entity. The case was published by Freud to demonstrate his own theoretical grasp of the condition as he then understood it, but the subject of obsessional neurosis was repeatedly discussed by Freud and others so that it is possible to find a large number of important works on the subject.[7] Moreover, the original explanation, although certain to be modified today, is still in general outline accepted by most present-day psychoanalysts. Reuben Fine, a nonmedical analyst, has stated in a recent book on Freud's work:

> The theoretical explanation which Freud gives of the obsessional neurosis on the basis of this case, is still essentially true today, although it would be expanded in a number of directions in terms of present-day concepts (1962, p. 114).

The case, then, seems to fulfill our general criteria. In addition, it has certain specific features to recommend it. First, the presentation of the case material is more clear-cut than in any of the other cases. There is at least some partial attempt to separate actual data from explanation and interpretation. Second, one gets the impression that Freud had a theoretical grip

---

[6] The label "rat man" is standard in the psychoanalytic literature. It is derived from the obsessional ideas concerning rats that were a major presenting symptom of the patient. Nevertheless, since the publishing of Freud's case notes the patient has had the pseudonymous name of Paul Lorenz, and we shall hereafter use this name for the case, rather than the older label "rat man." Further historical and textual comments on the Lorenz case will be found in the appendix.

[7] See historical note on p. 76.

on this case in a way not always apparent in the others. Finally, we have the unique opportunity to make use of some of the actual clinical notes made by Freud, those recorded during the first four months of the 11-month analysis. Freud's habit was to burn all drafts and preliminary writings once finished material was published (1909b, Editor's Note, p. 253; Jones, 1955, p. 230), but for some unknown reason this portion of his actual clinical notes remained among his papers and was discovered after his death.[8] These notes, often written immediately after each session, are the sole extant record of Freud's actual analytic methods during the crucial years when psychoanalytic theory was developing. Moreover, they extend our knowledge of the patient's history and on both counts are therefore quite invaluable.

For all these reasons, then, the Lorenz case has been selected to serve as our basic text. We shall present a summary of the actual case history and follow this with a synopsis of Freud's explanation of the case. In so dividing the presentation between history on the one hand, and Freud's explanation on the other, we depart from Freud's own approach and that common to most psychoanalytic case presentations. Nevertheless, for our purposes such separation is essential, if we are to be able to examine the logical aspects of this psychoanalytic explanation.

In relating the patient's history we shall follow a roughly chronological order, but there will also be an attempt to group together, for ease of understanding, certain incidents (e.g., those connected with a certain individual or those illustrating a typical pattern of behavior) which occurred at different periods. It must be emphasized that we are presenting a summary of the original material. While we have attempted to include most of the important biographical facts, selection has been inevitable; a reading of this summary, then, ought not be taken as an adequate substitute for familiarity with the published records.

Two caveats discussed in the introduction must again be mentioned. We are not asking the questions: "Did these events, etc., really occur, or

---

[8] These notes appear only in the Standard Edition (S.E.), Volume 10, not the Collected Papers (C.P.), Volume III, which contains only the original published case. In the following discussions we shall always use the Standard Edition text, which is in a new translation. However, because this edition is less readily available, the following conversion table may be helpful to locate the identical passages in the Collected Papers edition:

S.E. page	Conversion factor	
155–173	138	To find the approximate page in the
174–192	137	C.P., add the proper conversion factor
193–211	136	to the S.E. page number; S.E. page
212–230	135	numbers over 249 refer to material
231–249	134	not found in the C.P.

was the patient mistaken, hallucinating, or deliberately lying?" "Did the patient say and believe the things he did 'of his own free will,' or was the material forced upon him through the influence of the psychoanalytic process itself?" The standard reply to the first question is that whether or not the events actually occurred is of secondary importance provided that for the patient they form a part of his "psychic reality."[9] From such a view follows the analyst's typical practice of not attempting any outside confirmation of the facts in a patient's history.[10]

As to the second possible source of distortion, the analyst's power of suggestion, we have Freud's own words written two years before his death:

> The danger of our leading a patient astray by suggestion, by persuading him to accept things which we ourselves believe but which he ought not to, has certainly been enormously exaggerated. An analyst would have had to behave very incorrectly before such a misfortune could overtake him; above all, he would have to blame himself with not allowing his patients to have their say. I can assert without boasting that such an abuse of 'suggestion' has never occurred in my practice (1937, p. 262).[11]

That these are by no means the final words on such issues is obvious. Indeed a different study could be written making use especially of the clinical notes and documenting the very real problems of distortion in the case. Nevertheless, in *this* study we are playing the analyst's game and accepting all material elicited as being part of the patient's true history. The only other possible distortion (hopefully negligible compared to the imponderables above) is that resulting from our own rearranging of data.

Finally, a word concerning the changes occurring in Freud's theories

---

[9] A similar argument is used for dreams: The distortions arising in recounting dreams, whether or not consciously intended, are quite as significant as the dream itself.

[10] In the present case we have a partial exception in that Freud had at least some outside connection with the patient's family. We know from the unpublished notes that Freud's brother Alexander (with whom Freud was quite close, as can be gathered from Jones' biography) was known to both the patient's sister Julie and his brother-in-law (1909b, p. 285). We also have two hints that Freud knew the patient's father in the following statements: "By *all* accounts our patient's father was a most excellent man. *In point of fact* [as opposed to what the patient sometimes implied] he was a very genuine, downright, kindly man, with a sense of humor . . ." (1909b, pp. 200, 294). Italics and brackets mine. There is, however, no evidence that Freud actually attempted to verify his patient's story through any interrogation of the family.

[11] It is intriguing that over 40 years before Freud twice answered the same challenge, each time in very similar language (see Freud, 1893, Part IV, p. 295; 1896c, pp. 204–205). In 1896, however, the claim is that "I have never yet succeeded in forcing on a patient a scene I was expecting to find. . . ." By 1937, in the above quotation, the significant difference is that Freud now admits that such persuasive conversion could occur, even though he has never been guilty of doing it.

about obsessional neuroses through the course of his career. We have said that one criterion of choosing our case has been the existence of commentaries and elaborations upon it in the psychoanalytic literature. Likewise, we pointed out that Freud repeatedly discussed obsessional illnesses and that his ideas underwent changes and development.[12] This material has been of great importance to us in our own understanding of this particular case and Freudian doctrines in general. Nevertheless, as with the alternative schools of thought, the decision has been taken *not* to present a detailed analysis of the changing theoretical explanations of obsessional neuroses found in Freud. Instead, following our exposition we have given a sketch of Freud's theoretical views at the time the case was presented.

We are not interested in the true explanation of obsessional disturbances, nor even in what would have been Freud's final explanation of these illnesses. Our question is: What does a Freudian explanation of an individual's behavior look like "through logical spectacles?" Whether the original explanation or later emendations are closer to the truth, it seems safe to assume that the logical features remain roughly similar, that the original explanation has the same logical characteristics at least, as later ones, even if it is not as accurate.

B. THE CASE HISTORY OF PAUL LORENZ

1. Family and Parental History

The patient came from a fairly wealthy but newly established family. The family was Jewish in origin, but the father was not practicing the faith and did not consider the family any longer to be Jewish. Both the mother and father were of relatively humble backgrounds, although the mother was reared by a wealthy family of industry, the Rubenskys, with whom she was distantly connected. The father had been a noncommissioned soldier before his marriage and one incident from that period was

---

[12] Freud's major writings on this subject (and some works of other investigators) are listed in the bibliography. Chronologically, the modifications are best seen in: "The Neuro-Psychoses of Defense" (1894a); "Obsessions and Phobias" (1894b); "Character and Anal Erotism" (1908b); "Notes upon a Case of Obsessional Neurosis" (the case now under study, 1909b); "The Disposition to Obsessional Neurosis" (1913); and *Inhibitions, Symptoms and Anxiety* (1925). In this last work Freud wrote:

> Obsessional neurosis is unquestionably the most interesting and repaying subject of analytic research. But as a problem it has not yet been mastered. It must be confessed that, if we endeavor to penetrate more deeply into its nature, we still have to rely upon doubtful assumptions and unconfirmed suppositions (p. 27).

important to the patient. Once the father had been in control of some official funds and had lost it gambling on cards. He would have been in a serious position had a friend not loaned him money to cover the debt. After leaving the army he had tried to trace the man to repay the debt, but never found him. The recollection of this lapse of his father is very painful to the patient.[13]

Prior to meeting the mother, the father had made advances to a pretty but penniless girl of humble origin, the daughter of a butcher. At the time of his marriage he was taken into the Rubensky family business and had thus gained a comfortable status and occupation. The patient's mother occasionally teased the father by suggesting that he had once been the suitor of a butcher's daughter. To the patient, who knew this history, it had always seemed an intolerable idea that his father might have abandoned his love in order to secure his future position.

The marriage was an extremely happy one. The father was a simple, genuine man with a good sense of humor. He had, however, a violent temper and sometimes did not know when to stop in meting out punishment to his children. The patient emphasized that he and his father had lived together as the best and most intimate of friends, a closer friendship than the son had ever known with other male friends. With the exception of a few subjects (never specifically mentioned by the patient) "which fathers and sons usually hold aloof from one another," there had been complete sharing of feelings.

2. Birth and Early Childhood

The patient, Paul Lorenz, was born in 1878, the first boy of a family including at the time two older sisters. Eighteen months later a younger brother was born, who was destined to be a great and continuing rival for the patient. Very early in the analysis several events were described concerning this jealousy. Around age eight there occurred an important incident. He had shot his brother with a toy gun (a "criminal act," he now called it) by tricking him into looking down the barrel.

> He was hit on the forehead and not hurt; but I had meant to hurt him very much indeed. Afterwards I was quite beside myself, and threw myself on the ground and asked myself how ever I could have done such a thing. But I *did* do it. . . . [We] used to fight a lot. . . . We were very fond of each other at the same time, and were inseparable; but I was plainly filled with jealousy, as he was the stronger and better-looking of the two and consequently the favourite (Freud, 1909b, pp. 184–185).

---

[13] Throughout this presentation in statements concerning the patient we shall often use past tense for "past for Freud" and present tense for "present for Freud," that is, at the time of the analysis.

This hostility lasted into adulthood. During a certain period Lorenz became intensely jealous of what he considered were his brother's advances toward his lady friend Gisela; eventually he challenged him, in all seriousness, to a wrestling match in front of Gisela and was in fact defeated by the brother, who had remained the stronger and more athletic of the two. On a later occasion Lorenz had seriously considered murdering a girl friend of his brother whom he believed would have been an unwise marriage choice. During the analysis Lorenz claimed to be very fond of his brother at that particular time, although he also admitted that he, the brother, was the least worthy individual of all the children.

When the patient was about three years old, a younger sister was born, Julie, with whom he was to be very close. Even after his father's death when he was 21 years old, the patient and his sister were still sleeping in the same room. He would uncover her bedclothes some mornings to look at her while she slept and even claimed to have tried to assault her once.

When he was about the age of four, an elder sister, Katherine, who was eight years old, died. This event seemed to have been important to the patient, who had several memories of asking "Where is Katherine?" and of his father and mother weeping. Moreover, at the same time another very important incident occurred.

> When he was very small . . . he had done something naughty, for which his father had given him a beating. The little boy had flown into a terrible rage and had hurled abuse at his father even while he was under his blows. But as he knew no bad language, he had called him all the names of common objects that he could think of, and had screamed: 'You lamp! You towel! You plate!' and so on. His father, shaken by such an outburst of elemental fury, had stopped beating him, and had declared: 'The child will be either a great man or a great criminal!' . . .
>
> The patient subsequently questioned his mother again. She confirmed the story, adding that at the time he had been between three and four years old and that he had been given the puishment because he had *bitten* some one. She could remember no further details, except for a very uncertain idea that the person the little boy had hurt might have been his nurse. In her account there was no suggestion of his misdeed having been of a sexual nature (Freud, 1909b, pp. 205–206).

Early in the analysis, even during the first session, the patient had begun to describe his sexual development; he had heard of Freud's theories before coming to him and knew of the emphasis on sexual matters, although he had not seriously studied any of Freud's writings. His very earliest memories (before age six, from which time he had continuous memories) usually were of sexual incidents. Thus at age four or five he had begged his nurse to let him crawl under her skirt. She consented to this as long as he would not tell anyone. He fingered her genitals; "after this I was left with a burning and tormenting curiosity to see the female body." He also remembered "intense excitement" at the public baths waiting for the governess to undress. He used to wait eagerly each night to observe secretly another maid squeezing sores she had on her buttocks. He used to get into his nurse's bed and touch her. Although she had strong sexual desires, she apparently never molested her charge. The patient, however, did not sleep with his nurses but usually with his parents (presumably in the same room, not bed, although this is not made clear). He remembered an incident at age five or six when he was in bed between his father and mother and wet the bed. His father beat him and threw him out. Already at age six the patient had erections and remembered going to his mother to complain of them.

> 'I know too that in doing so I had some misgivings to get over, for I had a feeling that there was some connection between this subject [the erections] and my ideas and inquisitiveness [about sex], and at that time I used to have a morbid idea *that my parents knew my thoughts; I explained this to myself by supposing that I had spoken them out loud without having heard myself do it.* I look on this as the beginning of my illness. There were certain people, girls, who pleased me very much, and I had a very strong wish *to see them naked.* But in wishing this I had *an uncanny feeling, as though something must happen if I thought such things, and as though I must do all sorts of things to prevent it.'*
>
> (In reply to a question he gave an example of these fears: 'For instance, *that my father might die.'*) 'Thoughts about my father's death occupied my mind from a very early age and for a long period of time, and greatly depressed me' (Freud, 1909b, p. 162).[14]

At age eight the patient began school and made the acquaintance of his girl cousin Gisela, who became the "lady," the woman whom the patient courted in later life. At age 13, he purposely exhibited himself to a maid and there were several other voyeuristic and exhibitionistic incidents, even in recent years.

3. Some Behavioral Characteristics of Early Childhood

Several important behavioral characteristics marked the patient's early life. The patient was a rather dirty child before puberty and called himself a regular "little pig." Then at puberty he became very conscious of dirt and was overcleanly. Since the beginnings of his severe neurotic illness, he had been fanatical about cleanliness, although he never seemed to develop the typical "hand-washing" rituals, a common obsessional symptom. During the illness there were at least two occasions when the patient felt the command never to wash again. But this prohibition was never acted upon.

---

[14] Italics and parentheses Freud's.

Up to the age of 14 the patient was intensely religious, but since puberty he gradually grew away from religion until at the time of analysis he was a freethinker. However, since the onset of illness religious compulsions of various sorts have plagued him, which will be described below.

From early years the patient was very conscientious about money. He dated this trait from the time when his father had egged him on to steal a few coins from his mother's purse. He had afterward felt very guilty about this. Associated with this incident was the memory of having once cheated in a card game when he was grown up. The patient had never taken over his inheritance but had left it with his mother from whom he still drew a small allowance at the time of analysis. He finds it very difficult to loan even his best friend money. Associated with this exaggerated miserliness was the fear of losing other valuables and an inability to part with or mislay any object that had belonged to either his father or Gisela.

Finally, the patient was very cowardly and terrified of physical punishment or beatings. He used to creep away whenever one of the other children was being beaten and hide in terror. He once said he was very pleased that his father had never had to beat him, as far as he could remember, although on other occasions he did confess to memories of punishments given him.

4. Adolescent Sexual Development

At age 11 his male cousin, whom he now detests, initiated him into the secrets of sex. He also told the patient that all women were whores, including the patient's mother and sister. The patient countered with the question: "Do you think the same of your mother?" At age 12 the patient developed a strong love for a little girl, the sister of a friend. It had not been a sensual desire; there was no wish to see her naked since she was too small. However, the patient's attentions were not reciprocated, and he at one point conceived the idea that she would be kind to him if only some misfortune, such as his father's death, were to occur to him. However, he at once rejected the idea vigorously.

At age 14 there were some homosexual incidents with a neighbor boy, but, as with several of the earlier events concerning women, these consisted solely of mutual exhibition—looking instead of doing. At the same age there was a period during which an older boy of 19 had been a close friend and had praised the patient and raised his self-esteem immensely. The boy had subsequently become the patient's tutor, and then his behavior toward the patient altered completely; he treated him now as an idiot. It turned out that the older boy had simply used the patient to gain admission to the household in order to court the patient's older sister. This realization had been the first great blow of his life. At the time of analysis the patient had another very close male friend who was a source of support and advice, especially concerning his compulsions. It was this friend who had eventually persuaded the patient to seek medical aid.

In spite of the varied sexual experiences and frequent erections of childhood, the patient was not sexually active after puberty, and he, himself, wondered at the reason for this. There was only very occasional masturbation during his whole adolescence, almost exclusively during the years 16 and 17. The first time he masturbated he had the fear that his cousin and love, Gisela, would be harmed because of it. After a few times the patient quit because of feelings of shame and guilt. At age 21, soon after the death of his father, the patient resumed masturbation. In the next few years there were various oaths taken and broken to give up the practice, and these will be elaborated on below.

5. Early Adulthood and the Death of his Father

By the time the patient was 20 years old he was already in love with his cousin Gisela, although there were various other flirtations during the next 10 years, that is, up to the time the patient consulted Freud in October, 1907, when he was 29 years old. Financial obstacles, however, seemed to make a serious proposal impossible. The thought once occurred to him that his father's death might make him rich enough to marry her. This idea appeared so shameful, however, that he countered it by immediately wishing his father would leave him nothing at all instead.

At the fourth session the patient began: "I have decided to tell you something which I consider most important and which has tormented me from the very first (Freud, 1909b, p. 174). He then proceeded to describe his father's death (in 1899 when the patient was 21 years old) and the events surrounding it. The father had been ill for a long time; on the day before his death, the patient had thought: "I may be going to lose what I love most." But then immediately came the contradiction: "No, there is someone else [Gisela] whose loss would be even more painful to you." This idea surprised him very much. The father on the following day had a crisis, and afterward the patient, exhausted, had lain down for a short nap. During the interval the father died. The patient reproached himself for not being present at the death, all the more so because the nurse said that he had asked for Paul. For nearly two years, however, the patient never fully accepted the death. When he would hear a joke, he would say: "I must tell Father that." He imagined any knocks at the door to be his father, and had fantasies of seeing him whenever he walked into a room.

Several months after the death of his father the patient once again

began to masturbate. A year or so later, however, he again made an oath
to stop masturbating: "I swear on my blessed soul to give it up." He also
proposed to Gisela for the first time after his father's death but was
rejected. During the same period Gisela had a gynecological operation.
The patient always believed she could, because of this operation, have no
children. Right up to the time of analysis some seven years later this belief
persisted and made him hesitant about marriage. Yet ostensibly he never
knew the name of the doctor nor actually found out if the operation did
indeed have this consequence.[15]

Ideas of suicide had occurred to the patient at various times before and
during this period. The patient remembered childhood fantasies of suicide,
when, for instance, he brought home a bad school report. At one point,
however, aged 18, he took an oath never to commit suicide, not even if
disappointed in love. He admitted that the suicide impulse was a serious
one even at the time of analysis, but that it was resisted for two reasons:
First, the idea that his mother would find his bloody remains; second, that
his sister had once said that if he died, she would kill herself.

One suicidal incident occurred about two years after his father's death
and was very important to the patient. He had been studying for his law
examinations and Gisela had to be away nursing her sick grandmother.
Her absence was a great source of disturbance to his studies. One day the
thought occurred: "What if you were commanded to cut your throat with
a razor?" He was immediately aware that such a command had in fact
been given and rushed to fetch a razor. Then the second thought occurred:
"No, it's not so simple as that. You must first go and kill the old woman
[Gisela's grandmother]." Upon thinking this, he fell to the ground in horror.

Finally Gisela's grandmother died, and the patient wanted to go to
join Gisela. But his mother said: "On my soul, you shall not go." The
similarity of this oath to his own earlier prohibition of masturbation,
quoted above, struck the patient. He told himself not to be more cowardly
on his own account than on other people's (i.e., not to look out for his
own soul more than his mother's) and that if he persisted in his intention
to join Gisela he ought also to take up masturbation again. Subsequently,
the visit did not occur, but masturbation was resumed on certain occasions.
He would masturbate only in rather peculiar circumstances, whenever he

---

[15] Neither the published account nor the notes settle this issue completely. On
p. 216 Freud relates that the patient claims Gisela is condemned to childlessness.
On p. 232 he states that "ostensibly" the patient did not in fact know if one or both
ovaries were removed. However, since we know (p. 317) that the patient was with
Gisela at the nursing home at the time and met the doctor, it seems probable that
he did know the truth (that Gisela would be childless), and that the "ostensible"
ignorance was simply a convenient way to preserve a hope for marriage and children.

experienced very fine moments or after reading certain passages in books. He gave two such instances: Once on a lovely afternoon in the middle of Vienna he heard a horseman blowing his horn, until the man was stopped by a police officer for disturbing the peace. The patient then masturbated. A second occurrence followed his reading in Goethe of how in a burst of tenderness Goethe had freed himself from the effects of a curse which a previous mistress had pronounced on whoever should next kiss his lips. He had suffered this curse to hold him back, but now he broke through his fears and kissed his new love joyfully again and again. At this point in his reading the patient masturbated.

6. Beginning of Continuous Symptoms of Illness

About two years after his father's death the patient lost an aunt. On paying a condolence visit to his uncle, the patient misinterpreted a remark of the bereaved widower as an aspersion cast upon the patient's own dead father's character. In reacting to this the patient for the first time seemed fully to accept his father's death. At the same time the recollection of his neglect and disobedience of the dead father began to torment him— including reproaches for his not being present at the final moment of death, and his failure to work hard enough at school in defiance of his father's wishes.

The patient dates the real beginning of his obsessional neurosis from this time, late in 1902, when there emerged severe feelings of guilt and of acting criminally toward the dead father. The immediate result was a serious incapacity to work. The only thing that kept him going was the consolations of his close friend, who tried to point out that the patient's self-reproaches were grossly exaggerated and unjustified.

In February, 1903, an uncle died about whom the patient felt indifferent. In the same period the patient's mother told him that she had discussed his future with her rich relations, the Rubenskys. One of her cousins had said that the patient might marry one of his daughters and a business opening would then be made for him. This family plan, with its parallel to his dead father's marriage, stirred up in the patient a conflict as to whether he should remain faithful to Gisela, who was poor, or whether he should follow in his father's footsteps and marry the rich girl chosen by the family. It also emerged that shortly before his death the patient's father, too, had warned him against pursuing Gisela, that it was imprudent and that the patient would only make a fool of himself.

At this time, spring of 1903, there was an exacerbation of the obsessional illness. There was a fresh onset of reproaches for having slept through his father's death, extreme despair, ideas of suicide, and horror at the thought of his own possible death. The patient, however, still continued to work hard for his examinations which he felt compelled to take in July, that being the earliest time possible. He himself understood this compulsion as being "deferred industriousness," arising out of guilt for not studying harder while his father was alive. He worked out a daily timetable for study and would quit by midnight. At this time each night he would take off all his clothes and examine his penis in the mirror, for which he felt some concern that it was too small. At the same time he had the illusion of his father knocking at his flat door and would go to open it. He felt that if the door were not open his father would not feel wanted and would go away.

At this time there also occurred a revival of religious piety and the extension of his obsessional thoughts to include the next world. All his fears that something would happen to Gisela or other people if he did various things were now extended to the next life. Thus, he eventually ended the ritual practice of undressing and examining himself described above by the device of a self-imposed threat that if he continued, something terrible would befall his father in the next world. One of the oldest and favorite obsessions was: If I marry Gisela some misfortune will befall my father in the next world. At the time of analysis, some four years after the onset of severe disturbances and about eight years after the death of his father, these fears were still vivid, and, indeed, were the patient's chief complaint. At an intellectual level he claimed to recognize the irrationality of his beliefs but was powerless to change.

The compulsive religious period lasted in varying degrees until the time of analysis. The patient took to making up prayers to protect those people or prevent those events about which he had compulsive fears. Gradually these prayers took up longer and longer time, eventually lasting one and a half hours a day. The reason was that something evil always seemed to insert itself into the prayers. Thus, "May God protect him" became "May God *not* protect him" when it was uttered. At one point he even considered uttering curses instead, believing that in that case the opposite words would be sure to creep in. Eighteen months before the beginning of analysis the patient devised a new method of constructing prayers. He took the first letters of various phrases or parts of prayers and joined them to form a single word, adding "Amen" on to it. The patient could say this word so fast that nothing could slip into it. One formula used was *"Glejsamen."* There was also a ritual defensive measure employed whenever an evil thought occurred: a rapidly pronounced "but" accompanied by a gesture of repudiation, and the phrase, "Whatever are you thinking of?"

During the summer of 1903 the patient was in the company of Gisela and her male cousin, of whom the patient was very jealous. Prior to leaving on the vacation Gisela had said something to the patient which he misconstrued as a desire on her part to embarrass and deride him in front of her cousin. Only after the vacation had begun was this misunderstanding cleared up; Gisela had, on the contrary, by counseling discretion and nonchalance, wished to save him from being laughed at, not to discourage him. During the holiday a whole series of obsessional ideas and activities emerged. Once, out in a boat with Gisela, the patient became obsessed with protecting her from unknown dangers; the command formed in his mind that he must do anything to insure that nothing happen to her. Another obsession was having to count to 40 or 50 between lightning bolts and the subsequent thunder. Still another was a compulsion to diet, which the patient pursued for a time in an almost suicidal manner. He also felt a compulsion to talk and spoke constantly at certain periods, passing from subject to subject and uttering much nonsense. There was also an obsession with understanding. He forced himself to ponder and analyze the precise meaning of whatever was said, as though he would otherwise be missing some priceless treasure. He would keep asking his friends to repeat what was spoken. Yet after being repeated he could not help thinking it had sounded different the first time, and so he would remain dissatisfied.

The patient's marriage proposal was rejected a second time on this vacation, although the couple continued to see each other. His fury against Gisela for this had been tremendous though unspoken, and he remembered suddenly thinking: "She is a whore," which thought made him greatly ashamed. On the day of her departure the patient kicked his foot against a stone lying in the road and felt obliged to put it out of the way, because the idea struck him that Gisela's carriage would come along the road in a few hours and might be overturned by this stone. But a few minutes later he felt compelled to go back and replace the stone in its original position in the middle of the road, because, he explained, his original action had been absurd. He admitted to other vindictive thoughts against her during the ensuing years. There were occasional impulses to do her mischief, mostly when he was away from her. He remembered various "fantasies of revenge" about her; e.g., to marry some beautiful woman and then take her to visit Gisela, to flout his new wife in front of her. Once, when Gisela was lying seriously ill in bed, he was deeply concerned for her, and the wish crossed his mind that she might lie like that forever. He explained himself by maintaining that he had only wished her to be permanently ill so that he might be relieved of his intolerable fear that she would have a repeated succession of attacks.

In 1904, at age 26, the patient had intercourse for the first time.

During this episode the thought occurred: "This is a glorious feeling! One might do anything for this—murder one's father, for instance!" Exactly the same idea was expressed on the occasion of another episode of intercourse. In the next three years, up to the start of analysis, the patient had sexual relations only infrequently. There was a disgust for prostitutes. Once, when he was with one, he made it a condition that she take off her clothes. When she demanded 50% extra for this he paid her and left, revolted by it all. The patient always tried to make a sharp distinction between relations which were only sexual and everything called love. In this regard he felt that he loved Gisela but did not have really strong sensual desires for her such as he had constantly felt for other girls in his childhood. At one point there occurred the idea: supposing Gisela said, "You must have no sexual pleasure till you have married me;" would he accept such a condition? A voice inside him said "Yes." Again at other times a prohibition of intercourse occurred; e.g., "If you indulge in coitus, something will happen to your little niece."

7. Some Behavioral Characteristics of Adult Life

In the published case Freud groups certain additional biographical facts in such a way as to illustrate some general habits of thought or attitudes. First, the patient was superstitious, and even though he understood that such beliefs were dependent on and related to his obsessional thoughts, at times he gave way to them completely. He believed in premonitions and in prophetic dreams. He also felt that he was constantly meeting people about whom, for some inexplicable reason, he had just been thinking; or he would receive a letter from someone whose name had suddenly come to mind after being forgotten for many years. On the other hand, the patient was honest enough to admit that on other occasions his forebodings had come to nothing. Moreover, he admitted that the great majority of his premonitions concerned trivialities, while all the really important events of his life, such as the death of his father, had not been foreseen. But such considerations had no effect on his convictions.

A second typical trait was the need for doubt and the desire to create uncertainties. For instance, the patient was extremely concerned over the possibility that Gisela could have no children; yet, although her operation was carried out several years before the analysis, he claimed that he had never spoken to her doctor to find out if his fear of her being unable to have children was justified. The patient likewise turned his mind to just those sorts of subjects upon which everyone is uncertain: Is there a life after death? Is my memory correct, Did I hear what was spoken to me?

Connected with this need for doubt was an inability to make decisions.

The patient developed the customary technique, whenever faced with a decision for which the alternatives had apparently equally good arguments, of "letting God decide." That is, he would forget the arguments and allow chance, or a casual outsider's suggestion, to settle the issue. For instance, when making a railroad journey for which two trains were available, the patient waited until a porter asked him whether he was taking the ten o'clock one, to which he answered "Yes," the decision being thereby settled by the hand of God. The patient would often find himself paralyzed between a compulsion and a prohibition to action, or else he would discover that his actions were never successful and had to be constantly repeated, as with his prayers. Particularly in his affair with Gisela, the patient showed this deep ambivalence and wavering.

The patient also had a rather peculiar attitude toward death. He showed the deepest sympathy whenever people died and always attended funerals, so much so that among his family he earned the nickname "carrion crow." In his imagination, too, he was constantly doing away with people in order to be able to show his sympathy to the relatives.

As another characteristic, Freud points out the patient's long-lasting fantasy of the omnipotence of his thoughts or wishes, that is, the belief that his wishes would come true. He believed, for example, that his hostile thoughts had been responsible for the deaths of two people whose paths had chanced to cross his. To gain support for both his belief in premonitions and this fantasy of thought omnipotence the patient occupied himself a great deal of the time with the inexplicable coincidences familiar to everyday life.

Finally, Lorenz displayed what he himself regarded as a "conscientiousness" and "carefulness with money" (Freud, 1909b, p. 266). This characteristic was one of several points discussed by Freud and his colleagues when he presented material from the analysis, which had just begun, at some meetings of the "Wednesday Psychological Society," which became in 1908 the Vienna Psycho-Analytical Society (Federn, 1948, pp. 14–20).[16] Lorenz could not easily bring himself to loan money, not even to his best friend. Then, too, there was the peculiar circumstance concerning his allowance. Although the patient had inherited a sum from his father, he had never taken it up but continued to receive all his spending money from a modest allowance given him by his mother. This trait, like the others mentioned, posed a real problem for Freud, for it did not seem to fit in with the patient's education and the financially secure family position. In Chapter 7 we shall examine Freud's explanation of this trait in detail.

---

[16] These notes are also found in Nunberg and Federn (1962).

8. The Events Leading to the Patient's Seeking Freud's Help

In the summer of 1907 the patient was out on army maneuvers, and at this time the rat obsession developed which eventuated in his seeking Freud's help in October, 1907, and which gave the original label to this case. These ideas were extraordinarily complex, and the account of this period emerged clearly only after many analytic sessions and much resistance. In this presentation we shall give only the essential details as they were finally understood.

It all began with the patient's losing his glasses and wiring back to Vienna for a new pair. That same day a "cruel captain" (the patient's own phrase) in the officer's mess defended corporal punishment and argued this issue with the patient. The captain went on to describe a specially horrible punishment used in the East. A criminal was tied up, and a pot of rats was turned upside down on his buttocks so that the rats could bore their way into the criminal's anus. At the moment of hearing the torture described the patient had the thought that this punishment was being carried out on two people who were very dear to him—Gisela and his father (the latter was dead some eight years by this time). He also had the illusion of the ground heaving in front of him as though there were a rat under it.

A day or two after this, another officer mentioned to the patient that a small package had arrived for him at the post office and that the delivery charges had been paid by a young lady working there, who had advanced the money on trust that the unknown addressee (the patient) would reimburse her. This fact was seemingly forgotten by the patient when he met still later that day the captain who had described the rat torture a day or so before. This captain, who had happened to have gone by the post office, delivered the package containing the glasses to the patient. But the captain, not knowing that the girl attendant had paid the fees, mistakenly assumed that the army officer regularly in charge there had done so. Accordingly, he told the patient that he must repay the postage to Lt. A. (Here a second error is made by the captain. The officer who had been in charge at the post office, Lt. A., had recently been replaced by Lt. B., but this change was not known by the captain.) The patient, seemingly forgetting the actual truth of the matter as had been related earlier to him, accepted the captain's word. But he immediately formed the prohibition: "You must not repay Lt. A. the money, or the rat punishment will come true for Father and Gisela." Then, in the familiar manner, the opposite command occurred: "You must pay back Lt. A."

The next two days, the last of the maneuvers, were spent agonizing over this situation. First, the patient tried to get someone else to pay the money, but this, he decided, would not satisfy the oath, since it would not be he himself who was repaying Lt. A. but some intermediary. Finally, the patient met Lt. A. who refused the money saying that he was no longer in charge at the post office and that it must have been Lt. B. who had paid the fee. In order to satisfy his oath the patient devised a new scheme: Lt. A. would give the proper amount to Lt. B. and then he, the patient, would repay Lt. A.

During the analysis an important new fact came out. At the inn of the town Z, where the post office was, a pretty barmaid had been decidedly encouraging to the patient, so much so that he had thought of returning after the maneuvers were over to try his luck with her. With the maneuvers ending, the patient was tormented by the decision: whether to return directly to Vienna, or to go to the town Z, near which Lt. A. lived, and to get Lt. A. to carry out the patient's scheme. If he disregarded his vow, he argued, he was simply being cowardly, trying to save himself from looking foolish in front of Lt. A. by asking Lt. A. to participate in the plan. On the other hand, if he fulfilled the vow, he was likewise being cowardly by giving in to one of his obsessional oaths. At the station the patient "let God decide" and ended up going back to Vienna. All along the trip, however, the patient thought that he might still get out at the next stop, return to Z, and carry out his plan. Finally he arrived at Vienna and went to visit his friend, in whom he confided the whole story. The friend was amazed that the patient could still be in doubt as to whether he was suffering from an illness. The next morning, knowing that the money must be owed to the postal authorities themselves, the friend went with the patient and sent off the correct amount. The friend also persuaded him to seek medical help. By chance, one of Freud's books happened to fall into the patient's hands, and this directed his choice of doctor.

9. The Patient's Analysis

The entire analysis lasted approximately 11 months, with an unknown number of sessions, certainly averaging several a week and being often daily in the early months. As to the outcome, Freud speaks of "the therapeutic success of the treatment," which led "to the complete restoration of the patient's personality, and to the removal of his inhibitions" (1909b, pp. 155 and 207). There was in addition at least some sort of long-term follow-up, as can be seen from the note Freud added in 1923:

> The patient's mental health was restored to him by the analysis which I have reported upon in these pages. Like so many other young men of value and promise, he perished in the Great War (1909b, p. 249).

During the analysis important additional events occurred that must be taken into account when we turn to examine Freud's psychoanalytic explanation of the case. One striking development was the rapid proliferation of the "rat" idea and imagery into a major factor in the patient's obsessional thinking. At various times he would wish the rats (i.e., the rat punishment) on different people, including Gisela, his older sister, and others. On the other hand, his old protective prayer formula *"Glejsamen"* became *"Glejsamen* without rats." But what were most intriguing were the connections that grew up between the rat idea and certain other thoughts. These appeared sporadically at different times; there was no gradual shift from one idea to the next, but only alternating appearances of first one, then another. One important meaning for rats came to be "money." Gradually, a whole rat currency developed. For instance, when speaking of Freud's fees, the patient would say: "So many florins, so many rats."

A second idea was that rats were the carriers of disease, particularly syphilis. There was a fear that either his or Gisela's father may have contracted the disease and passed it on to them. A very important associated memory emerged of a "terrifying" experience occurring before his illness. Once, when visiting his father's grave, he had seen a beast, which he had taken to be a rat, gliding along the top of the grave. The patient assumed that it had actually come out of his father's grave, and had just had a meal off the corpse.

The patient's family doctor took ill during the analysis, and this caused a great deal of concern. The doctor physically resembled the patient's dead father; moreover, the two had been intimate friends and the doctor had the same mortal illness. The patient seemed to go through the same feelings as when his father had died. His regrets were, however, mixed with fantasies of revenge, i.e., that the doctor be subjected to the rat punishment. The belief persisted that he had not done all he should have for the father, had not insisted strongly enough on the father's retiring. This doctor, shortly before the father's death, had spoken of turning the case, which he saw to be hopeless, over to someone else, since it affected him too deeply because of his friendship with the family. The patient had thought at the time: "The rats are leaving the sinking ship." He had the notion during the doctor's present illness that it was his (the patient's) wish which was killing him—another example of the patient's belief in the omnipotence of his thoughts. Finally the doctor died. The patient found himself smiling in his typical, peculiar way at the funeral (the "carrion crow"), and he said "So many kreuzers, so many rats" when he dropped money on the collection plate there.

During the analysis there were also various developments in the patient's sex life. One incident concerned an engaged girl who made some sort of approach to the patient. He responded by kissing her, and this immediately aroused in him the idea that the rat torture was going to happen to Gisela, in this world and the next. The patient during this period also went back to masturbation, but there seemed to be no compulsive fears any longer connected with this. After a few months of analysis a new love affair was begun with a dressmaker. This affair tended to displace and compete with the long-standing love for Gisela. In the beginning at least there were successful and frequent sex relations. The patient would think: "For every copulation, a rat for my cousin [Gisela]." The later history of this affair is not recorded.

At times the patient's resistance to the analytic process grew very strong, and old symptoms reappeared. Several months after the analysis began, when his resistance was at a height, the patient once more felt the temptation to return to Z, look up Lt. A., and go through the ritual of paying back the money. Freud comments:

> Whenever in the course of the treatment he was faced by the necessity of taking some step which would bring him nearer the successful end of his courtship [of Gisela], his resistance usually began by taking the form of a conviction that after all he did not very much care for her—though this resistance, it is true, used soon to break down (1909b, p. 194).

Finally, a number of interesting ideas and events also occurred that we can group under the label of "transference phenomena." Our use of this term is the standard one, referring to those events which are centered upon some aspect of the patient's relationship to the analyst, Freud, as opposed to being events occurring in his outside life and simply recounted to the analyst during the therapeutic session.[17] A typical feature of such phenomena is that the attitudes and habits of behavior characteristically exhibited by the patient in his outside life or to significant figures in his past tend to be recreated, or repeated, within the transference situation.

During a certain period the patient became extremely hostile to Freud and heaped vile abuse upon him. At this time the patient could not remain lying on the couch but would stalk around the room. He admitted that he was afraid Freud would beat or even murder him. In this connection he remembered his father's passionate temper and that the dead man sometimes had not known when to stop in his punishments. These feelings were expressed in dreams, fantasies, and waking thoughts and associations. At the same time there was a great deal of guilt over having such feelings, and the patient showed difficulty in expressing them. The patient also admitted that his sister Julie had suggested that Freud's brother Alex would make the best match for Gisela and that this was a further source of anger. There was an interesting dream that Freud's mother had died:

---

[17] Transference is discussed briefly in the next section of this chapter.

[The patient] was anxious to offer me his condolences, but was afraid that in doing so he might break into *an impertinent laugh,* as he had repeatedly done on similar occasions in the past. He preferred, therefore, to leave a card on me with 'p.c.' [*pour condoler*] written on it; but as he was writing them the letters turned into 'p.f.' [*pour feliciter*] (1909b, p. 193).

Later in the analysis various fantasies developed concerning Freud's daughter. These began after the patient met a young woman on the stairs to Freud's flat and took her to be Freud's daughter. The patient came to believe that Freud was so kind to him only because he wanted the patient for a son-in-law; in his mind he exaggerated the wealth and position of Freud's family to make a greater contrast with the station of Gisela. There were fantasies of sexual relations with Freud's daughter, and of her performing *fellatio* on him. At the same time there were guilt feelings connected with the fantasy of being unfaithful to Gisela. This led to hostility against both Freud (for luring him away from Gisela) and Freud's daughter. Thus, there was one fantasy of Freud's wife licking the patient's anus. A significant dream image was of Freud's daughter standing with two patches of dung for eyes.

This completes our exposition of the case history of Paul Lorenz. In order to understand the explanation Freud put forth about this patient, we must have at least some familiarity with his theories as they were formulated during this period. In the next section, therefore, we present a sketch of Freud's views around the time of the Lorenz analysis.

C. An Outline of Freud's Theories, 1905–1909

In presenting a brief sketch of certain aspects of Freud's theories we are obviously in danger of being both inadequate and imprecise, simply by virtue of compression. But there are also, perhaps less obviously, additional dangers peculiar to the present undertaking. We must always remember that Freud's psychoanalytic career spanned about 45 years, during which time there occurred an almost constant process of theoretical development. Cutting across such a sequence to give an instantaneous view is therefore bound to be rather arbitrary and distorting. The texts themselves involve additional difficulties. First, in the early period with which we are concerned many important ideas were adumbrated in the correspondence with Wilhelm Fliess several years prior to their publication; publication dates are therefore apt to be misleading for judging changes and new developments. Moreover, it would be agreed that Freud did not pay great attention to the careful definition of terms, or even to consistent usage. Like the Bible, he can be quoted to prove opposing theses.

Nevertheless, some attempt at a historical reconstruction of his views must be undertaken in order that his analysis of the Lorenz case can be understood. In the following account an effort has been made to use only those ideas that were actually at hand by 1909 when the Lorenz case was published.[18] Since our concern is simply to become familiar with the basic ideas, we shall avoid the difficult and somewhat unrewarding task of elucidating the exact meanings of certain terms, notably "instinct," "libido," and "unconscious." Insofar as the terms occur at all, it is hoped that their usage will be made clear by the context in which they appear. It must also be remembered that in presenting a fairly unified and consistent out-line, certain vague points and inconsistencies must be passed over without comment.

1. Infantile Sexuality

The fact of infantile sexuality, together with its importance in account-ing for psychopathology, formed an unchanging foundation for Freud. The basic observation is that:

---

[18] In effect this means confining ourselves to papers *written* no later than 1909. Our main texts are the *Three Essays on the Theory of Sexuality,* published in 1905 (1905b) and first revised in 1909, and the *Five Lectures on Psycho-analysis* (1909c), delivered in September, 1909, and written up by December of that year, although not published until April, 1910, first in an English translation in the *American Journal of Psychology,* Vol. 21, No. 2. With regard to the actual writing of these lectures, Ernest Jones is not consistent. In Vol. II, p. 211, he states:

They were finished in the second week of December. His memory in such matters was so good, however, that they did not depart much from the original delivery.

Jones refers to an unpublished letter to Jung of December 12, 1909, for confirmation of this date. However, later on p. 346, he states:

Before the end of the year he had written three of the five lectures he had delivered *ex tempore* in America that autumn, but he now put them aside for three months to work at his more absorbing theme [the Leonardo essay].

Since all five lectures were published in April, 1910, in English translation, it seems most probable that Freud did in fact finish them in December, rather than in the spring of 1910 as the second quotation from Jones would suggest. Moreover, Jones gives no source for this second statement. Freud had spoken about the Lorenz case to various groups no fewer than six times from October, 1907, to April, 1908, during which time the analysis was still going on. On five occasions he addressed his Wednesday evening psychoanalytic meetings. The minutes of these sessions are available in the *Minutes of the Vienna Psychoanalytic Society*—Oct. 30, Nov. 6, and Nov. 20, 1907; and June 22, and April 8, 1908. Later in April the Lorenz case was Freud's subject for his paper given at the Saltzburg International meeting. But the case was not written up for publication until June, 1909, about a year after the analysis was completed (Jones, 1955, p. 264). The *Five Lectures on Psycho-analysis,* therefore, follow the case by only three months, and we feel justified in using them as an additional source.

> A child has its sexual instincts [libido] and activities from the first; it comes into the world with them; and, after an important course of development passing through many stages, they lead to what is known as the normal sexuality of the adult (Freud, 1909c, p. 42).

In order to understand this theory we must appreciate the fact that Freud expands the concept of "sexual" in three ways. He uses the word, first, to refer to physical pleasure of different varieties obtained through bodily stimulation of any sort, and he applies the term "erotogenic zone" to those parts of the body or organs especially capable of yielding such pleasure. As the theory evolved and observations increased it became apparent that virtually any part of the skin or any organ could become such a zone. Nevertheless, "there are some particularly marked erotogenic zones whose excitation would seem to be secured from the very first by certain organic contrivances" (Freud, 1905b, p. 233). These are the mucosal-cutaneous junctures, the oral, anal, and genital zones.[19]

Sexual pleasure, then, refers to pleasure resulting from the stimulation of any area of the body, not simply the genitals. But the concept is also extended in another way.

> . . . in spite of the preponderating dominance of erotogenic zones, [infantile sexuality] exhibits components which from the very first involve other people as sexual objects . . . which appear in a sense independently of erotogenic zones; these instincts do not enter into intimate relations with sexual [that is, genital] life until later, but are already to be observed in childhood as independent impulses, distinct in the first instance from erotogenic sexual activity (Freud, 1905b, pp. 191–192).

Among these component instincts Freud listed sadism, masochism, scopophilia (voyeurism), and exhibitionism.[20] Activities displaying such impulses also yield physical pleasure for the infant and can thus be termed "sexual."

Freud summed up these points in characterizing the infant as "polymorphously perverse." By this he emphasized, first, the variety of activities and types of stimulation whereby sexual pleasure is obtained, and, second, the fact that these modes of behavior normal to the child are just what we shall call "perverted" when found in adults. Voyeurism, exhibi-

---

[19] It is important, and not always remembered, that the "classical" temporal sequence of psychosexual development through oral, anal, and genital stages was not described completely until 1915 (see note p. 110). In the period we are considering, Freud recognizes the importance of these areas but not their exact sequential and developmental characteristics. His emphasis at this time is primarily on the genital stage with its oedipal conflict.

[20] The fact that the component instincts actually listed in the *Three Essays on the Theory of Sexuality* (the ones stated above) were only intended as examples from a more extensive group was explicitly affirmed by Freud in a 1910 letter to Ernest Jones (Jones, 1955, p. 449).

tionism, sadism, masochism, homosexuality, coprophilia—all such perversions of adults are expressions of "partial instincts," normal components of infantile sexuality. The frequency of homosexual experience in infancy is, moreover, one indication of bisexuality, which Freud regarded as a "decisive factor" in understanding sexual development (1905b, p. 220).[21] Thus, the "disposition to perversions is an original and universal disposition of the human sexual instinct" (1905b, p. 231).

Freud also emphasizes other characteristics of infantile sexuality besides this complex or polymorphous feature. One of the "essential characteristics" is that "it has as yet no sexual object, and is thus auto-erotic" (1905b, p. 182). Satisfaction is obtained through self-stimulation. In fact, however, Freud is not consistent on this point, since he makes it clear in other passages that the infant is only primarily, not exclusively, autoerotic, that relations with external sexual objects are possible even during infancy.

> At a time at which the first beginnings of sexual satisfaction are still linked with the taking of nourishment, the sexual instinct has a sexual object outside the infant's own body in the shape of his mother's breast. It is only later that the instinct loses that object, just at the time, perhaps, when the child is able to form a total idea of the person to whom the organ that is giving him satisfaction belongs. As a rule the sexual instinct then becomes auto-erotic, and not until the period of latency has been passed through is the original relation restored (1905b, p. 222).

A third feature is that infantile sexuality is "still independent of the reproductive function, into the service of which it will later be brought" (1909c, p. 43). Freud described this infantile period as corresponding to the first stage of cultural development when "the sexual instinct may be freely exercised without regard to the aims of reproduction" (1908c, p. 189).

A fourth characteristic of libido is its flexibility, or "plasticity" to use Freud's word (1909c, p. 54). In its first sense this is simply another way of pointing out that a variety of activities and sorts of body stimulation can yield sexual gratification. But libido is flexible in another way, in contrast to instincts like hunger.[22] Less than a year after publishing the Lorenz case Freud explicitly differentiated between the race-preserving (sexual) and

---

[21] Bisexuality was a notion suggested to Freud by Fliess. Freud used the concept often and discussed it in detail in several places besides the *Three Essays on the Theory of Sexuality,* notably "Hysterical Phantasies and their Relation to Bisexuality" (1908a) and "A Child is Being Beaten" (1919). He did not, however, accept the thesis that it could, by itself, account for the various forms of psychopathology.

[22] The comparison of hunger and the sexual instincts was a subject for discussion at one of the Wednesday evening meetings in Freud's home in this same period, January 23, 1907. (Nunberg and Federn, 1962, pp. 81–91.)

the self-preserving instincts. The distinction had, however, been implicit much earlier, for instance in Freud's speaking of the sexual insinct and the need for nourishment in the quotation above.[23] In 1910 Freud wrote:

> . . . a quite specially important part is played by the undeniable opposition between the instincts which subserve sexuality, the attainment of sexual pleasure, and those other instincts, which have as their aim the self-preservation of the individual—the ego-instincts (1910c, p. 214).

Freud in this passage and elsewhere lumps under the term "ego-instincts" both instincts determined by biology—hunger, thirst, etc.—and the very different drives determined by social forces, by the demands of civilization. However, for the purposes of explicating the flexibility of libido we need only be concerned with the biological instincts of self-preservation. These latter instincts, such as hunger, are fixed in their aims (i.e., the obtaining of food) and must be satisfied at fairly regular intervals; their intensity, therefore, cannot build up beyond certain limits before satisfaction must take place.

The libido, in contrast, besides being variable in its modes of satisfaction, is also flexible in its outcome or expression. It need not be gratified either directly or at regular intervals. In the *Three Essays on the Theory of Sexuality* Freud distinguishes four methods of dealing with libido in the face of the conflicting demands of family and society. While these become most important after puberty, when adult relationships are established, these same methods are employed by the child in dealing with his sexual conflicts. We can, therefore, outline them at this point. The first is simply direct expression, the immediate acting out of the various component instincts. The second is direct repression, where the impulses "are prevented by psychical obstruction from attaining their aim" (1905b, p. 237).[24]

---

[23] On February 20, 1907, Freud reviewed a book, *The Hopelessness of all Psychology,* by a German psychiatrist and neurologist, Paul Moebius. In the discussion, Freud speaks approvingly of the view that there are two basic divisions of instincts— the self-preserving and the race-preserving (sexual). (Nunberg and Feden, 1962, pp. 119–127.)

[24] The concept of repression has a long history. In the early papers on hysteria, repression and defense both occur interchangeably. By 1905 Freud explicitly substitutes "repression" for "defense" (see 1905c, p. 276). An attempt to differentiate between types of repression does not begin until the 1911 Schreber case and is continued in 1915 with "Instincts and their Vicissitudes." In 1925, in *Inhibitions, Symptoms and Anxiety,* Freud reverted back to the use of defense as the general mechanism and repression as a variety of defense. For good historical reviews of these changes see James Strachey's Appendix to the Standard Edition text of this last book, and also Peter Madison's *Freud's Concept of Repression and Defense* (1961).

Sublimation is the third method of dealing with libido.[25] The fourth
method, reaction-formation, Freud in the *Three Essays on the Theory of*
Sexuality calls a subspecies of sublimation (1905b, p. 238). In this period
Freud believed that both these methods begin to be employed during a
child's period of latency (1905b, pp. 178, 232, and 238). These two ways
of handling libido are brought into operation for the most part "with the
assistance of education" (1905b, p. 232). But this development is
"organically determined" and can sometimes occur "without any help at
all from education" (1905b, pp. 177–178). Sublimation

> . . . enables excessively strong excitations arising from particular sources
> of sexuality to find an outlet and use in other fields, so that a not incon-
> siderable increase in psychical efficiency results from a disposition which in
> itself is perilous (1905b, p. 238).

Insofar as certain activities represent sublimations of an original sexual
motivation, they too can be referred to as "sexual," and this is Freud's
third extension of the use of this term. In the case of reaction-formation
the original impulses, under the direction of social pressures, evoke opposing mental forces—feelings of disgust and shame over sexual matters, and
a sense of morality—which effectively block the expression of the original
sexual instincts.

2. Psychosexual Development

These four methods of dealing with sexual instincts are all employed
to varying degrees in the course of normal psychosexual development, and
having outlined Freud's views about sexuality itself, we can now turn to
this theory of development. Freud held that psychosexual development fell
into three periods, determined primarily by the human constitution. The
first period, infantile sexuality, ends in an "early efflorescence" around the
third to sixth years of life (1905b, p. 177). This is followed by the so-called
latency period, in which sexual manifestations are at a minimum and little

---

[25] Sublimation, like repression, is a subject in itself. The concept first appears in
Freud's letter of May 2, 1897 to Fliess, and its first published use is in 1905, both
in the Dora case and the *Three Essays on the Theory of Sexuality*. From then on the
word is used often, but in a loose manner, and one important distinction is not yet
made by 1910. Indeed, it might be argued that Freud is never clear on this point.
This distinction is between "displacing," "diverting," "deflecting" an instinct the
"proper ends" of which remain sexual; and completely withdrawing a sexual aim and
"replacing," "substituting," "exchanging" a new nonsexual aim. According to the
English texts of the Standard Edition, these terms and others are used interchangeably
in the period we are discussing (for examples, see 1905a, pp. 50, 116; 1905b, pp. 156
and 178; 1908a, p. 161; 1908b, p. 171; 1908c, pp. 187, 189, and 193; 1909c, pp. 28
and 54; 1910a, pp. 78 and 80).

or no psychosexual development occurs. The third stage of adult sexuality is ushered in by puberty.

One of the important developmental trends in the period of infantile sexuality is the progress from autoerotic pleasure seeking to sexual gratification through a relationship with an external object. The infant begins, during the period of breast feeding, with sexual pleasure closely associated to the satisfaction of hunger.

> But even after sexual activity has become detached from the taking of nourishment, an important part of this first and most significant of all sexual relations is left over, which helps to prepare for the choice of an object and thus to restore the happiness that has been lost . . . children learn to feel for other people who help them in their helplessness and satisfy their needs a love which is on the model of, and a continuation of, their relation as sucklings to their nursing mother. There may perhaps be an inclination to dispute the possibility of identifying a child's affection and esteem for those who look after him with sexual love. I think, however, that a closer psychological examination may make it possible to establish this identity beyond any doubt. A child's intercourse with anyone responsible for his care affords him an unending source of sexual excitation and satisfaction from his erotogenic zones (1905b, pp. 222–223).

Freud emphasizes that the child's early development culminates in the problem of object-choice.

> Its choice is directed in the first instance to all those who look after it, but these soon give place to its parents. Children's relations to their parents . . . are by no means free from elements of accompanying sexual excitation. The child takes both of its parents, and more particularly one of them, as the object of its erotic wishes. In so doing, it usually follows some indication from its parents, whose affection bears the clearest characteristics of a sexual activity, even though of one that is inhibited in its aims. As a rule a father prefers his daughter and a mother her son; the child reacts to this by wishing, if he is a son, to take his father's place, and, if she is a daughter, her mother's. The feelings which are aroused in these relations between parents and children and in the resulting ones between brothers and sisters are not only of a positive or affectionate kind but also of a negative or hostile one. The complex which is thus formed is doomed to early repression; but it continues to exercise a great and lasting influence from the unconscious. It is to be suspected that, together with its extensions, it constitutes the *nuclear complex* of every neurosis, and we may expect to find it no less actively at work in other regions of mental life. The myth of King Oedipus . . . (1909c, p. 47).

Here is perhaps the best early statement of the Oedipus complex, occurring within about three months of the publication of the Lorenz case.[26] The

---

[26] The first published use of this actual phrase occurs in 1910, in the first paper of Contributions to the Psychology of Love, "A Special Type of Choice of Object made by Men." The gist of this paper was, however, reported in May, 1909, before

oedipal or nuclear complex represents the culmination of the period of infantile sexuality and is in fact a "crisis" of object-choice. The child typically develops intense, often sexual love for the opposite parent and a feeling of rivalry with the parent of the same sex. Yet at the same time there is a love for that parent who also seems to be a rival. Moreover, the child recognizes its dependence upon both parents for care, and hence the need to remain on good terms with both. This might prove impossible if feelings of hostility were openly displayed; thus is born the oedipal conflict.

A number of factors will determine the magnitude of this conflict. Of prime importance is the strength and precocity of the libido in the child. One determinant of this is simply genetic constitution,

> . . . spontaneous sexual precocity, whose presence at least can be demonstrated with certainty in the aetiology of the neuroses though, like other factors, is not in itself a sufficient cause (1905b, p. 240).

In addition to heredity, sexual precocity can also result from early experiences with nurses and parents.

> It is true that an excess of parental affection does harm by causing precocious sexual maturity and also because, by spoiling the child, it makes him incapable in later life of temporarily doing without love or of being content with a smaller amount of it . . . neuropathic parents, who are inclined as a rule to display excessive affection, are precisely those who are most likely by their caresses to arouse the child's disposition to neurotic illness (1905b, p. 223).

> A neurotic wife who is unsatisfied by her husband is, as a mother, over-tender and over-anxious towards her child, on to whom she transfers her need for love; and she awakens it to sexual precocity (1908c, p. 202).

Other important factors include the birth of younger siblings who become very real threats insofar as they are competitors for the parents' attention and affection. Specific sexual incidents with older persons may also play a part.

Ideally the oedipal situation arouses only a moderate amount of hostility and conflict in the child, and such feelings as do exist are allowed adequate expression by understanding parents. Where adequate release is not allowed, neurosis may result.

> [The child's] strict upbringing, which tolerates no activity of the sexual life that has been aroused so early, lends support to the suppressing force and

---

the Lorenz case was written up, to the Vienna Psycho-Analytical Society (see 1910b, Editor's Note, p. 164). The idea of the oedipal conflict goes back much earlier, however, and appears explicitly in a letter to Fliess of October 15, 1897. Hints occur even earlier, in the letter of September 21, 1897 and Draft N (notes enclosed with letter of May 31, 1897). These letters are all found in *The Origins of Psychoanalysis* (Freud, 1954).

this conflict at such an age contains everything necessary for bringing about lifelong nervous illness (1908c, p. 202).

Generally, the sexual desires of this oedipal period, insofar as they are expressed at all, are released through masturbation rather than any activities involving the parents. Thus, although there is in this period of infantile sexuality a trend from autoerotic to object-related sexual expression, the end of this period tends to show a resurgence or "second phase" of auto-eroticism (1905b, pp. 189–190). It is only after puberty that the trend to object-related sexuality is successfully completed with the establishment of adult sexual relationships.

If the family situation prevents or punishes expression of feelings, then repression may be the only solution, since the child "at that time [is] still imperfectly organized and feeble" (1909c, p. 53). This repression may cause an interruption in development.

> For the extirpation of the infantile wishful impulses is by no means the ideal aim of development. Owing to their repressions, neurotics have sacrificed many sources of mental energy whose contributions would have been of great value in the formation of their character and in their activity in life. We know of a far more expedient process of development, called 'sublimation,' in which the energy of the wishful impulses is not cut off but remains ready for use. . . . It is probable that we owe our highest cultural successes to the contributions of energy made in this way to our mental functions. Premature repression makes the sublimation of the repressed instinct impossible; when the repression is lifted [through psychoanalysis], the path to sublimation becomes free once more (1909c, pp. 53–54).

It is therefore important to have relatively unhindered expression of sexual wishes earlier on. Provided this occurs, development continues and the child soon learns through his social education during the latency period a more adequate method of dealing with his sexual instincts, namely, sublimation. A wide range of new interests and activities tend to become sufficient outlets for sexual energies. It is only with the onset of puberty that sexual problems once more come into prominence as the final development of adult sexuality becomes necessary.

Freud emphasized two over-all trends that mark the sexual development from childhood to adulthood, and which both dominate the time following puberty.

> This widespread and copious but dissociated sexual life of children, in which each separate instinct pursues its own acquisition of pleasure independently of all the rest, is now brought together and organized in two main directions, so that by the end of puberty the individual's final sexual character is as a rule completely formed. On the one hand, the separate instincts become subordinated to the dominance of the genital zone, so that the whole sexual life enters the service of reproduction, and the satisfaction of the separate

instincts retains its importance only as preparing for and encouraging the sexual act proper. On the other hand, object-choice pushes auto-erotism into the background so that in the subject's erotic life all the components of the sexual instinct now seek satisfaction in relation to the person who is loved (1909c, pp. 44–45).

Both of these trends must be elucidated. As to the subordination of component instincts to genital primacy, Freud points out that in fact certain instincts, notably the coprophilic ones, have actually been energetically repressed before adulthood and may even give way to opposing reaction-formations. Others, such as those involving the oral erotogenic zone, are subordinated and become admissible only as fore-pleasures leading up to genital gratification. Still others no longer find direct expression but are sublimated into a wide variety of activities. Indeed, Freud suggests that an individual's character traits can be accounted for by examining the typical methods he has adopted for dealing with his instincts.

> The sexual behavior of a human being often *lays down the pattern* for all his other modes of reacting to life (1908c, p. 198).

> We can at any rate lay down a formula for the way in which character in its final shape is formed out of the constituent instincts: the permanent character-traits are either unchanged prolongations of the original instincts, or sublimations of those instincts, or reaction-formations against them (1908b, p. 175).

The second trend of sexual development is from the autoerotic to mature object love. It is, in fact, a continuation of a trend seen in the period of infantile sexuality, at which time, however, a successful conclusion within the family situation could not be reached. But the influence of that early period remains. Freud argues that the original object relationship was to the breast. And not only can we trace general character traits back to methods of dealing with sexual instincts as we pointed out above, but mature methods of dealing with object choices can similarly be traced back to that first relationship with the breast:

> . . . a child sucking at his mother's breast [becomes] the prototype of every relation of love. The finding of an object is in fact a refinding of it (1905b, p. 222).

Once objects of love come to be regarded as whole persons, then the next development is the choice of the opposite parent, and eventually the opposite sex, as is the usual case during the oedipal period:

> It is inevitable and perfectly normal that a child should take his parents as the first objects of his love. But his libido should not remain fixated to these first objects; later on, it should merely take them as a model, and should make a gradual transition from them on to extraneous people when the time for the final choice of an object arrives (1909c, p. 48).

The detachment from the parents is thus an important aspect of the development of mature sexuality.

> At every stage in the course of development through which all human beings ought by rights to pass, a certain number are held back; so there are some who have never got over their parents' authority and have withdrawn their affection from them either very incompletely or not at all (1905b, p. 227).

Conversely, there may also be individuals who have never successfully resolved their hostility toward their parents, and who therefore will also remain "fixated" at the oedipal level of rivalry. This concept of "fixation" brings us to Freud's views on psychopathology, as they are based upon the libido theory we have now outlined.

3. Psychopathology

The developmental scheme so far presented contains within itself a definite theory of neurosis, which Freud elaborated during this same period.

> There is a dictum in general pathology . . . which asserts that every developmental process carries with it the seed of a pathological disposition, insofar as that process may be inhibited, delayed, or may run its course incompletely. The same thing is true of the highly complicated development of the sexual function. It does not occur smoothly in every individual; and, if not, it leaves behind it either abnormalities or a predisposition to fall ill later, along the path of involution (i.e., regression) (1909c, p. 45).

Freud calls inhibitions of development "fixations;" he also uses this term in two other related ways. First, instincts can be fixated upon a particular aim or mode of expression. In this meaning fixation is opposed to sublimation, which is the capacity for displacement onto, or substitution of, new objects and new activities. Second, an individual can also be said to be fixated upon one unchangeable method of dealing with his impulses or at a particular stage of psychosexual development. In this sense, fixation is the opposite of flexibility in an individual, the capacity to adopt new methods of dealing with instincts in the face of changing conditions.

Often the inhibitions of development are not complete but only partial and not noticeable unless the individual is placed under stress.

> . . . an excessively strong manifestation of these [component sexual] instincts at a very early age leads to a kind of partial *fixation*, which then constitutes a weak point in the structure of the sexual function. If in maturity the performance of the normal sexual function comes up against obstacles, the repression that took place during the course of development will be broken through at the precise points at which the infantile fixations occurred (1909c, p. 46).

If, because of environmental frustrations or a developmental lack of adaptation, sexual needs are not satisfied in reality, then the patient may

> . . . take flight into *illness*. . . . The flight from unsatisfactory reality into what, on account of the biological damage involved, we call illness (though it is never without an immediate yield of pleasure to the patient) takes place along the path of involution, of regression, of a return to earlier phases of sexual life, phases from which at one time satisfaction was not withheld (1909c, p. 49).

We can see that this theory allows for at least two varieties of psycho-sexual developmental pathology, "two kinds of harmful deviation from normal sexuality" (1908c, p. 189). In the first, development ceases at a certain point. In the second, development proceeds, but the previous stages may not have been successfully resolved and the conflicts simply repressed. In this case under stress the individual may regress back to the earlier stage before the conflict was repressed. In fact, however, these two varieties overlap. Nevertheless, to some extent they can be distinguished in the difference between perversions and neuroses.

It may occur that the component instincts fail to be united and brought under the domination of the genital zone. Such components may remain even into adulthood independent of mature sexual and procreative impulses, and the result is a perversion such as exhibitionism. Likewise, there may be a failure in the oedipal period to focus sexual desires upon the sex of the opposite parent, and the original bisexuality may persist as a tendency to homosexuality.

Besides the "coalescence" of the component instincts, there must also occur a shift in aim from autoerotic pleasures to gratification through relation to other persons. This development is first met in the oedipal period in the child's relation to his parents. If fixation occurs at this time a mature choice of love object after puberty may prove impossible since the unresolved and repressed feelings of hostility and jealousy may transfer themselves onto any new individuals who might otherwise become love objects.

In neuroses the fixation of sexual development occurs in the same periods, but the solutions adopted are different from those in the perversions.

> Neuroses are related to perversions as negative to positive. The same instinctual components as in the perversions can be observed in the neuroses as vehicles of complexes and constructors of symptoms, but in the latter case they operate from the unconscious (1909c, p. 46).

> [If repression occurs] the excitations [of the component instincts] continue to be generated as before; but they are prevented by psychical obstruction

from attaining their aim and are diverted into numerous other channels
till they find their way to expression as symptoms (1905b, pp. 237–238).

In both neuroses and perversions, then, we see inhibited sexual development and a dissociation of the component instincts. Where these impulses
remain active and immediately expressed we see perverse tendencies.
Where they are repressed into the unconscious, instead of being adequately
dealt with, they remain and express themselves in indirect ways through
neurotic symptoms.

4. Transference

Finally, we complete our sketch with mention of Freud's concept of
transference. This refers to the patient's recreating within the analytic
situation old attitudes and conflicts dating back to infancy. These trans-
ferences are characteristically not governed by the realities of the analytic
relationship but by ancient conflicts in which the analyst often assumes the
roles of various important figures. Transference is in fact only a variety of
"response generalization," the tendency of organisms to give a response
originally associated with an old stimulus to a new stimulus which may
resemble the old one in some particular way. In psychoanalysis these trans-
ferences are for the most part unnoticed by the patient.

> Thus the part of the patient's emotional life which he can no longer recall
> to memory is re-experienced by him in his relation to the physician; and it
> is only this re-experiencing in the 'transference' that convinces him of the
> existence and of the power of these unconscious sexual impulses (1909c,
> p. 51).

The phenomenon of transference "arises spontaneously in all human relationships"; psychoanalysis "merely reveals it to consciousness and gains
control of it in order to guide psychical processes towards the desired
goal" (1909c, p. 51). Unconscious impulses are beyond the reach of any
inhibiting reasons that the patient might consciously use to counteract their
influence. In analysis, and especially in the analysis of the transference
relationship, these unconscious impulses are demonstrated. By bringing
them into conscious recognition, they can be mastered; *"repression* is
replaced by a *condemning judgment* carried out along the best lines"
(1909c, p.53).

This sketch presents a somewhat inadequate and certainly incomplete
view of Freud's theories in the period when the Lorenz case appeared.
Nevertheless, our purpose is to examine a particular psychoanalytic explanation, not psychoanalytic theory itself. The outline given should be
sufficient for the reader to grasp the essential themes of Freud's explanation
of Paul Lorenz's illness, to which we can now turn.

D. Freud's Psychoanalytic Explanation of
the Paul Lorenz Case

1. The Presumptions of Explanation

In Chapter 2 we pointed out that certain specific conditions must be fulfilled in any situation before one can properly ask for an explanation. The mere description of one or a long series of events, no matter how complex, may not constitute such an explanatory context; that is, one or more of the four necessary presumptions may be absent. Therefore, before presenting Freud's explanation of the case of Paul Lorenz it behooves us to demonstrate briefly that those presumptions discussed earlier are in fact discernible.

Freud's interest, and our own, in this case is in the unusual and at times seemingly irrational behavior exhibited by the patient. One gets the impression that this behavior is "apart from," does not fit into, or even contradicts our usual understanding of human activities. Within this field of interest Freud finds particular incongruities or puzzles that require explanation. The patient's behavior, even in childhood, presents us with "an apparent absurdity" (1909b, p. 164). What is needed is not simply a filling in of missing information, but rather an explanatory reorganization of the data into some meaningful whole. Indeed, any incongruities may become even greater once further information is discovered. For instance, commenting on the fact (which had not emerged at first) that the patient had been told previously that the money was owed to the post office authorities, yet still persisted in his belief of owing money to Lt. A., Freud states: "I must admit that when this correction has been made his behavior becomes even more senseless and unintelligible than before" (1909b, p. 173). Also connected with this same incident, Freud again clearly expresses his appreciation of an incongruity in the patient's behavior:

> Obviously the first problem to be solved was why the two speeches of the Czech captain—his rat story, and his request to the patient that he should pay back the money to Lt. A.—should have had such an agitating effect on him and should have provoked such violently pathological reactions (1909b, p. 210).

Thus there seems no doubt that the patient's behavior, at least for Freud, presented an incongruity, both as an over-all life history and, within that history, as a series of incongruous incidents each demanding to be explained. For us, too, a great deal of the patient's behavior does not fit in with what we, as common men, know of human activities: the exaggerated guilt about sleeping through the death of his father, for example. Also, within that life history many pieces of behavior fail to fit in with each other. How, for instance, can the variety of superstitions be reconciled with his good intelligence? It is to such incongruities that Freud addresses himself.

The first two presumptions, of interest and of incongruity, seem therefore to be present. Likewise with the third, the presumption of knowledge, which is the counterpart of the presumption of incongruity. It is just because Freud, simply as a plain man living in this world, had a body of more or less accurate knowledge about human behavior that Paul Lorenz's behavior seemed so peculiar, disturbed, and in need of special investigation and explanation. Thus, in discussing the feelings of love and hatred existing in the patient Freud states:

> We know that incipient love is often perceived as hatred, and that love, if it is denied satisfaction, may easily be partly converted into hatred. . . . But the *chronic* co-existence of love and hatred, both directed towards the same person and both of the highest degree of intensity, cannot fail to astonish us (1909b, pp. 238–239).

Freud asks in effect: How, in the face of all we know of human nature, is such a situation possible? Clearly then, Freud's explanation functions within a body of common-sense understanding about human behavior— understanding which may nevertheless on the basis of further investigation prove to be misinformed.

As to the fourth presumption, the use of standards of appropriateness, one need only note that Freud repeatedly speaks at different points of "rationalization," "poor explanation," "partial explanation," and "more cogent explanation"—all terms implying the use of criteria for evaluating possible explanations. To what extent we can elucidate these standards and to what extent such criteria form a consistent and useful set are important issues. But the present point that some such standards *are* presumed does not seem open to question.

The four presumptions inherent in any explanatory context seem to be present in the case of Paul Lorenz. We are, then, justified in asking for an explanation of the patient's behavior, as did Freud; and we can now present his proposed psychoanalytic explanation. In the following account we shall emphasize the general explanation of the patient's behavior as a whole; the explanation of specific actions, beliefs, and the like will be presented only insofar as they bring out the general explanatory principles Freud suggests. In later chapters a number of specific explanations of particular pieces of behavior will be discussed, but all of these will rely heavily on the general factors now to be elucidated. We shall employ Freud's own words as much as possible in order to become familiar with the actual methods of expression and patterns of reasoning used.

2. First Foundation: Unresolved Oedipal Conflict

The Lorenz case appeared to Freud to fit in well with his belief that the roots of neurotic illness lay in problems of early sexual development. He explained the case in terms of "two foundations," the first of which was an unresolved oedipal conflict. He suggested that there was an underlying hostility in the patient directed toward his father and that this hostility was connected to sexual impulses. Even in the early sessions of the analysis several hints were given about the existence of such feelings; for example, the fear that something terrible might happen to his father if the patient did certain actions or thought certain things (e.g., the wish to see girls naked), or the twice-repeated idea about intercourse: "This is a glorious feeling! One might do anything for this—murder one's father, for instance!"

> There can be no question that there was something in the sphere of sexuality that stood between the father and son, and that the father had come into some sort of opposition to the son's prematurely developed erotic life (1909b, p. 201).

Of course the patient repeatedly denied any interpretations that suggested hostility toward his father. The gradual recognition of these feelings occurred only in the course of a number of sessions, and a review of this process will be very instructive for our understanding of Freud's methods. Early in the analysis, in recounting the story of the childhood attachment to a 12-year-old girl, the patient reported that she had not been very responsive. Thereupon the idea occurred to him that if his father were to die she would be kind to him. He at once strongly rejected the idea and under analysis could not at first admit even the possibility that it was a wish; it had clearly been, he claimed, no more than a "train of thought." Freud then pointed out that if such an idea had been only an association of thought it seemed strange that an emotional rejection would be necessary; why should one feel obliged to reject so vehemently a thought or feeling to which one had never assented in the first place? To this comment the patient had no answer.

In the following session the patient returned of his own accord to this subject and again denied the possibility of his ever having had hostile feelings directed against his father. He then went on to tell a story he had once read: A woman, who sat by her sister's sickbed, felt a wish that her sister might die so that she could marry her sister's husband. The woman thereupon committed suicide, thinking she was not fit to live after being guilty of such base thoughts. The patient went on to say that he understood this woman's sense of guilt and agreed with her. It would only be right, he said, if his own thoughts were the death of him for he deserved nothing less. Freud did not at this point comment to the patient on this admission of guilt; but he does so in a note:

> This sense of guilt involves the most glaring contradiction of his opening denial that he had ever entertained such an evil wish against his father. This is a common type of reaction to repressed material which has become conscious: the 'No' with which the fact is first denied is immediately followed by a confirmation of it, though, to begin with, only an indirect one (1909b, p. 183).

The patient then went on to recount what he called a "criminal" act, the "shooting" of his younger brother with a toy gun at age six. He quoted Nietzsche: " 'I did this,' says Memory. 'I could not have done this,' says Pride and remains inexorable. In the end Memory yields." But, said the patient, on this point (of remembering a hostile act) my memory has *not* yielded. Soon after this he began to recognize his hostile feelings toward his father.

The problem of resistance to interpretations is clearly brought out by the above examples, as is the process whereby awareness gradually comes to the patient. The concatenation and movement from explicit denial to the story of the woman wishing for her sister's death, then to the admission that he deserves to be punished for his thoughts, and finally to the memory of another incident in which hostility *was* shown toward someone else in his family—this seems a good example of the fascinating complexity of the analytic situation and the unfolding process occurring in it.

At a later session Freud once again suggested that the patient had a great deal of hostile feelings within him:

> . . . I ventured to put forward a construction to the effect that when he was a child of under six he had been guilty of some sexual misdemeanor connected with masturbation and had been soundly castigated for it by his father. This punishment, according to my hypothesis, had, it was true, put an end to his masturbating, but on the other hand it had left behind it an ineradicable grudge against his father and had established him for all time in his role of an interferer with the patient's sexual enjoyment. To my great astonishment the patient then informed me [at the following session] that his mother had repeatedly described to him an occurrence of this kind which dated from his earliest childhood and had evidently escaped being forgotten by her on account of its remarkable consequences. He himself, however, had no recollection of it whatever. The tale was as follows . . . (1909b, p. 205).

The patient then related the "beating" incident which we quoted earlier in our exposition. In the light of this incident the patient's hostility toward his father takes on a more specific nature. In addition to the general source within the oedipal situation, our patient had also experienced a particular instance of his father's power and opposition. This event occurred at an especially vulnerable period of development, and through constant retelling by his parents its moral had been drilled into the patient. An additional factor emphasizing the importance of this incident was the circumstance of his sister's death in this same period.

> A deeper interpretation of the patient's dreams in relation to this ["beating"] episode revealed the clearest traces of the presence in his mind of an imaginative production of a positively epic character. In this his sexual desires for his mother and sister and his sister's premature death were linked up with the young hero's chastisement at his father's hand (1909b, p. 207).

With the exposure of this beating incident the patient's resistance was much reduced. Yet he still wondered how he could possibly have had such hostile wishes, considering that he loved his father more than anyone else in the world, indeed, so much so that he had not been able to accept the fact of his father's death for nearly two years.

> [Freud] answered that it was precisely such intense love as his that was the necessary precondition of the repressed hatred. In the case of people to whom he felt indifferent he would certainly have no difficulty in maintaining side by side inclinations to a moderate liking and to an equally moderate dislike. . . . In the case of some one who was closer to him, of his wife for instance, he would wish his feelings to be unmixed, and consequently, as was only human, he would overlook her faults, since they might make him dislike her—he would ignore them as though he were blind to them. So it was precisely the intensity of his love that would not allow his hatred— though to give it such a name was to caricature the feeling—to remain conscious (1909b, pp. 180–181).

It might be asked why some other solution of this oedipal conflict was not adopted, for the persistence of conflicting emotions is not the only possibility. Indeed, it seems on the face of it highly unlikely.

> . . . the *chronic* co-existence of love and hatred, both directed towards the same person and both of the highest degree of intensity, cannot fail to astonish us. We should have expected that the passionate love would long ago have conquered the hatred or been devoured by it. And in fact such a protracted survival of two opposites is only possible under quite peculiar psychological conditions and with the co-operation of the state of affairs in the unconscious. The love has not succeeded in extinguishing the hatred but only in driving it down into the unconscious; and in the unconscious the hatred, safe from the danger of being destroyed by the operations of consciousness, is able to persist and even to grow. In such circumstances the conscious love attains as a rule, by way of reaction, an especially high degree of intensity, so as to be strong enough for the perpetual task of keeping its opponent under repression. The necessary condition for the occurrence of such a strange state of affairs in a person's erotic life appears to be that at a very early age, somewhere in the prehistoric period of his infancy, the two opposites should have been split apart and one of them, usually the hatred, have been repressed (1909b, p. 239).

A great number of factors had intensified the oedipal conflict in the patient. The first was constitutional—sexual precocity. Freud speaks of the patient's "prematurely developed erotic life" and feelings that were "from constitutional causes . . . exceptionally strongly developed" (1909b, pp. 201 and 240).[27] Another group of factors involved the family situation. The birth of a younger brother, especially one who was perceived as such a great rival for the parents' affection, was important. So, too, was the apparently domineering and strong-tempered father who ruled his family kindly but allowed little freedom to his children. Finally, a number of specific incidents occurred which reinforced the conflict. The beating incident was crucial, especially as the patient admitted that he

> . . . attributed to this experience a part of the change which came over his own character. From that time forward he was a coward—out of fear of the violence of his own rage (1909b, p. 206).

Here is direct evidence that as a result of his father's attitude and actions the patient was afraid to express his feelings, particularly hostile ones. Then, too, the incident of having been thrown out of bed by his father, of being forcibly separated from his mother, underlined the rivalry in the family situation.

The oedipal conflict was intensified, then, by a variety of factors. On the other hand, the family situation apparently allowed for even less overt display of feelings than is usual. There was a demand for love and obedience to the father in spite of any feelings to the contrary. At such an early age a child may be unable to deal effectively with his emotions, may be "incapable of making a clear decision," and repression of the illicit hostility may be the result (Freud, 1909b, p. 183). Eventually a reaction-formation develops, over-accentuated love is established whose strength is made necessary by the very power of the feelings being repressed.

> . . . the neurotic phenomena we have observed arise on the one hand from conscious feelings of affection which have become exaggerated as a reaction,

---

[27] It must be remembered that what was considered precocious by Freud in 1909 might well have been regarded as normal in his later writings. We see as Freud's theories develop, definite tendencies (1) to emphasize ever earlier stages of development, (2) to keep dating stages earlier, and (3) to find various mechanisms being employed at earlier periods. Thus, the "classical" oral, anal, and genital stages of infantile sexuality were in fact posited in reverse order, the genital stage in the present period, the anal stage in 1913, and the oral stage in 1915. Indeed, the process has continued in the work of Melanie Klein, where pre-oedipal stages are postulated. Again, the oedipal conflict is first considered to occur from ages four to six; later, it is placed around age three. Finally, as a third example we can again refer to the mechanism of sublimation, which in Freud's early writings was said to be employed only in latency. In later writings Freud considered this a possible mechanism even in the pregenital stages of development.

and on the other hand from sadism persisting in the unconscious in the form of hatred (1909b, p. 240).

For the patient, then, the oedipal situation resulted in an unresolved love–hate conflict with regard to his father, and we can, hereafter, use this as a convenient label.

We remember that very early in the analysis the patient had described his childhood wish to see girls naked, his "uncanny feeling" that something would happen to his father if he thought such things, and his belief that he must do all sorts of things to prevent this occurrence. Summarizing Lorenz's development in this early period, Freud states:

> We find, accordingly: an erotic instinct and a revolt against it; a wish which has not yet become compulsive and, struggling against it, a fear which is already compulsive; a distressing affect and an impulsion towards the performance of defensive acts. The inventory of the neurosis has reached its full muster. Indeed, something more is present, namely, a kind of *delusion* or *delirium* with the strange content that his parents knew his thoughts because he spoke them out loud without his hearing himself do it (1909b, pp. 163–164).

This last belief reflects the child's guilt and fear that his secret evil wishes may be found out. Later on, various protective or defensive measures became some of the most striking features of the patient's behavior. A good example of such symptoms are the prayers for safety and the fear that certain tortures would occur unless he did or did not perform certain actions. Such exaggerated and unrealistic precautions were reaction-formations that disguised unconscious wishes, for example, that father *would* have the rat torture done to him. It is just because these maneuvers are reactions against strong opposing wishes that they are never completely successful. The "not," for instance, always seemed to slip into Lorenz's prayers because unconsciously it was always there. Hence these protective measures easily degenerate into rituals whose repetition is necessitated by the fact that they can never be satisfactorily carried out with the proper motivating feelings.

The patient's intellectualizing tendencies are another form of protective measure. His emphasis on symbolic words, on counting procedures, on abstract philosophizing about the afterlife—these were not signs of true intellectual development but rather of emotional regression to a sort of word-magic which, by naming and conceptualizing, attempts to master the underlying emotional conflict. Freud speaks of the regression whereby

> . . . preparatory acts become substituted for the final decision, thinking replaces acting, and, instead of the substitutive act, some thought preliminary to it asserts itself with all the force of compulsion (1909b, p. 244).

Precisely because of this regression the patient's thoughts take on the emotional import of the original instincts. Hence, Lorenz's fantasy of the omnipotence of his thoughts was only an elaboration of the very real fact that his thoughts did indeed have an abnormal potency—the full emotional import of the displaced instinctual drives composing his love–hate conflict. It is as if the "thought-process itself becomes sexualized" (1909b, p. 245).

Freud saw this basic love–hate conflict, originating well before the age of six and persisting into adulthood, as the underlying cause of the patient's obsessional neurosis.

> We may regard the repression of his infantile hatred of his father as the event which brought his whole subsequent career under the dominion of the neurosis (1909b, p. 238).

As the patient grew up and became aware of the norms governing the parent–child relationship, the hostile feelings were completely repressed until by adulthood the patient had no recollection of any such wishes— only memories of unimportant "trains of thought" or "fears" that some harm might come to his father.

3. Death of Father and the Sense of Guilt

Although the ambivalent[28] relationship with his father was one of the underlying causes of the patient's neurosis, the actual course of the illness was determined by other circumstances and events. Thus, the patient emphasized that the various symptoms became intensified only after his father's death.

> [Freud] regarded his sorrow at his father's death as the chief source of the *intensity* of his illness. His sorrow had found, as it were, a pathological expression in his illness (1909b, p. 186).

The father's death freed the patient from one source of domination and obstruction to his sexual activities in general, and especially his romance with Gisela. The father, it will be remembered, frequently counseled the patient against this attachment. Freud believed that the unusual absence of masturbation during almost all adolescence and its emergence soon after the father's death reflected the fact that the father was regarded as an obstacle to sexual gratification. Once the father was dead sexual activities could be undertaken. However, the death also fulfilled the patient's unconscious desires to harm his father. Thus the patient's sense of the potency of his wishes was reinforced; moreover, the death triggered off a terrible

---

[28] The term "ambivalence" was not used by Freud in the published version of this case; it was apparently introduced into psychoanalysis by Bleuler in 1910 (see 1909b, p. 239).

sense of guilt for having had such wishes. This "pathological mourning" found expression in all those various symptoms which implied a refusal, indeed an inability, to accept the father's death: the fantasies that father was in the next room, or knocking at the door; the idea that he must tell father the latest jokes; the compulsive inability to put aside objects once owned by father, even years after his death.

But side by side with an inability to *accept* the death was a desire to *undo* it. This was manifested in the belief that father was still living (and hence could still be hurt and punished), but in the "next world." This simultaneous affirmation of contradictory ideas ("I do not believe father is dead"; "I must attempt to undo his death") is a common feature of neurotic, and even fairly normal, behavior. We find other evidence of such disturbed and compartmentalized ("isolated") thinking in the fact that the patient, a bright university-educated man, recognized certain of his beliefs (e.g., the omnipotence of his thoughts) as being superstitious; yet he still acted upon such beliefs and was quite helpless to abandon them. Thus, irrationality existed side by side with intellectualization. It was as if certain ideas existed in a special compartment in the patient's mind, insulated from the need to accommodate to other beliefs that might be inconsistent with them.

This irrationality or, perhaps more accurately, insusceptibility to rational argument, is an important feature of an obsessional neurosis. Freud explains it by reference to the "mechanism of displacement."[29] By this, Freud meant the mechanism whereby the "affect" or complex of associated emotions is separated from the memory of the original event which gave rise to those emotions and instead is attached to a new, un-related and consciously more acceptable idea or memory. In the case of our patient we can see several good examples of this mechanism.

---

[29] The concept of displacement presents another example of the difficulties encountered in clarifying Freud's early theories. The first extended discussion of the mechanism described above occurs in "The Neuro-Psychoses of Defence" (1894a). The actual phrase "mechanism of defence," however, is not used there. In the Lorenz case this mechanism is described and employed; but where this actual phrase occurs, it is quite clear that Freud means what we might call "response generalization" and not displacement at all (1909b, p. 241). This interpretation is confirmed when, five pages later (p. 246), the same mechanism is again mentioned, this time explicitly in terms of generalization. Second, as we pointed out earlier, Freud frequently used the term "displacement" as a synonym for the separate mechanism of "sublimation" and even spoke of the latter as the "process of displacement" (1908c, p. 188). Thus, three different mechanisms are sometimes referred to as displacement and must all be distinguished from each other. The mechanism we describe above is the one usually labeled "displacement," and it is discussed again in the quotation regarding *mésal-liance* on p. 114.

When the father died the patient denied the fact, at least emotionally, for nearly two years. Then, following another death in the family, the father's death was forcefully driven home to the patient, who became weighed down with guilt. Indeed, he was so incapacitated that he could no longer study and was kept going only by the encouragement of his friend, who reassured him that his self-reproaches were grossly exaggerated. But the fascinating question is: What exactly was the sin for which he felt such guilt? Ostensibly, it was that the patient had been asleep at the final moment of his father's death. Here is a good example of what Freud calls a *"mésalliance"* or "false connection," a displacement of affect:

> When there is a *mésalliance* . . . between an affect and its ideational content (in this instance, between the intensity of the self-reproach and the occasion for it), a layman will say that the affect [the guilt] is too great for the occasion—that it is exaggerated—and that consequently the inference following from the self-reproach (the inference that the patient is a criminal) is false. On the contrary, the [analytic] physician says: 'No. The affect is justified. The sense of guilt is not in itself open to further criticism. But it belongs to some other content, which is unknown (*unconscious*), and which requires to be looked for. The known ideational content has only got into its actual position owing to a false connection. . . . Moreover, this fact of there being a false connection is the only way of accounting for the powerlessness of logical processes to combat the tormenting idea (1909b, pp. 175–176).[30]

People suffering such illnesses are unaware of the real meaning of their symptoms or the real cause of their feelings. Thus, the patient felt deeply guilty; yet he consciously displaced this feeling of guilt onto the memory of his sleeping through his father's death. But it was in fact the unconscious hostility that was the original impulse against which the guilt was a reaction. For this reason rational argument against the conscious reason for guilt—sleeping through his father's death—had no result, since the real source of guilt remained untouched.

The patient's suicidal impulses can be understood as being caused by this same sense of guilt over hostile, aggressive feelings directed at someone else. One is reminded of the patient's self-reproaches as an adult over the shooting of his brother with a toy gun in early childhood. It was remembered as definitely being a "criminal act" even some 25 years after the incident.

> Afterwards I was quite beside myself, and threw myself on the ground and asked myself how ever I could have done such a thing. But I *did* do it (1909b, p. 184).

---

[30] Parentheses and italics, Freud's; first bracket, mine; second bracket, editor's.

Here, too, the emotional reaction is totally out of proportion to the ostensible causal incident. Although first denying that he ever felt hostile feelings toward his father, the patient then proceeded to admit that "it would be only right if his thoughts were the death of him, for he deserved nothing less" (1909b, p. 183). In a third incident described earlier the patient was angered that Gisela had to be away spending time with her sick grandmother. Then the command to slash his throat occurred and he rushed to the cupboard for the razor. But the thought came: "No, it's not so simple as that. You must [first] go and kill the old woman [Gisela's grandmother]." With that, he fell to the floor in horror.

In each of these examples the self-destructive thought involves a situation in which either a hostile act or hostile thoughts are originally directed against someone else: the brother, father, or Gisela's grandmother. In the first incident, shooting his brother, there is an overt act followed by remorse. In the second, there is no conscious admission of just what the hostile thoughts were but only the belief that they were of such a nature as to warrant "the death of" the patient. In the last case, the whole order is reversed in the patient's mind: the punitive command comes first, then the expression of the hostile wish against Gisela's grandmother.

4. Ambivalence in the Relationship with Gisela

In the relationship to Gisela this same love–hate conflict was reenacted, and the old methods of dealing with the father situation were transferred into that new love relationship. Here too, as at that earlier time, a very intense love and desire exist alongside "fantasies of revenge," feelings of hostility. To be sure, the girl, in her rejections and perhaps in other ways, gave good reason for such anger on the part of the patient. The point is not that the patient's hostility might not have been reasonable or justified; it is rather that the patient in this new situation, as in the distant past, failed to accommodate himself to these conflicting feelings and instead adopted his ancient obsessional defense—displacement of affect or its denial by repression.

From such a refusal to recognize the ambivalence of his own feelings arises the pervading sense of doubt which characterized so much of the patient's behavior. The doubting of evidence, the inability to come to decisions or to initiate actions—when carried to abnormal lengths these are all intellectualized, verbalized manifestations of a basic emotional conflict.

> The *doubt* corresponds to the patient's internal perception of his own indecision, which, in consequence of the inhibition of his love by his hatred, takes possession of him in the face of every intended action. The doubt is in

reality a doubt of his own love . . . and it becomes diffused over everything
else. . . . A man who doubts his own love may, or rather *must,* doubt
every lesser thing.

It is this same doubt that leads the patient to uncertainty about his protective measures, and to his continual repetition of them in order to banish
that uncertainty; and it is this doubt, too, that eventually brings it about that
the patient's protective acts themselves become as impossible to carry out as
his original inhibited decision in connection with his love. . . . [For instance
in the case of the prayer reversals.] If the 'not' had remained mute, he would
have found himself in a state of uncertainty, and would have kept on
prolonging his prayers indefinitely. But since it became articulate he
eventually gave up praying. Before doing so, however, he, like other
obsessional patients, tried every kind of method for preventing the opposite
feeling from insinuating itself. He shortened his prayers, for instance, or
said them more rapidly. And similarly other patients will endeavor to
'isolate' all such protective acts from other things (1909b, pp. 241–243).

The patient was himself aware, at least to some extent, that such
ambivalence of feeling existed. Yet he had no insight at all into the depth
of this ambivalence, nor into its connection with a whole array of obsessional symptoms. The stone incident is another good example, like the
prayer reversals, of this ambiguity of feeling.

A battle between love and hate was raging in the lover's breast, and the
object of both these feelings was one and the same person. The battle was
represented in a plastic form by his compulsive and symbolic act of removing the stone from the road along which she was to drive, and then of
undoing this deed of love by replacing the stone where it had lain, so that
her carriage might come to grief against it and she herself be hurt. We shall
not be forming a correct judgment of this second part of the compulsive act
if we take it at its face value as having merely been a critical repudiation
of a pathological action. The fact that it was accompanied by a sense of
compulsion betrays it as having itself been a part of the pathological action,
though a part which was determined by a motive contrary to that which
produced the first part (1909b, pp. 191–192).

The patient's habit of "letting God decide" is another expression of
his ambivalence and emotional conflict. It is analogous to the consulting
of an oracle, or the practice of drawing deep significance from everyday
coincidences—another feature of Lorenz's behavior. These are typical
means, not of warding off danger, but of escaping the responsibility for the
danger that comes of giving in to repressed instinctual urges. It is as if God
were allowing him, just this once, to express his real feelings, or that
having expressed them, he is excused from any ensuing consequences,
because God, the oracle, or fate told him to do so.

Still other aspects of the patient's behavior can be explained, not as
manifesting the ambivalence itself, but rather as obsessive reactions to the
repressed hostility that makes up one part of that ambivalence. The com-

pulsions, for instance, are attempts "at a compensation for the doubt and at a correction of the intolerable conditions of inhibition to which the doubt bears witness" (Freud, 1909b, p. 243). Included in this group would be the fear that something might happen to Gisela during that summer holiday of 1903 and the compulsion to do everything possible to protect her (such as *forcing* her to put on the patient's hat when a wind blew up). The counting between lightning and thunder strokes can also be understood as a protective ritual to ward off danger.

5. Second Foundation: Object-Choice Conflict

We have now discussed one major foundation of the patient's neurosis—the ambivalent relationship to his father together with the guilt engendered by the hostile feelings involved in that relationship. This love–hate conflict originated in an unresolved oedipal complex dating back to the early period of infantile sexuality. We have seen how this conflict explained various aspects of the patient's behavior, and especially his attitude toward Gisela. But in this relationship Freud also saw evidence of the second major conflict underlying the illness—the conflict over a choice of love object. This conflict

> . . . corresponds to the normal vacillation between male and female which characterizes every one's choice of a love-object. . . . But normally this opposition [between love of 'Mummy' or 'Daddy'] soon loses the character of a hard-and-fast contradiction, of an inexorable 'either–or' (1909b, p. 238).

Ideally, this process begins in the resolution of the oedipal conflict. The boy identifies with his father and fixes his sexual hopes on getting a woman like mother. Eventually however, on reaching maturity, he is forced to choose a specific object, a certain woman as the loved person. This choice must always be a difficult one, but in Lorenz's case the problem became insuperable because of the additional burden of the unresolved oedipal conflict.

It will be remembered that the father had opposed the relationship with Gisela and stood for a marriage of security, especially since this had been his own choice with regard to the patient's mother.

> The conflict at the root of his illness was in essentials a struggle between the persisting influence of his father's wishes and his own amatory predilections (1909b, p. 200).

A number of pieces of behavior can be explained as symbolic or real efforts to break this authority, to defy this influence that remained psychically, emotionally potent even after the man had actually died. Remember the two peculiar incidents that the patient recalled when masturbation occurred—after reading how Goethe broke through his fears about a previous girl's curses, and after seeing a policeman stop a man playing a horn in a park. In both cases there was a prohibition to emotional display, and the masturbation could be interpreted as the defiance of such a command. Likewise the strange ritual of hearing the dead father knocking at the door late at night, opening the door, and exhibiting his penis. Here too, an act of rebellion against the father is apparent. At the same time, Freud points out, another motive, one not relevant to the present discussion, is at work in this ritual. The patient was plagued by guilt about not studying hard enough while the father was alive. In this one act, then, there is an element of penance, showing the father that the patient is now studying very late at night, and also an element of rebellion.

If the underlying psychological defect in the patient (the love–hate conflict) involved an unresolved oedipal situation, the "precipitating cause" of the actual neurosis can nevertheless be located in this second, object-choice conflict. Freud emphasizes this point in a section entitled "The Precipitating Cause of the Illness." The patient had long known that his dead father had once been in love with a poor girl and gave her up to marry into the wealthy family of his mother. Then in 1903 the patient's mother broached her own plans for marrying her son into a wealthy family. Now the identification with his father was reinforced.

> This family plan stirred up in him a conflict as to whether he should remain faithful to the lady he loved in spite of her poverty, or whether he should follow in his father's footsteps and marry the lovely, rich, and well-connected girl who had been assigned to him. And he resolved this conflict, which was in fact one between his love and the persisting influence of his father's wishes, by falling ill; or, to put it more correctly, by falling ill he avoided the task of resolving it in real life (1909b, pp. 198–199).

It was the suggestion of this marriage plan, and not the death of an uncle as the patient thought, that accounted for the exacerbation of his illness during 1903.

6. The Rat Obsession

Certainly the most complex pieces of behavior to be explained predominantly by reference to this object-choice conflict concerned the rat obsession. Freud admits that his own account is neither complete nor even certain as far as it goes. Moreover, his explanation suffers because he fails to back up certain interpretations with any actual statements of the patient. Therefore in our presentation we shall use primarily those parts of Freud's account that actually refer either to the biographical material published or to that found in the clinical notes.

The first factor is the identification of the "cruel captain" with the patient's father.

> When . . . the captain had told him about the rat punishment, the patient had only been struck at first by the combined cruelty and lasciviousness of the situation depicted. But immediately afterwards a connection had been set up with the scene from his childhood in which he himself had bitten some one. The captain—a man who could defend such punishments—had become a substitute for his father, and had thus drawn down upon himself a part of the reviving animosity which had burst out, on the original occasion, against his cruel father. The idea which came into his consciousness for a moment, to the effect that something of the sort might happen to some one he was fond of, is probably to be translated into a wish such as 'You ought to have the same thing done to you!' aimed at the teller of the story, but through him at his father (1909b, p. 217).

A second factor was that the patient tended always to identify himself with his father, particularly with regard to the military situation, since the father had been an officer for many years. A certain incident occurring during the father's service had been of special significance to the patient— the gambling episode in which the father was saved only by a loan from a friend, a loan which he was never able to repay. The patient related this story during a discussion of the rat obsession and noted its connection. His father had been a gambler, a *Spielratte* in colloquial German, a "playrat." The patient went on to say that the recollection of this debt was painful to him (the patient), and he felt ashamed of his father's behavior.

> The captain's words, 'You must pay back the 3.80 *kronen* to Lt. A.', had sounded to his ears like an allusion to this unpaid debt of his father's (1909b, p. 211).

The relation of the object-choice conflict to the whole rat punishment is made explicit by Freud in the following quotation:

> . . . the information that the young lady at the post office at Z had herself paid the charges due upon the packet, with a complimentary remark about himself, had intensified his identification with his father in quite another direction. At this stage in the analysis he brought out some new information, to the effect that the landlord of the inn at the little place where the post office was had had a pretty daughter. She had been decidedly encouraging to the smart young officer, so that he had thought of returning there after the maneuvers were over and of trying his luck with her. Now, however, she had a rival in the shape of the young lady at the post office. Like his father in the tale of his marriage, he could afford now to hesitate upon which of the two he should bestow his favors when he had finished his military service. We can see at once that his singular indecision whether he should travel to Vienna or go back to the place where the post office was, and the constant temptation he felt to turn back while he was on the journey, were not so senseless as they seemed to us at first. To his conscious

mind, the attraction exercised upon him by Z, the place where the post office was, was explained by the necessity of seeing Lt. A. and fulfilling the vow with his assistance. But in reality what was attracting him was the young lady at the post office, and the lieutenant was merely a good substitute for her, since he had lived at the same place and had himself been in charge of the military postal service. And when subsequently he heard that it was not Lt. A. but another officer B., who had been on duty at the post office that day, he drew *him* into his combination as well; and he was then able to reproduce in his deliria in connection with the two officers the hesitation he felt between the two girls who were so kindly disposed towards him (1909b, pp. 211–212).

The association of rats with money is accounted for by Freud in various ways. First, there are two linguistic associations:

$$Ratten = \text{rats}$$
$$Raten = \text{installments}$$
$$Spielratte = \text{gambler}$$

The installment word *Raten* was given by the patient when asked by Freud to associate to the idea *Ratten*. The patient even tended to pronounce these words identically, and had in fact once been corrected by a lawyer on this point. After giving Freud this association, the patient then went on to speak of his father's legacy to him, which was kept by the mother, while the patient received monthly installments or allowances. The second meaning has already been mentioned in connection with the father's unpaid debt resulting from a gambling loss. Thus, both these associations led through the father to money.

Freud also points out another of "the earliest and most important roots" of the rat obsession (1909b, p. 215). This was the incident in which the patient, while visiting his father's grave, saw a large beast that he took to be a rat (Freud suggests it was a weasel, which were very common in the locale) gliding along the top of the grave. The thought occurred that it had just eaten a meal off the corpse.[31]

Lastly, Freud emphasizes the general conditions existing within the patient at the time of the army maneuvers, during which the rat obsession began.

---

[31] One cannot help commenting that this incident is precisely the sort that a behavioristically inclined psychiatrist might pick up as the origin of the whole rat obsession. It is interesting to remember that the same sort of incident, brushed over by Freud, became the crux of an alternative, behavioristic explanation of the "Little Hans" case: Hans saw a horse-drawn bus fall over; it gave him a bad fright, and that is when his "nonsense" began (see Wolpe & Rachman, 1960). It is not our purpose to develop any such alternative explanation, but it is striking to notice how the focus of attention and the weighting of events is so very dependent upon one's theoretical commitments.

His libido had been increased by a long period of abstinence coupled with the friendly welcome which a young officer can always reckon upon receiving when he goes among women. Moreover, at the time when he had started for the maneuvers, there had been a certain coolness between himself and his lady. This intensification of his libido had inclined him to a renewal of his ancient struggle against his father's authority, and he had dared to think of having sexual intercourse with other women. His loyalty to his father's memory had grown weaker, his doubts as to his lady's merits had increased. . . . And when at the end of the maneuvers he had hesitated so long whether he should travel to Vienna or whether he should stop and fulfill his vow, he had represented in a single picture the two conflicts by which he had from the very first been torn—whether or no he should remain obedient to his father and whether or no he should remain faithful to his beloved.

[Freud adds in a note] It is perhaps not uninteresting to observe that once again obedience to his father coincided with abandoning the lady. If he had stopped and paid back the money to Lt. A., he would have made atonement to his father, and at the same time he would have deserted his lady in favor of some one else more attractive. In this conflict the lady had been victorious—with the assistance, to be sure, of the patient's own normal good sense (1909b, p. 219).

All of the factors mentioned so far added to the formation of the rat obsession.[32] There was the patient's identification with his soldier-father, and the simultaneous rebellion against such identification and shame over the father's "crime" of failing to repay a debt. At the same time there was

---

[32] Freud mentions another factor—anal erotism—which we have not included in this discussion for several reasons. In the first place are historical considerations. In 1909 when the Lorenz case was published Freud had not yet distinguished any definite "pregenital" stages of development; as mentioned earlier, footnote 27, these were added to his theories over a period of several years and in reverse order. In 1908, in "Character and Anal Erotism" (1908b), the "anal personality" was described, but there was as yet no reference to a particular anal-sadistic pregenital stage. This idea, together with the connection of obsessional illnesses to fixation at the anal-sadistic level, was not posited until "The Predisposition to Obsessional Neurosis" (1913). The oral stage was not described until the third, 1915, edition of the *Three Essays on the Theory of Sexuality*.

Second, in the present case Freud's use of the concept of anal erotism is quite minimal. It is put forth only as one of several possible factors accounting for the rat obsession, and the evidence from the patient's testimony seems particularly weak and open to the charge of being elicited by Freud's suggestions. Moreover, in the second, theoretical portion of the Lorenz case, where Freud discusses the general mechanisms and characteristics of obsessional illnesses as he then understood them, there is no mention at all of anal erotism. Thus, on the grounds of both the historical development of the concept and because of its minimal role in the actual case, anal erotism will not be introduced at this point. Nevertheless, it must be kept in mind that it is precisely this aspect of the case that is often focused upon and enlarged by present-day analysts.

the object-choice conflict, which was first cast as the choice between loyalty to the father and love for Gisela. During the maneuvers this same conflict became extended to cover a choice between loyalty to Gisela and sexual attraction for a new girl. In such a state of mind the idea of the rat punishment had immediate appeal as a new method of giving vent to hostile feelings—those directed at the dead father and also at the absent Gisela. But in the fashion typical of the patient such wishes could reach consciousness only as reaction-formations, fears that the rat punishment would occur to his father and Gisela unless certain protective measures were adopted.

The exact content of the original prohibition can, perhaps, offer further insight into this behavior: "You must not repay Lt. A. the money, or the rat punishment will come true for father and Gisela." In this way the patient attached a supposedly dire consequence onto an almost inevitable action, the repaying of a public debt. Thus, in repaying the debt the responsibility for the unconsciously desired consequences in Lorenz's fantasy could be removed; he could say in truth that he had no choice. Here was a form of wish fulfillment which avoided the recriminations of a guilty conscience. However, once the true state of affairs, which had been consciously repressed by Lorenz, is brought out, then the opposing compulsion can be at least partially understood. The original prohibition was against repaying Lt. A., but the truth was that the money was not owed to him, so there was no necessity at all for breaking the obsessional prohibition. Yet the patient then found himself bound by a compulsion: "You must repay Lt. A." This compulsion had no reality basis in any debt, but it did tie into Lorenz's fantasies in two different ways. Because of the patient's identification with his father, repaying Lt. A. symbolized repaying his father's old gambling debt and, in a sense, forgiving him by removing this old disgrace. This, of course, was good reason for the patient *not* to repay Lt. A. Then, a useful rationalization would be the fear, based on the previous prohibition, that repaying Lt. A. would bring a horrible torture down on his dead father. On the other hand, this same obsessional connection between the repaying of Lt. A. and the rat torture offered a good reason to Lorenz *for* carrying out the compulsion, thereby giving vent to his deepest feelings of hostility. In this case, however, the rationalization was that if he failed to carry out this command he would be acting cowardly, a trait both he and his soldierly father detested. Thus, in obeying the command, far from harming father, he would be fulfilling his noble ideals.

The upshot of all these extraordinarily complex interconnections was that whether Lorenz obeyed or broke either the prohibition or the compulsion, various deep and for the most part unconscious feelings would be expressed. And this, of course, is a primary purpose that obsessional thinking serves.

These considerations certainly seem to go some way toward explaining the origin of the rat obsessions of Lorenz. However, it is important in this case, as with all other sorts of neurotic behavior, to separate the factors leading to that behavior's adoption or development, and the factors which perpetuated or exaggerated that behavior as the individual grows up or changes his life situation. Thus, during the course of the analysis the rat punishment remained a favorite device for expressing hostility. For instance, when the patient was having the affair with a dressmaker he thought: "So many copulations, so many rats for Gisela." Here, the vindictive, punishing theme, the desire to get back at Gisela, is unmistakable. The reasons for this continuing prominence of the rat ideas are not entirely clear. One important factor, however, must have been the punishment's terrifying novelty and its peculiar personal verbal associations. Then, too, Freud's own emphasis on this material during the analysis must have contributed to its continuing development and elaboration. These questions, however, may remain outside our discussion since they were not taken up by Freud in any detail in his explanation of the patient's illness.

7. Transference Phenomena

A psychoanalytic explanation should be able to account not only for the history of the patient's neurosis before coming to the analyst, but also it should explain the course of development during the analytic process itself. This is simply an application of the distinction mentioned above, between the explanation of the origin and the explanation of the changes and developments of a piece of behavior. In the present case Freud isolates two basic conflicts, and each offers insight into the events we described as transference phenomena. Thus, early in the analysis a period occurred in which each session was marked by great outpourings of abuse directed toward Freud. The patient alternated between overt hostility and abject shame for showing such feelings. These phenomena can be understood as the result of gradually bringing into consciousness the patient's latent hostility previously directed against his father. In the transference relationship Freud became the patient's father in that feelings once felt about the father were reenacted in the therapeutic situation with the analyst.

Later in the analysis another group of phenomena occurred. Having brought to awareness his ancient ambivalence toward his father and having at least partially "worked through" these emotions, the patient went on to form a second transference, this time focusing on his second conflict—the choice of a love object. Several incidents occurred centering on a young girl the patient once met outside Freud's rooms, whom the patient immediately assumed to be the doctor's daughter. Thus, there was the idea that Freud was so kindly and good to the patient only because he desired the patient for a son-in-law. At the same time there were fantasies about the wealth and position of Freud's family. Freud was in this way cast in the same role as the Rubensky family who had lured the patient's father from his true love for a poor girl into the wealthy marriage to the patient's mother. Freud also represented the patient's mother and her own plan to marry off her son to yet another Rubensky girl and so secure for him a financially bright future. The dream of Freud's daughter with dung for eyes symbolizes this conflict between marrying for "filthy lucre" or for "beautiful eyes." On the other hand, this daughter of Freud also presented an attractive aspect. Hence the fantasy of having sexual relations with her, of getting revenge on Gisela in this way.

Still later in the analysis the affair with the dressmaker repeated this same conflict over choice of love object. It was only when the original conflict and the original ambivalence of feelings were reenacted within the transference situation, or within a new reality situation such as the dressmaker affair, that these emotions could be recognized for what they were and demonstrated to the patient. In this way unconscious patterns of behavior and repressed feelings first escape the censors of consciousness by being recreated within the transference situation. The analyst is then in a position to study them and to gradually bring the patient to an awareness of these original sources of his disturbance.

This completes our formal presentation of the case of Paul Lorenz. A number of additional explanations of particular pieces of behavior will be given in the following chapters, but these will all be derived by the application of the general explanation which has been discussed. Our task now is to examine the logical characteristics of this explanation and to discover the similarities and differences between it and explanations in other fields.

Chapter 5/THE THESIS OF THE SEPARATE DOMAIN

In this chapter we shall be concerned with an analysis sometimes put forth of psychoanalytic explanations which emphasizes the differences between them and explanations in the natural sciences; then, in the following two chapters we shall attempt to develop an alternative account emphasizing the similarities and showing the extent to which the methods and procedures developed for other sciences can be applied in psychoanalysis. The various philosophical arguments comprising this issue will be examined first in general terms and then in their specific application to Freud's explanation of Paul Lorenz's behavior.

It has been argued that explanations of human behavior, especially in psychoanalysis, are wholly, or at least partially, of a peculiar kind, rational certainly, and perhaps even scientific in some sense, yet of a radically different type from the typical explanations of physical events. This radical difference has two components: There is first of all a difference of subject matter in that psychoanalysis is said to deal with human "actions" instead of "mere body movements." Second, there is a difference in the sorts of factors used in explaining this peculiar subject matter, in that psychoanalysis is said to refer to purposes, motives, intentions, reasons, etc., instead of physical causes. From the many examples possible, one might take the following as an unambiguous statement of the thesis:

> One may ask 'Why?' and expect an answer in terms of reasons, intentions, purposes and the like; or one may ask 'Why?' and expect an answer in terms of physiological or psychological determining antecedent conditions. This dichotomy remains untouched when the misleading character of other dichotomies such as that between the mental and the physical, or the inner and the outer aspects of human behavior, has been noted (MacIntyre, 1958, pp. 51–52).

We can, very roughly, epitomize this position, which can be called the "thesis of the separate domain," by saying that the psychoanalyst (or psychologist, etc.) explains human actions in terms of reasons, while the neurologist (or physical scientist, etc.) explains body movements in terms of causes.

The historical background and development of this position would make a fascinating study, but we shall not pursue it. Nevertheless, it seems evident that one important factor in its present popularity has been the desire to defend psychoanalysis from what has sometimes seemed to be a very unfavorable and possibly unjust comparison to other behavioral sciences, let alone to the natural sciences. Occasionally, this sort of defense has been adopted by psychoanalysts; Guntrip's discussion of the concept of "overdetermination" in *Personality Structure and Human Interaction* (1961) seems to be an example of this, and we shall discuss it in Section D of this chapter. However, apart from a few such instances, it seems fair to say that this position has been predominantly an "outsider's" argument, a defense put forward for the most part by philosophers who are favorably disposed to psychoanalysis. Such a characterization, it should be understood, is not meant to be pejorative but only descriptive. Clearly, two options are available to any defender: He can try to show that psychoanalysis does in fact, or at least can in principle, measure up to the standards of the natural sciences, or he can try to show that psychoanalysis is entirely separate from these other fields with its own methods and its own canon of procedure. The thesis of the separate domain is a form of this latter defense with the implicit aim being the marking off of a private preserve, however circumscribed, within which the analyst can reign supreme.

This position has a number of variations. For one thing there is the problem of just how circumscribed the preserve is to be, whether all human behavior or only parts of it fall into the separate domain. Again, different philosophers emphasize different aspects of this thesis, some concentrating on the action-movement distinction and others on the reason-cause distinction. In this chapter we shall not be concerned with the question of the extent of this separate domain but with the possibility that the whole thesis is mistaken in principle. Our discussion will be divided into four sections. In Section A, we shall present one account of the movement-action distinction as it is presented by a philosopher with specific reference to psychoanalytic explanations. In Section B the cause-reason distinction will be discussed. Obviously, the various arguments cannot be separated so neatly into these two groups; nevertheless, it will be informative to approach the problem in this way. It must be emphasized, however, that we are *not* attempting to deal adequately with the manifold complexities of the philosophical concepts of "action," "movement," "reason," and "cause." Our purpose is to examine these problems only insofar as to show that certain formulations of these concepts have been wrongly used to support an unwarranted interpretation of psychoanalytic explanations, to place them within a separate domain divorced from all other physical sciences. Our major focus, however, remains on psychoanalytic explanations, not on the philosophical analysis of causation or motivation.

In Section C, we shall try to show that in Freud's writings, and especially in the Lorenz case itself, there appears no foundation whatever for either the movement-action or the cause-reason forms, or indeed any other variation of the thesis of the separate domain. Finally, in Section D, we shall discuss how some analysts have mistakenly taken over these philosophical distinctions in an attempt to establish their own peculiar form of separate domain.

A. MOVEMENTS AND ACTIONS IN *The Concept of Motivation*

For the sake of argument we shall confine ourselves at this point to a single philosopher's use of the separate domain thesis, namely, Professor R. S. Peters in *The Concept of Motivation*.[1] Peters states his basic thesis simply:

> . . . human actions cannot be sufficiently explained in terms of causal concepts like 'colourless movements.' Indeed to claim that we are confronted with an action is *ipso facto* to rule out such mechanical explanations, as being sufficient (1958, p. 8).

The reason why causal explanations cannot be sufficient soon emerges:

> To give a causal *explanation* of an event involves at least showing that other conditions being presumed unchanged a change in one variable is a *sufficient* condition for a change in another. In the mechanical conception of 'cause' it is also demanded that there should be spatial and temporal contiguity between the movements involved. Now the trouble about giving this sort of explanation of human actions is that we can never specify an action exhaustively in terms of movements of the body or within the body (Hamlyn, 1953). It is therefore impossible to state sufficient conditions in terms of antecedent movements which may vary concomitantly with subsequent movements. 'Signing a contract,' for instance, is a typical example of a human action. . . . A very general range of movements could perhaps

---

[1] We have chosen this book to begin with since it uses Freudian examples and in general seems more concerned with explicitly psychoanalytic explanations than, say Melden's *Free Action* (1961), where a somewhat similar view is put forth. For a more recent discussion, see Hamlyn (1964) and Smart (1964). It is interesting to note that in his 1964 paper Hamlyn explicitly rejects his earlier position which is cited approvingly by Peters in the argument now under discussion. Also, Professor A. J. Ayer's Auguste Comte Lecture "Man as a Subject for Science" (1964) contains some excellent criticisms, from a somewhat different point of view, of these same arguments. Our debt to these and other writers should be apparent.

be specified [for signing a contract], but no specific movements of the
muscles, limbs, or nervous system, which *must* occur before it would be
conceded that a contract had been signed. . . . So we could never give a
sufficient explanation of an action in causal terms because we could never
stipulate the movements which would have to count as dependent variables
(1958, pp. 12–13).[2]

The argument of this passage can be outlined, almost entirely in Peters'
own words, as follows:

1. Causal explanations of events must at least show that a change in
   one variable, with other conditions presumed unchanged, is a sufficient condition for a change in another variable.
2. The ability to give a sufficient condition presupposes the exhaustive, complete specification of the event in question.
3. It is impossible to give a complete specification of any action in
   terms of body movements.
4. Therefore, it is impossible to "give a sufficient explanation of an
   action in causal terms . . .," i.e., in terms of body movements
   (1958, p. 13).

This argument must now be analyzed in detail.

1. Necessary and Sufficient Conditions, and Causal Explanations

The first premise given above involves a partial definition of what is
meant by the concept of "causal explanation," namely, a causal explanation "involves at least showing that a change in X is a sufficient condition
for a change in Y." This statement, however, seems mistaken, at least as an
analysis of the usual meaning of the term "causal explanation." Let us
confine ourselves to a single meaning of "cause" that seems to be central
to our common-sense understanding of the term. The meaning we have in
mind is that in which it is true to say:

a. The radiation exposure caused this plant to wither.
b. The nail puncture caused the tire to blow out.

The first question to be asked concerning these examples is whether
the logical concepts of necessary and sufficient conditions seem to have any
application. Let us take each of these concepts in order. To say that A is
a necessary condition for B is to say that if B occurs, or has occurred, then
A must have occurred prior to B. Given both the occurrence of a B and
the assertion that A is a necessary condition of B, we can infer the occurrence of A:

---

[2] Peters' italics.

1. B has occurred.
2. A is a necessary condition for B's occurrence.

3. Therefore, A has occurred prior to B.

But it is quite plain that this analysis would not normally fit either of our examples above. In applying this idea of a necessary condition to our examples we get the following:

a1. If the plant withered, then it must have been caused by radiation exposure, since radiation exposure is a necessary condition for withering.

b1. If there were a tire blowout, then it must have been caused by a nail puncture, since a nail puncture is a necessary condition for a tire blowout.

Certainly it is clear that a1 and b1 do not *mean* the same thing as a and b, respectively. Moreover, these new statements a1 and b1 are not even entailed by the originals; that is, one could assert a and deny a1; assert b and deny b1. In fact, in all but the most contrived of situations this is just what would occur. Under normal circumstances many other factors might have been sufficient to cause the event in question (the plant's withering) without necessarily including the particular factor stated (the radiation). A lack of water or of sunlight might have been sufficient to cause the plant's withering without any radiation being necessary at all. Of course, it *might* be the case that one would want to assert just such a statement as a1 or b1; that is, to give a necessary condition for an event. Our point is only that the meaning of such a statement is quite different from the meaning of the ordinary causal assertion as exemplified by a and b.

Much the same argument can be given against the use of the concept of "sufficient condition." To say that A is a sufficient condition for B is to say that if A occurs (or did occur) then B will occur (or must have occurred) after A. Expressing our original examples in terms of sufficient conditions we get:

a2. If the plant were given the radiation exposure, then the plant must have withered, since radiation exposure is a sufficient condition for withering.

b2. If there were a nail puncture, then a tire blowout must have occurred, since a nail puncture is a sufficient condition for a tire blowout.

But it is obvious that many other conditions had also to exist in order that these events should have occurred. In restating the original examples in terms of sufficient conditions we end up with statements that would be false in most contexts. And whatever their truth value as they stand, a2 and b2, like a1 and b1, express meanings quite different from the original statements a and b.

It might be objected at this point that we have ignored the author's statement that:

> . . . other conditions being presumed unchanged a change in one variable is a *sufficient* condition for a change in another (1958, p. 12).[3]

In fact, however, this particular caveat does not recur as Peters' argument progresses, and there is good reason for its omission. To add the "all other things being equal" clause would be to break down the entire necessary-sufficient distinction on which the argument relies. To assert "When all other things are equal (i.e., under certain conditions), A is a necessary condition of B" is actually to *deny* that A *is* a necessary condition pure and simple. That is, under certain *other* conditions (i.e., when other things are not equal), A may *not* be necessary. Likewise with "sufficient condition." To introduce this clause would undermine the term's meaning. To assert "When all other things are equal, A is a sufficient condition of B" is in fact to admit that A is *not* sufficient by itself. We have interpreted Peters as using the concepts of necessary and sufficient conditions as integral parts of his argument, and we have offered criticism directed to this point. Far from refuting our own objections, the reference to "other things being equal" seems incompatible with his main argument and hence can offer no support to it.

The discussion above has centered upon individual occurrences and has attempted to show that causal statements given in such contexts cannot usually be analyzed into statements about necessary or sufficient conditions. There is an important related issue, not touched upon so far, concerning statements about classes of events such as "plants withering." The vital questions are: (1) What is the relationship between asserting causal statements about individual occurrences, like examples a and b above, and asserting general laws about classes of events? (2) Specifically, does the assertion of a statement like a (i.e., "This radiation exposure caused this plant to wither.") commit us to some form of generalization or causal law about the class of events "plants withering" (i.e., "Radiation exposure causes plants to wither.")? (3) Do the arguments about necessary and sufficient conditions we used regarding statements a and b hold also for laws about classes of events? These questions will be left unexamined at this point since they do not affect our discussion of the separate domain thesis as Peters develops it. We will, however, take them up in Chapter 7

---

[3] Peters' italics.

when we examine the use of laws in psychoanalytic explanations of behavior.

What, then, are we to conclude from this discussion of Peters' analysis of causal explanation? Are we no longer to be allowed to say that the radiation caused the plant to wither, or that the nail caused the tire blow-out? Far from it. We do not imply that it was necessarily wrong to assert a or b, to assert that such and such was indeed the cause of the event in question. Rather the proper conclusion is that in such typical situations some other criteria for selecting causes are in operation than those for choosing necessary or sufficient conditions. The cause pointed out in each assertion may not be a necessary condition, for other circumstances might have been sufficient for the event's occurrence even in the absence of that cause. Nor must the cause be a sufficient condition, for many other factors might be necessary in addition for the event's occurrence. The first premise, then, of Peters' argument seems to be untenable. It rests upon the faulty definition of causal explanation as the giving of logically sufficient conditions for an event's occurrence.

2. Logically Sufficient Conditions and Sufficient Explanations

If one compares the first premise of the argument as outlined earlier with the conclusion it can be noted that a crucial shift has occurred: from "causal explanation" in statement 1 to "sufficient explanation . . . in causal terms" in statement 4. The two phrases are not synonymous, and in order for the argument to be valid a further assumption is necessary: that a sufficient explanation of an action involves at least a knowledge of the sufficient conditions for that action's occurrence. Without such an assumption the conclusion would simply be that no *causal* explanation is possible of an action in terms of movements, but *not* that a sufficient explanation is impossible. That is, by Peters' definition a causal explanation must give the sufficient conditions in terms of movements; yet, he claims, it is impossible to state the sufficient conditions in terms of body movements for any action; hence, a causal explanation of actions is impossible. But this is not the same as saying that a sufficient explanation is impossible.

Obviously, there is something paradoxical both about the assertion that a sufficient explanation involves giving the sufficient conditions, and the denial of this assertion. Clearly, we are conflating two meanings of the word "sufficient":

1. The logical meaning as used in the phrase "sufficient conditions" and discussed in the previous section.
2. The more general meaning of "adequate" or "proper," as used in speaking of a "sufficient explanation."

To say that an explanation of an action in terms of sufficient conditions of movements (meaning 1) is impossible is *not* to say that a sufficient explanation of an action (meaning 2) in terms of movements is likewise impossible—unless one stipulates that a "sufficient explanation" *means* a "statement of sufficient conditions"; that is, unless one chooses to define an adequate or sufficient explanation (meaning 2) by reference to "logical sufficiency" (meaning 1). In our first criticism we attempted to show why Peters' analysis of causal explanation in terms of sufficient conditions was wrong. But even granting his analysis, granting premise 1 of the argument, the conclusion still follows only if this second definition is added, that of "sufficient explanation" in terms of "sufficient conditions." Of course, if one insists on defining an adequate explanation in this way there can be no objection. One simply notes the definition and then goes on to observe that many explanations judged to be sufficient or adequate both by scientists in laboratories and by laymen in everyday experience fail to meet this definition; they just do not give the sufficient conditions for their subjects. This failure is interesting, but neither arresting nor condemning, for the important issue is to bring out just what *other* criteria of sufficiency or adequacy *are* in fact being employed.

The statement "sufficient explanations of an action involve at least the giving of the sufficient conditions for that action's occurrence" is therefore definitely not a linguistic observation, since our ordinary usage, as we have seen, of "sufficient explanation" is something rather different. Nor is there any reason why we should make this statement true by definition. As we have seen from the previous section, one important variety of explanations, causal explanations of particular events, do *not* in fact supply the logically sufficient conditions for an event's occurrence. Indeed, it seems more and more apparent with the development of science that there are few, if any, categorical statements which could include *all* the conditions sufficient for an event's occurrence. It appears that the quest for sufficient conditions may be an illusory one, impossible in practice ever to be successful. Yet it would be quite wrong to draw from this observation some metaphysical conclusion as to the impossibility of certainty or objectivity in science. Instead, this observation casts grave doubts upon the utility, indeed the self-consistency of analyses of explanation which involve such criteria. If the criteria can never be met, then they will be useless as an aid to distinguishing adequate from inadequate explanations. There are other criteria for sufficiency or adequacy of an explanation than giving the "logically sufficient conditions," be they physical or purposive conditions, and this is the point of the present criticism. The examination of what such criteria may be will be taken up in Chapter 7.

3. Exhaustive Specification of Movements and Actions

Our third criticism of Peters' argument is that there is a logical muddle involved in premise 3. This can best be seen by reviewing the author's exact words:

> . . . we can never specify an action exhaustively in terms of movements of the body or within the body. . . . [there are] no specific movements of the muscles, limbs, or nervous systems which *must* occur before it would be conceded that a contract had been signed (1958, pp. 12–13).[4]

There is first of all an ambiguity here as to whether one is referring to a particular class of actions, such as "signing a contract," or to a particular instance of that kind of action. From the above quotation it appears that it is a class of actions that is meant, so we can examine this interpretation first.

The argument is that one could never specify completely the movements that might conceivably be involved in actions of a certain type or class. This assertion seems true. One can think of all sorts of movements that might in a particular situation be considered part of the action of signing a contract. For instance, there would be arm movements in the usual cases, but an amputee holding a pen between his toes or in his mouth could certainly sign a contract. Pen and paper are of course the most common instruments, but one can easily imagine various others, which would necessitate different movements. But this observation can easily be taken to be more impressive than it actually is.

In fact, one can never specify exhaustively the class of actions "signing a contract" in terms of other *actions,* let alone in terms of body movements. The analogous question can be posed: What *actions* must take place "before it would be conceded that a contract had been signed"? Is it always drawing complex lines on a piece of paper, or writing a name in a blank space? What of the fact that the signing of a contract might at the same time also be the action of "selling one's house" or "buying a boat," or "joining the Foreign Legion?" A class of actions, for instance "buying a boat," may contain virtually an unlimited number of other actions: handing money to John Smith, writing a check for $15,000, signing an order form, etc. It seems clear that there is no limit to the possible actions that might, on a particular occasion, be a part of an instance of "signing a contract" or "buying a boat." Conversely, there is no particular action, let alone particular body movements, which must on every occasion be executed before one would admit that a contract had been signed or a boat purchased.

---

[4] Peters' italics.

Finally, still another analogous question can be asked: What *neuro-logical events* must occur before it would be conceded that a body movement of the class "arm rising" had occurred? Could any neurologist give a listing of such events? Conversely, is there any particular neurological event the occurrence of which is sufficient to guarantee that there is an instance of "arm rising"? The conclusion appears obvious: not even a class of body movements can be exhaustively specified in terms of other physical movements.

It seems that we have now reduced to absurdity the argument as it is proposed about classes of events. Not only can a class of actions not be exhaustively specified in terms of movements, such a class cannot even be exhaustively specified in terms of other actions. Nor can any class of body movements be exhaustively specified in terms of all the possible neurological events that could compose it. But this observation that classes of events have indefinite numbers of differently describable instances composing them, while interesting, is irrelevant from the standpoint of Peters' argument. We do not hold it against the neurologist that he cannot give an exhaustive list of the neurological events comprising all possbile instances of "arm rising." The essential question is whether or not, given the *particular* instance of an "arm rising" or "signing a contract," complete specification in terms of movements is possible.

It is not the lack of exhaustive specification of classes of actions, but of particular *instances* of actions that is essential to Peters' argument. The argument as presented gains a specious plausibility by trading on the easy confusion of an obviously true assertion about classes of actions with an independent one about particular instances of actions. The real issue is, first, whether or not in a particular instance one can exhaustively specify an action in terms of body movements and, second, if not, what conclusions follow as to the possibility of explaining that action. For the continuity of our argument, however, we shall delay this problem until we have discussed several further errors in the argument as originally presented.

4. Insufficient versus Inappropriate Explanations

Peters' argument can be criticized quite apart from the previous three points concerning certain of its premises; for even if the particular argument given seems faulty, the conclusion might still be true on other grounds. There is, however, a confusion in the conclusion itself. Consider the following two statements:

> Such physiological knowledge [about the brain and nervous system] *might* enable us to predict *bodily movements*. And *if* we had bridging laws to correlate such physiological findings with descriptions of actions we might

indirectly predict actions. But we would *first* have to grasp concepts connected with action like 'knowing what we are doing' and 'grasp of means to an end.' As such concepts have no application at the level of mere movement, such predictions would not count as sufficient *explanations* of *actions* (Peters, 1958, p. 14).[5]

If the question is 'Why did Jones walk across the road?' a *sufficient* explanation can only be given in terms of the rule-following purposive model—if this is a case of an action rather than of something happening to him. Answers in terms of causal concepts like 'receptor impulses' and 'colourless movement,' are either not explanations because they state not sufficient but only necessary conditions, or they are ways of denying that what has to be explained is a human action (1958, p. 15).[6]

These two quotations show a basic confusion as to which is the operative word—"sufficient" or "explanation." The shift in the use of italics in the last sentence of the first quotation and the first sentence of the second clearly shows this problem. The question is whether explanations of actions in terms of movements are: (1) simply not *sufficient* (adequate) explanations or (2) whether they are not really *explanations* of the actions *at all* but only "physiological knowledge" explaining "bodily movements." It seems that either alternative raises difficulties.

With regard to the first interpretation, in Section 2 we have already discussed the thesis that explanations of actions in terms of movements cannot be sufficient. We pointed out that Peters' argument for this assertion rests upon a particular definition of sufficiency or adequacy, namely, that a sufficient explanation must at least provide the logically sufficient conditions for an action's occurrence. This definition, however, is not the normal usage, at least with regard to certain explanations, for instance, those of the causal variety. Moreover, we argued that to adopt such a criterion for a sufficient explanation would be unwise, since there is good reason to believe that such a standard could never in practice be attained.

It is, however, the second, more extreme interpretation of the conclusion that seems to emerge during the course of Peters' book, namely, that there is a logical gap between movements and actions which renders explanations of actions in terms of movements not simply insufficient but inappropriate. As is evident from the second quotation above, to give such movements as explanation for an action is either no explanation at all, or alternatively it is to deny that the event in question was in fact an action.

Movements *qua* movements are neither intelligent, efficient, nor correct. They only become so in the context of an action. There cannot therefore be a sufficient explanation of actions in causal terms because, as Popper has put

---

[5] Peters' italics.
[6] Peters' italics.

> it, there is a logical gulf between nature and convention. . . . There is, however, no objection to [causal] explanations of what *happens* to a man; for happenings cannot be characterized as intelligent or unintelligent, correct or incorrect, efficient or inefficient. *Prima facie* they are just occurrences (1958, pp. 14–15).[7]

Here the logical distinction between movements and actions and the explanations of each is very clear-cut. It will be shown in Section 6 that the author is not consistent on this point of whether statements about physical movements are simply insufficient or logically inappropriate. Yet in passages such as that just quoted this extreme interpretation seems evident, and this assertion is repeated elsewhere:

> For my case is not simply that causal explanations are otiose when we know the point of a person's action. . . . It is also that if we are in fact confronted with a case of a genuine action (i.e. an act of doing something as opposed to suffering something), then causal explanations are *ipso facto* inappropriate as sufficient explanations. Indeed they may rule out rule-following purposive explanations (1958, pp. 11–12).

The difficulty is that no reasons at all are given to support this view. The argument outlined earlier, even if its premises were valid, proves only that explanations of actions in terms of movements alone could not be sufficient, according to a certain definition of "sufficiency." But this is very different from contending that such explanations are completely inappropriate. This conclusion does not follow from Peters' argument. Moreover, it is a very extreme and doubtful assertion. To say bluntly that causal factors are "not explanations because they state not sufficient but only necessary conditions" (1958, p. 15) just seems wrong. Consider for instance Paul Lorenz's supposed sexual precocity. It is one thing to say that such a constitutional factor is insufficient to account for his childhood inability to cope with his sexual feelings and hostility toward his father. This contention is one that Freud himself admitted. But it is quite different and far more radical to assert that sexual precocity is completely inappropriate to, and out of place in, our explanation of Lorenz's problem of adjustment during the oedipal period. Is it really inappropriate to take note of and introduce such physical factors into our explanation? I think the answer is obviously "no." It is one of our purposes to suggest that information concerning physical states and movements may often be highly relevant to and indeed be a part of explanations of human actions.

5. *Criteria for Distinguishing Movements from Actions*

A fifth criticism of Peters' argument rests upon the author's own criteria for distinguishing between movements and actions. Although

---

[7] Peters' italics.

there may be good reasons against our drawing a hard and fast distinction between actions and movements, nevertheless, it will be illuminating to accept this dichotomy for the sake of argument. The obvious question then arises: How, in practice, in a particular instance of an event's occurring is one to decide if this is a case of a "genuine action"? There seem to be three criteria which Peters offers at different times and which might be used separately or in conjunction (numbering mine):

(1) . . . if we are in fact confronted with a case of a genuine action (i.e. an act of doing something as opposed to suffering something) . . . (1958, p. 12).

(2) Movements *qua* movements are neither intelligent, efficient, nor correct. They only become so in the context of an action . . . for happenings cannot be characterized as intelligent or unintelligent, correct or incorrect, efficient or inefficient. *Prima facie* they are just occurrences (1958, pp. 14–15).

(3) Indeed to claim that we are confronted with an action is *ipso facto* to rule out such mechanical explanations, as being sufficient (1958, p. 8).

If these criteria are to be at all useful in practice, they will have to be interpreted not as definitions but as referring to definite observable characteristics by virtue of which one can distinguish between actions and movements. Criteria (1) and (2) clearly can be interpreted in this way. Each of these criteria, however, raises difficulties.

In the case of (1) the contrast between doing something and suffering something can be grasped from an example Peters uses of behavior that would *not* be an action, i.e., a case of someone suffering something.

[Behavior] may go wrong by being deflected towards a peculiar goal as with a married man who suddenly makes an advance to a choir boy. In such cases it is as if the man suffers something rather than does something. It is because things seem to be happening to him that it is appropriate to ask what made, drove, or possessed him to do that. The appropriate answer in such cases may be in terms of a causal theory (1958, p. 10).

It seems this locution of "suffering something" is a very peculiar and artificial one. It gains whatever plausibility it may have from the related usage of "suffering from" something. We might say that the person in the example "suffers from" a frustration of his sexual life. The man was, perhaps, unable to gain adequate satisfaction of his needs for a passive, dependent relationship within his marriage, and therefore he sought out a homosexual relationship. One might even say after careful study that the man in question "suffers from" strong, compulsive desires for young boys. But does it follow that he "suffered" the particular seduction attempt in question? It seems almost impossible to put such a notion into meaningful language. People do "suffer from" hunger pangs, or the pain of renal colic; and one could also say that people suffer or undergo hunger pangs, or even that a person suffers or undergoes spasmodic retchings or tonic-clonic seizures. Even these cases seem odd, but beyond such examples it seems to make little sense to speak of suffering or undergoing complex movements or behaviors such as a seduction of a choir boy. We may do things without being aware of them, as in sleepwalking and all sorts of habitual and compulsive activities; yet this does not mean that we "suffer" these actions. And this contention remains true even if one goes on to point out that because a person "suffers from" certain conditions he may act in certain ways. The feelings, emotions, and delusions from which people might be said to suffer will certainly affect their behavior and must be taken into account in any explanation. These considerations, however, do not affect the question of what actions are done, but only the problem of explaining those actions.

Peters' first criterion, then, involves a very misleading and dubious dichotomy between "doing" and "suffering" some piece of behavior. But even if we accept this division a further problem remains: How are we to know whether a given piece of behavior is a case of a "doing" or of a "suffering"? Presumably any overt, observable behavior, a seduction, for instance, could be either one, as the example given implies. This rules out our using observation of behavior as evidence for a "doing" or a "suffering." The alternative is to see how the event in question is to be explained. Apparently, if the seduction is explained by a compulsion, a "possession," then it was a "suffering" and not an action. But now we have reversed our criterion. We began by considering "suffering" as a sign that a causal explanation would be appropriate. It turns out, however, that only if we first know that a causal explanation is appropriate can we assert that the event was a "suffering."

Criterion (2) in contrast to (1) offers three separate characteristics by which actions are to be distinguished from movements: intelligence, efficiency, and correctness. That is, actions can be judged along these three parameters whereas movements cannot. If we can find pieces of behavior of which it is true to say they are somewhat intelligent, or efficient, or correct, then such pieces of behavior must be actions. The problem now becomes: How does one make judgments concerning these characteristics? What is the evidence upon which such judgments are based? There must be certain features on the basis of which an action is said to be more or less intelligent, efficient, and correct.

There are two possibilities here. The first is that one bases such judgments upon the observation of bodily changes or motions in the individual under study. But of course this will not do at all, since all such changes are simply pieces of "physiological knowledge" which might at best "enable us to predict *bodily movements*" (Peters, 1958, p. 14).[8] From such move-

---

[8] Peters' italics.

ments, by Peters' own argument, one could never get to the action itself. Two events might be characterized by the same outwardly observable movements, yet only one might be a "genuine action." Whatever evidence we use to determine whether an event shows "intelligence, efficiency, and correctness," such observations could, on this account, not be of physical movements.

So the second alternative emerges. The properties which make an action something more than mere movements are not physical properties at all. But this conclusion seems to solve one problem by creating two mysteries. First, what is the evidence that there *are* any such properties which are not physical? Second, if there are such properties what is the evidence that they are observable to our senses? Or, alternatively, what is the evidence that we possess some special sense of intuition or immediate awareness by which such properties can be directly grasped? Simply posing all these questions seems quite enough to cast grave doubts upon the applicability of criterion (2).

At this point, however, the objection can be made that we are confusing "physical" with "observable." The relationship between these two concepts is a complex one and deserves some study. There are, in fact, difficulties with either answer to the question of whether or not to equate "physical" with "observable." Consider the problem of deciding whether a metal artifact found among a primitive people is actually an idol, a child's toy, or an implement for preparing a peculiar food unique to this group. Certainly such a problem is straightforward and could be answered by careful observation of the group in question (provided any members were still alive). The use of this artifact is certainly observable, discoverable, at least in principle, but we may hesitate to say that there is some physical characteristic of the artifact which differentiates these alternative uses. There can be no argument with those who would insist that the object's use is observable but not "physical" in the strict sense. However, for our present purposes, we are using "physical" in a broader sense to be roughly equivalent to "observable." Our reason for this is that an argument like Peters' concerning actions and movements gains a specious plausibility because it is obviously true that actions are *not* just physical movements in the strict sense. However, as long as we admit the essential point that our criteria for identifying actions depend upon properties which are observable, and hence amenable to scientific investigation, there is no problem. In order for the action-movement distinction to provide the basis for a real dichotomy between the physical and the behavioral sciences, actions would have to be essentially nonobservable, and this position is, I suggest, untenable.

The third criterion by which one might distinguish actions and movements is different from the first two, which at least appear to give observable features that could mark actions—"doing" versus "suffering"; or "intelligence, efficiency, and correctness." The third criterion, in contrast, simply provides a definition: Any piece of behavior which cannot be sufficiently explained in terms of movements is an action. But this procedure is overtly circular. The whole point of Peters' argument is that if we are dealing with a "genuine action" then it cannot be sufficiently explained in terms of movements. But now it turns out that one cannot know if what one is dealing with is in fact an action until one determines whether a sufficient explanation in terms of movements is impossible. Furthermore, it is not enough simply to realize that the *present* movement explanation is not sufficient; it is essential that one also know that such an explanation, no matter how far science advances, could *never be* sufficient. And such a claim seems very rash indeed, regardless of whether one adopts the author's definition of "sufficient explanation" or some other.

In the case of the first two criteria the problem was that one could find no observable properties which distinguished the particular actions under study from apparently identical body movements. In the case of the last criterion the situation is just the opposite. One has a definite logical feature that characterizes all actions; yet one can never be sure in a particular case if the event in question is in fact an instance of an action. It seems one can be clear about the existence of actions, yet unclear as to what if anything distinguishes them from observable movements. Alternatively, one can, by defining "action," be clear as to their distinguishing features, yet at the risk of never being sure whether one has a particular instance in view. And yet there certainly *is* a difference between actions and movements; Peters is pointing at some logical truth. Just how to characterize this difference will be examined further on in this chapter.

6. Movements and Actions in Actual Instances of Human Behavior

In the discussion of Freud's concept of motivation by Peters a further inconsistency becames apparent in his formulation of the separate domain thesis. Peters makes the point that Freud's theory of unconscious wishes as the motivating forces behind certain behaviors is in fact a causal-mechanical theory applicable just in those cases where there is no action but only a happening, an occurrence.

> The wish is a current in the mind that arises from unpleasure and ends in pleasure, achieved by the discharge of tension through the motor apparatus. If movements do not alter the source of stimulation unpleasure persists, though temporary satisfaction may be obtained by activating a memory trace of a previous perception associated with satisfaction (1958, pp. 66–67).

[For example], if a man is unintentionally rude to his employer, the explanation might be that the sight or thought of a man who was emotionally
equivalent to the father initiated tension which must persist until some kind
of discharge is found. . . . The explanation is of causal type; he is, as it
were, pushed into being rude by the wish or current seeking some form of
discharge (1958, p. 68).

The matching of unconscious wishes with causal-mechanical factors is
quite explicit in this example.

It would follow, according to the earlier argument, that where such
an explanation is appropriate there could not be a "genuine action."
Explanations in terms of wishes are of a causal type; hence, they are
appropriate only to movements, as the example of the rude man emphasizes. Unfortunately, Peters is not consistent on this point:

But there are cases when we would be perfectly agreeable to say that both
conscious reasons and unconscious motives were relevant. For instance a
doctor might decide to operate very quickly on an abscess on the grounds
that it was essential to stop the poison spreading in the patient's system; this
would be a perfectly satisfactory conscious reason. Yet he might also be
acting out of unconscious sadism . . . (1958, p. 58).[9]

There are then actions, like that of the surgeon, where good explanations in
terms of conscious reasons can be supplemented either by other motives or
by postulating unconscious wishes as well (1958, p. 61).

Peters' justification for this view is that

Plurality of causes is common enough in the natural world. There is no
reason to suppose that actions must have only one motive (1958, pp. 58–59).

But this will not do. It is quite true that more than one cause may be
operating; that is not the point. The issue is rather over the *kinds* of causes
that Peters, at this juncture, seems prepared to accept. For on his own
earlier argument, if unconscious wishes are appropriate in a particular
case, then it follows that the explanation is of a causal type and that the
subject of that explanation is a body movement. Yet the appropriateness
of a reason explanation implies that the subject is an action. To agree that
both types of factor can be relevant in the same instance is to contradict
the whole earlier argument that distinguished actions from movements. It
is not the plurality of causes that is the problem, but the fact that the
different causes Peters is prepared to allow in certain cases imply that the
behavior is simultaneously an action and a movement, a situation that by
his own argument is logically impossible.

It is important to note that even in such a simple case as the surgeon,
once confronted with a specific example of human behavior, the author

---

[9] Peters' italics.

himself is forced to obliterate the movement-action distinction, at least insofar as it is used to separate different types of explanations. How much more so would this be necessary with a whole case history such as that of Paul Lorenz. Here it is quite impossible to think that one could divide the mass of behavior into the happenings and the actions, and that two different sets of explanations could be given to cover each group.

7. Movements and Actions: Comments on an Alternative Formulation

In the previous sections we have given a critique of the separate domain thesis as presented in *The Concept of Motivation*. The first three points (Sections 1–3) attempted to show logical errors within certain of the premises of the basic argument. These included a faulty analysis of "causal explanation," a confusion over two distinct meanings of "sufficient," and a failure to distinguish between the application of the argument to classes of actions and to particular instances of actions. In Section 4 an ambiguity in the conclusion was pointed out: the problem of whether Peters is arguing that explanations of actions in terms of movements could never be entirely adequate, or whether such explanations were completely inappropriate. Section 5 posed the question: If there were a rigid division between actions and movements, by what criteria could one know that any event under consideration was in fact an action? Three possible criteria were examined, and each was found to be unusable. Finally, in Section 6 it was pointed out that the author himself, when faced with certain typical examples of human behavior, contradicts his previous position and merges the two types of explanation, those applicable to actions and those applicable to movements.

It might well be questioned whether such a belabored critique was necessary. Certainly it is quite true that a disproof of one particular formulation of a thesis is rather unimportant unless its arguments have wide acceptance. And this is precisely our justification; for it is hoped that the criticisms lodged against the particular form of the separate domain thesis presented in *The Concept of Motivation* will be equally valid with regard to various other versions of the position that are presently in circulation.

At this point it is essential to clarify just what is being affirmed and what denied. We are *not* asserting that there is no logical difference between the concept of "action" and the concept of "movement." It is quite true that the criteria for identifying an action are different from those for identifying a movement; that is, the same body movement may in different circumstances be part of different actions, and the same action may in different circumstances be composed of different body movements. Having determined that certain body movements have occurred, the question still remains open as to whether a particular action has likewise occurred. Such assertions are unobjectionable and represent the basic truths behind Peters' argument.

The concept of an action is context-dependent; that is, dependent to varying degrees upon how we apply certain social norms and conventions. Moreover, what we consider an action will depend not only on the actual situation but also upon the various possible interests of the observer. One thinks of such classic examples as Miss Anscombe's man pumping poisoned water into a house (1958, p. 37). He may be pumping water, killing the house's occupants, saving the Jews, or perhaps making the world safe for democracy—all or none of these actions, depending upon how we want to regard the situation. Again, did little Johnny swing his leg, kick the ball, or break the window? It takes little imagination to see that father and Johnny might easily disagree on just where the action ended and the consequences began.

Another striking example of how one's concept of an action varies with one's purposes can be seen in the following statement of Alasdair MacIntyre:

> . . . writing one's name is never merely by itself an action; one is either signing a document or giving information or perhaps just doodling. All these are actions, but writing one's name is not (1962, p. 56).

It is interesting that for other supporters of the rigid action-movement dichotomy signing one's name, as opposed to certain complex hand and finger movements, is an example *par excellence* of an action. Certainly the conclusion should be that actions are context-dependent, and that this context includes the observer's (or philosopher's) interests on the one hand and the situational and social aspects on the other. In any given situation the number of actions a particular piece of behavior may exemplify is indeterminate, limited only by the number of descriptions, the number of points of view, available.

The important issue, first stated earlier, is whether there can be complete specification of particular instances of actions in terms of body movements; and if not, what conclusions can be drawn about the type of explanation necessary for actions. The first of these questions has now been answered in the negative by our ready acceptance of the obvious fact that the criteria for identifying an instance of a particular action are not necessarily the same as those for identifying an instance of a particular body movement. But it does not follow that actions are in some sense "unobservable." Nor does it follow that the explanation of the action will be independent of the explanation of the movement.

We have already seen that there are various types of explanation possible for any given subject, depending upon the context in which an explanation is desired. Moreover, we have emphasized that these explanations are logically independent of each other. For instance, knowing the function of a particular object need not have any bearing on its explanation in terms of genesis or significance. But this sort of independence is not what is meant by the assertion that the explanation of a particular action is independent of the explanation of the body movements comprising that action. The claim is not that different types of explanations are independent of each other, but rather that the explanation in terms of genesis of an action is independent of the explanation in terms of genesis for the body movements comprising that action. Our contention, in contrast, is that a particular action *is* comprised of observable body movements and nothing else. But this does not contradict our previous assertion that the *criteria for identifying* actions and body movements are different.[10]

If our language describing human behavior has different criteria for application than that for describing everyday physical occurrences, this does not make it unique; the language of physical science, like that of behavioral science, shows this same logical gap, although we may sometimes fail to notice it. This mistake is shown clearly in arguments such as this:

> The evidence required to justify the assertion that 'salt is soluble in water' is simply that it has so dissolved; whereas the evidence required to justify the assertion that 'Smith is ambitious' is always more than that he has behaved in an ambitious fashion. . . . For it always makes sense to say that Smith seems to be ambitious, because he behaves in certain ways, but that he may not in fact be ambitious; it would be nonsense to say of salt that it dissolved and would therefore seem to be soluble but might not be (MacIntyre, 1958, pp. 57–58).

The author loads his argument at this point by using the word "dissolve" as if it were a part of our relatively noncommital language of physical occurrences. In fact, however, in using this word to describe the salt we have *already applied* a theoretical language, and it is our tendency to forget this which gives the author's argument its plausibility. The word "dissolve" is "theory-laden" and carries a certain logical commitment,

---

[10] There is a special group of behavioral phenomena which are usually called "actions" that are clearly *not* comprised of body movements, nor may they be observable in practice. An example is the act of "making a decision." Their proper analysis is exceedingly complex and has ramifications far beyond the present study. Nonetheless, whatever logical analysis we wish to apply to these "nonperformative acts," it seems clear that their existence does not affect the present discussion one way or the other, since the focus of both Peters' and our own arguments is on the great bulk of "performative acts" where observable behavioral performances are involved.

namely, the equivalence of "dissolve" and "soluble," which makes it inconsistent to say both "X dissolves" and "X may not be soluble." If we rephrase the statement, the mistake becomes quite evident:

> It always makes sense to say that Smith seems on the basis of what we observe of his behavior, to be ambitious, but that he may not in fact be ambitious. In the same way, it always makes sense to say that this compound seems, on the basis of its disappearance in the water, to be soluble, but that it may not in fact be soluble.

Rock salt, in contrast, will not disappear in water during a fairly brief period of agitation; powdered gelatin will. Yet the former is chemically soluble, while the latter is not (it forms a colloidal suspension). Thus, our criteria for saying "X disappeared in water" are not the same as those for saying "X is soluble in water." In the case of both the white powder and Smith, we need to know much more about their construction and performance in other circumstances before we commit ourselves to saying either "This white powder is soluble" or "Smith is ambitious."

We can now complete the argument by returning to our case history and considering some behavior of Lorenz's in which it might seem to make sense to distinguish the physical movements from the action. Let us take as an example the incident in which he got up from his books and ran to get a razor. Given that we know only this much we are still completely in the dark as to what, if any, further action he was executing. Various additional information would have to be known before we were convinced that this was a piece of any goal-directed behavior other than "fetching a razor." Then, once this was established, we might still be uncertain whether it was an instance of "suicide gesture" or not. On the other hand, given that we are told Lorenz tried to commit suicide, we are still completely in the dark as to what particular body movements comprised the action in question. Did he try to take poison, shoot himself, or slash his throat? Nevertheless, in this particular case the action of attempted suicide was comprised of "nothing more than" the movements of fetching a razor, etc. Actions are goal-directed activities, and both the goals themselves and the activities necessary for attaining them are often defined by social norms and conventions. Thus it may well be that in a particular situation we are unsure whether certain activities are actions of a certain sort. But it is a mistake, as we have seen, to think that because our criteria for identifying certain movements as an action involve reference to rules and norms of behavior, that the action itself must therefore be composed of something other than body movements.

We can pursue this example by asking how Lorenz's behavior might be explained:

Q1a: Explain how it came about that Lorenz was holding a razor to his throat.

Q1b: Explain how it came about that Lorenz attempted suicide (made a suicidal gesture).

Both of these are demands for explanations in terms of genesis, and it seems clear that both might be answered by a single explanation:

A1: Lorenz was under great tension because of his coming examinations. He wished that Gisela might be with him and resented her having to spend time with her sick grandmother. He wished the old woman would die so that Gisela could return to him, but because of his habitual refusal to acknowledge hostile feelings this wish was not consciously recognized. Instead, the hostility was self-directed out of a sense of guilt and a desire to punish himself for having such evil thoughts. This led to the conscious command to slash his throat, which caused him to fetch a razor and put it to his throat.

This may or may not be an adequate explanation. But the essential point is that there is only *one* explanation that need be given for both of our original questions. Thus, it does not matter how we form the requests for explanations, in terms of a body movement or in terms of an action like a suicide attempt; Lorenz himself did not do two different things. He did not go through some body movements and also commit an action, and there is no reason why there should be two different explanations given. There are body states, emotions, thoughts, perceptions—all of these figure in the explanation, but it would be quite wrong to divide these between two types of explanation.

There is of course a chain of neurological occurrences which comprise the causal factors themselves, that is, the thoughts, perceptions, emotions, etc. This being so, there must inevitably be a neurological story to go along with every piece of behavior and every state of the organism, but usually we are not interested in elucidating these neurological occurrences, for in an important sense, as we shall see in the following section, these are not causes at all. In the explanatory context they form part of our presumption of knowledge—certainly not because we do in fact *know* these details, but rather because we *presume* that they can be known, and because they are not involved in the incongruity presently demanding explanation.

B. Causes and Reasons in *Causation in the Law*

The book, *Causation in the Law* (Hart & Honoré, 1959), presents an excellent examination of the concept of causation as it occurs in legal practice and theory. In contrast to Peters' book, the distinction between causes and reasons which the authors outline plays a relatively minor role in their study, and there is no attempt to relate it to psychoanalysis. Nevertheless, because their account is generally so cogent, it provides an ideal basis from which one can then go on to consider the problems specific to psychoanalytic explanations, for their distinction between causes and reasons is a good example of the sort of argument that could be used to support the thesis of the separate domain.

The authors begin, as we have done in Chapter 3, with a strong emphasis on the explanatory contexts in which causal terminology occurs. They contrast the interests of the lawyer and the historian (and we might add the psychoanalyst) with that of the typical scientist.

> The lawyer and the historian are both primarily concerned to make causal statements about *particulars,* to establish that on some particular occasion some particular occurrence was the effect or consequence of some other particular occurrence. . . . Their characteristic concern with causation is not to discover connections between types of events, and so not to *formulate* laws or generalizations, but is often to *apply* generalizations, which are already known or accepted as true and even platitudinous, to particular concrete cases (1959, pp. 8–9).[11]

The contexts within which we employ causal statements are in fact of two kinds. The first are explanatory contexts, where

> . . . we ask for the cause of something because we are *puzzled* and do not understand how something has happened, and so ask for the cause because we want an *explanation* (1959, p. 22).[12]

In the second type of situation we are involved in an "attributive inquiry," attempting to establish responsibility, liability, or blameworthiness. For our own purposes we shall ignore this second variety and concentrate only on the explanatory contexts.

1. Causally Relevant Factors

We can begin with the authors' concept of a necessary condition, and their use of this concept in defining the class which they call "causally relevant factors"—a class which may include, but is definitely much more extensive than, "causes." Hart and Honoré distinguish among three different ways in which a factor can be said to be a necessary condition of some consequence:

1. One of a set of jointly sufficient conditions.
2. A necessary member of every set of sufficient conditions.

---

[11] Authors' italics.
[12] Authors' italics.

3. A condition necessary on the particular occasion in question, a *sine qua non* that but for which the event would not have occurred.

The authors first state that "a condition which is necessary in any of the above three ways is a *causally relevant factor*" (1959, p. 107).[13] But they immediately go on to modify this view. Their conclusion, which is certainly correct, is that "to be a condition *sine qua non* of some event on some given occasion and to be causally connected with it are not the same thing" (pp. 121–122). This is, of course, precisely the point taken against Peters in Section A,1. Hart and Honoré argue, first, that being a condition *sine qua non* is not sufficient to guarantee being a causally relevant factor. Thus, for example, having previously been married is a *sine qua non* of being a widow, but causally irrelevant to any particular woman's actually being a widow. Again, unless a car had been driven excessively fast earlier in a journey, it would not have been standing in the intersection at the moment at which it was hit by another vehicle. Nevertheless, speeding earlier in the trip, while a *sine qua non,* is not causally relevant to this particular accident. These sorts of conditions *sine qua non* which are *not* causally relevant are labeled "analytic" or "incidental" conditions by the authors.

Conversely, it can be shown that causally relevant conditions need not always be conditions *sine qua non;* for example; in those cases where there is an additional set of sufficient conditions present: When two men simultaneously shoot a bullet into the brain of their victim. Or the similar situations in which there is an alternative cause present, such that had A not in fact been sufficient to cause the event, then B would still have caused it. In such cases the event would have occurred even without the causally relevant factor A; hence, this factor was not a condition *sine qua non.*

The authors' conclusion, then, is that being a condition *sine qua non* is neither necessary nor sufficient for being a causally relevant factor in our normal use of this concept. Nevertheless, apart from the various admittedly exceptional situations of the sort outlined above, the question "Would X have occurred if Y had not?" will usually tell whether or not Y is a causally relevant factor. Again, it must be remembered that not all these causally relevant factors are causes.

The next point is that these causally relevant factors form in everyday experience and language a much more varied group than is generally recognized. Not only physical events and acts can be causal factors, but also all sorts of properties and states of affairs. Moreover, all of these include "positive" and "negative" examples. That is, not only a positive commission of an act can be a causal factor but also a negative omission,

[13] Authors' italics.

a failure to act. Likewise, the absence of certain properties can be as much a causal factor as the presence of others.

The authors ascribe the difficulty in accepting such "negative" causal factors to the influence of certain specious analogies or models. One of the most important is the terminology of "active forces," which has its parallel in human actions where causes are seen as active "manipulations" or "interventions" or "interferences." Such terminology makes it difficult to see how something that is *not* done, how a force that *fails* to act, could be a cause. Another misconception, not specifically mentioned by the authors but one we might add, is the belief that causes must be events or occurrences; because of this belief it seems hard to understand how a failure to do something, a nonoccurrence, could be a causal factor. The corrective for such difficulties is simply

> . . . to realize that negative statements like 'he did not pull the signal' are ways of describing the world, just as affirmative statements are, but they describe it by *contrast* not by *comparison* as affirmative statements do (Hart & Honoré, 1959, p. 35).[14]

Statements like "he failed to pull the signal" describe the situation by contrasting it with the presumably standard or usual situation in which the signal is pulled. But this failure may be a causally relevant factor as surely as anything else. The statement: "If he had not failed to pull the signal, the accident would not have happened" is an understandable and unexceptional causal statement.

2. Causes and Causally Relevant Factors

We now have some understanding of just what the authors call a causally relevant factor, and this brings us to the second issue. Given that we understand what is a causally relevant factor, how do we further distinguish among these between the factors which are "mere conditions" and those which are "causes"? Hart and Honoré emphasize that this decision is dependent upon careful appraisal of the actual situation, including the interests of the parties involved, a point we have discussed under the term "context-dependence." They are likewise very insistent on the related point that

> . . . in making this distinction [between causes and conditions] it is plain that our choice, though responsive to the varying context of the particular occasions, is not arbitrary or haphazard (1959, p. 10).

Yet it is not the case that every causally relevant factor, every necessary condition or condition *sine qua non,* is equally entitled to be called a cause. In fact,

---

[14] Authors' italics.

. . . neither the plain man, nor the historian, [nor the psychoanalyst] uses the expression 'cause,' or any related expression, in this way. For the contrast of cause with mere conditions is an inseparable feature of all causal thinking, and constitutes as much of the meaning of causal expressions as the implicit reference to generalizations does (1959, p. 11).

Thus, the set of all necessary conditions for an event, or all the causally relevant factors, can be ascertained without regard to social norms or to the knowledge and interests of the individuals concerned. However, once we attempt to distinguish from among these factors the causes, as opposed to the conditions, we enter a new, interpersonal dimension. In precisely the same way we have seen that when we ask for an explanation, con-textual, interpersonal considerations are inevitably brought to bear. But if this distinction between causes and conditions is context-dependent, can it nevertheless be nonarbitrary: What are the criteria being applied?

The central notion in the typical situation is to look for that factor which *made a difference* to the usual outcome and hence created the incongruity, the puzzle demanding a causal explanation. Often this factor is considered in a literal sense as an intervention, intrusion, or interference by some natural phenomenon or else by a human action. The basic model seems to be that of a human manipulation bringing about some physical event. Even where the cause is not a physical intervention, the influence of the original analogy remains, leading to the problems mentioned earlier about accepting "negative" causes. In practice the factors which "make a difference" generally contrast in one of two ways with those other causally relevant factors which are only conditions.

The first contrast that Hart and Honoré discuss is that between normal and abnormal conditions. Clearly, those factors which are present un-changed in the standard or usual situations as well as in the puzzling ones could not be the factors which made the difference. The factors we designate as causes will, most often, be in some way abnormal. Thus, tires are always under high pressure when in use, so this causally relevant factor probably was not what made the difference, and hence was not the cause, in the unusual situation where a blowout occurred.

It must be understood that "abnormal" is a relative term, in the sense of being what we call context-dependent; that is, in different contexts or situations what is abnormal may change. Remember, for instance, the contaminated bacterial culture plates example from Chapter 2. In most situations the ordinary air in the normal room would be a condition, not a cause of an occurrence such as a fire. On the other hand, in the example where supposedly sterile plates developed bacterial cultures, the room air *was* the cause, since it was abnormal in the supposedly germ-free room; it was the unusual contaminant that made the difference.

The authors also discuss a second sort of context-dependence which refers not to different situations but to the same situation; that is, what we will see as being abnormal in a given situation will depend partly on our purposes, interests, and prior knowledge:

> The cause of a great famine in India may be identified by the Indian peasant as the drought, but the World Food authority may identify the Indian government's failure to build up reserves as the cause and the drought as a mere condition (Hart & Honoré, 1959, p. 33).

In Chapter 2 similar examples were discussed under the heading of the presumption of interest.

The authors qualify the term "abnormal" in still another way. What is considered normal in a given situation is not necessarily the brute, physical situation unaffected by any human intervention. This is clear from examples like that of the bacterial cultures mentioned above. What is normal in given circumstances may well include certain normally completed human actions or precautions such as the sterile conditions that are normally maintained. Thus, what is abnormal may be either an unusual physical event, the breakdown of the sterilizing equipment, or an unusual human act, the deliberate contamination by an unauthorized person. Moreover, the abnormal factor may be a negative one; that is, the absence of some physical condition which is normally present or, more often, the absence or failure or omission of some normally completed human action such as shutting the safety doors properly. Thus, abnormality is one criterion for distinguishing causes from conditions, but what is considered normal: (1) may be a natural event or a human action of either a "positive" or "negative" sort, (2) may vary from one situation to the next, and (3) may vary within a particular situation depending upon our interests.

In addition to the contrast between abnormal and normal, there is a second rule often employed to distinguish between causes and conditions among the causally relevant factors. This rule is to look for a voluntary human action. For instance, in a case of arsenic poisoning, the presence of arsenic is certainly the immediate cause of death, the abnormal factor without which death would not have occurred. Yet we would in most cases search for another cause which would explain how the arsenic came to be given to the victim. We would probably not stop our inquiry until we found a human act, the act of giving the poison to the dead man. And having found such an act, our causal explanation would be completed.

> A deliberate human act is therefore most often a barrier and a goal in tracing back causes in such inquiries: it is something *through* which we do not trace the cause of a later event [that is, we do not look any further for the cause of the death, although we might well inquire into why the murderer committed the crime] and something *to* which we do trace the

cause through intervening causes [such as the arsenic itself] of other kinds (1959, p. 41).

Of course, nonvoluntary human actions may also be causes, but then they may be discovered by the previous criterion of abnormality.

The general position can be summarized as follows. We can say, following Hart and Honoré, that there are numbers of causally relevant factors, by which we mean, roughly, factors which are necessary parts of sets of jointly sufficient conditions. This criterion would, of course, have to be modified along the grounds discussed earlier to avoid the special problems raised by alternative or additional sets of sufficient conditions being present in the same situation. It would also have to be modified, again as we have already discussed, to remove those factors which are necessary simply because of what Hart and Honoré call "analytic" and "incidental" relations. From among these causally relevant factors we distinguish causes and reasons. This does not mean, however, that we must first know all these factors before we can distinguish causes and reasons. It seems clear that in some cases we never know all the necessary conditions, let alone that we know them before we know the causes and reasons. Instead, because we have various other criteria, we can use these to discover the causes and reasons before we know even the majority of necessary conditions. Indeed, with certain factors it is only *because* we *already* know the cause that we can then go on to pick out certain other factors as necessary conditions. For instance, consider a case of poisoning using crystals of potassium cyanide. Certainly a multitude of physiological factors will be necessary in order that the poison works. But we cannot know which ones are necessary until we know the proposed method of poisoning. Thus, is it necessary that the pH of the humors of the eye be within a certain range in order that the cyanide take effect? Probably not, if the cyanide is administered by mouth. On the other hand, if cyanide poisoning occurs because the crystal is placed against the cornea of the eye (a not impossible method), then clearly it is necessary if the poison is to have effect that the pH of the eye be between certain values, a range within which the normal pH falls. In such cases it is not until we know the mechanism of action that we can pick out the rest of the necessary factors from our knowledge of human physiology.

This is the reason why, as we mentioned earlier, neurological or chemical information is often out of place in an explanation. It is certainly not that this information is too well known; often, it may not be known at all, especially where human behavior is concerned. The point, as Hart and Honoré state, is that we do not consider our explanation that

> . . . the cause of a particular fire was the dropping of a lighted cigarette, as strengthened when we learn from science that without the presence of oxygen the fire would not have occurred (1959, p. 44).

This sort of scientific information, while essential for a complete account of all necessary conditions, all the causally relevant factors, may be beside the point in the particular explanatory context.

Consider another set of examples—explanations of voluntary human actions. The observation that human beings can announce goals, can form intentions, and often can act in such a way as to fulfill them is a central fact of the human experience and the bedrock upon which our understanding of behavior is based. All such activities, the admitted goals and the hidden motivations, are ultimately functions of the nervous system. There is no good evidence to the contrary; indeed there is every reason to expect that the infinite complexities of human behavior will eventually find their explanation in the workings of what is unquestionably the most complex-functioning physical system so far discovered in the universe—the human brain. Moreover, it is another basic fact of our experience that we can alter an individual's behavior, transiently or permanently, by telling him something or by giving him a drug, through a process of conditioning or by performing a cingulectomy. It is equally obvious that a parent's "tender loving care" is as much a factor in a child's development as the deoxyribonucleic acid which he inherits. At present we simply lack the theoretical understanding that would allow us to write TLC and DNA into a single formula for human behavior. But this *conceptual* failure in no way negates the *experiential* fact of the psychophysiological unity of the human organism. Thus, the neurological explanation of how it is that people can form intentions and act so as to carry them out is still far beyond us. Yet in a particular explanatory situation, when faced with puzzling behavior, it is not the gap in our neurological understanding with which we are concerned. The incongruity, rather, concerns just what the person's intentions were. Once we discover this, our explanation is complete, since it is part of our presumed knowledge that people can act in such a way as to carry out their intentions. It is just because explanations have this contextual, situational aspect that satisfactory explanations are possible in the face of incomplete scientific knowledge of all the necessary conditions.

3. Causes and Reasons

So far we can agree with the analysis of causation that Hart and Honoré offer, at least in its general outline; our own discussion earlier has emphasized many of the same points. The real divergence comes on the issue of causes and reasons, for the authors put forward a modified form of what we have called the "thesis of the separate domain." To be sure, their discussion is rather sketchy since their main concern is with the concept of causation as it is used in legal proceedings. Nevertheless, I think the basic arguments are distinguished enough so that we can examine them.

The authors adopt the term "interpersonal transactions" to cover the relationships between two human beings. In this area, they say:

> . . . we have to deal with the concept of *reasons* for action rather than *causes* of events; yet there are many transitional cases for, while the contrast between these concepts is important, it shades off in many directions (1959, p. 48).[15]

The standard case for examination is when one individual says something and thereby brings about another individual's action. The authors go on to point out that there is in fact a whole spectrum here, from "He made me do it" through "He persuaded . . .," and finally a simple "He advised, or suggested . . . ." All of these statements concern interpersonal transactions, and all show certain similarities. There are, however, "*radical* differences which separate 'He induced me to do it' from 'His blow caused the victim's death'" (p. 49).[16]

What arguments are given in favor of this "radical difference"? There is one minor argument which can be called linguistic, and one major argument which deals with the lack of any commitment to general statements. The linguistic argument is not gone into in any detail, but because it is common in discussions of this sort, it is worth examination:

> It would be somewhat unnatural in the informal discourse of ordinary life to describe any of this [interpersonal] range of cases by saying that one person *caused* another to act; and in some cases this description would be positively misleading. 'He caused me to act' would be merely unnatural (and 'He made me do it' natural) in those cases where one person is induced to act by threats, coercion, the exercise of authority, or false statements; it would be positively misleading in those cases where one person merely advised, or tempted, or requested another to act, or procured his action by offering a reward (1959, pp. 48–49).[17]

It must be admitted that there is indeed something unnatural or misleading about these statements. But the source of the confusion does not lie where the authors believe. It is not a case of mistaking a reason for a cause; it is rather a case of mistaking a weak factor for a strong one.

The authors themselves recognize a continuous range or spectrum regarding the strength of reasons, from coercion to mere suggestion. Moreover, they admit that the "gross forms of persuasion" where "the first person 'works on' the feelings of the second come very close to cases of ordinary causal connexion" (p. 50). The very fact that there is such a spectrum seems incompatible with the idea of a "radical difference" existing between causes and reasons. Consider Peters' example of the married

---

[15] Authors' italics.
[16] Authors' italics.
[17] Authors' italics.

man who attempted on a particular occasion to seduce a young choirboy. The question is whether his desires were the reason or the cause of his behavior. It could be said that his desires became so strong that at some point they ceased to be strong reasons and became weak causes of his behavior. But is this really credible? At what point does the desire for sexual intercourse cease to be a reason for one's actions and become a cause of one's movements? How radical, for instance, is the difference between holding a gun to someone's head and asking him to do something, and holding a hundred dollar bill to his eye and asking him to do something? If we insist upon a radical difference, then we must be prepared to face such questions, questions which seem quite wrong-headed and confused.

On the other hand, if we believe that causes and reasons are the same sorts of entities, then we must accept that they can be of varying strengths. Common speech, of course, gives ample evidence of our treating reasons in just this way: We often speak of powerful or unconvincing reasons for actions. Yet it seems at first odd to speak of strong and weak causes. However, I think we can make good sense of such notions. First, we should remember that it is quite common to speak of more or less important factors, especially in complex areas like medicine and psychology. Nor is this incompatible with the idea that all the causal factors are necessary. For instance, if A and E are jointly sufficient to cause event R, and if B, C, and E are also jointly sufficient to cause R, then I think it makes sense to speak of A as being a more important or stronger factor than B or C, even though all the factors named are equally necessary.

Actual cases of this sort of situation are quite common. For instance, in regard to the determinants of various physical body traits we know that a number of factors can all contribute, in varying degrees, to the final outcome. Consider general body physique and stature. Geographical area is a minor factor in determining body somatotype; race is a more important factor; parental body type is extremely important; environmental influences during childhood of medium importance, and so on. Not only is this varying influence of a number of causal factors quite understandable, it is also quantifiable in the sense that statistical methods are available to evaluate and rank their influences. It seems, therefore, that the concept of the varying strength of causes and reasons is quite understandable. The apparent oddity is because once we raise the question of strength or importance we tend to drop the limited terms cause and reason entirely and employ a richer vocabulary with such terms as "overriding" versus "minor" factors, and "strong" threats versus "tentative" suggestions. Thus in interpersonal transactions the essential thing is to get clear on just how important was the factor involved. In order to do this we shall have to use

such words as "forced," "induced," and "advised." But once we understand, for instance, that a person held a gun to the man's temple, then it
does not really matter whether we speak of this as a cause or a reason for
the victim's action.

The authors' second and "most important" argument for the cause-
reason distinction is that the relationships between interpersonal transactions, "though often and intelligibly called causal connexion, . . . do
not depend upon 'regular connection' or sequence as the causal relations
between physical events do" (1959, p. 48).

> The statement that one person did something because, for example, another
> threatened him, carries no implication or covert assertion that if the cir-
> cumstances were repeated the same action would follow; nor does such a
> statement require for its defence, as ordinary singular causal statements do,
> a generalization of the kind discussed [to the effect that what did in fact
> occur is what always or usually occurs in such situations] . . . (1959, p.
> 52).

This is an important contention, and we shall divide our discussion of it
into two parts.

a. The authors are quite correct in asserting that there is at least one
important sense in which reason statements are not explicitly or implicitly
general. But in the above quotation they have lumped together two very
different varieties of generalizations and claimed that the reason statement
implies neither. Consider the following statements:

1. His offering me $5 if I would do it was the reason I stole the bread.
2. If ever (or usually when) I steal bread, then I have previously been
   offered $5 for doing so.
3. Whenever (or usually when) people offer me $5 for doing it, I steal
   bread.
4. If the circumstances were the same I would again steal the bread.
5. His blow was the cause of the bruise on my arm.
6. If ever (or usually when) I get a bruise on my arm, then I have
   previously had a blow on my arm.
7. Whenever (or usually when) people hit me, I get a bruise.
8. If the circumstances were the same I would again have got a bruise.

Statements 1 and 5 represent basic reason and causal types of assertion,
respectively. Statements 2 and 6 represent the assertions that each of the
first events are necessary antecedents of the second, according to the
analysis of "necessary condition" given earlier: if ever B, then always A
previously. Statements 3 and 7 represent the assertions that the first events
are sufficient conditions for the occurrence of the second events, again
applying the analysis presented earlier: whenever A, then always B. State-

ments 4 and 8 are what can be called the "repetition" assertions. The problem is to understand the relationship between the reason and cause statements, 1 and 5, and the three other types of related statements that could be made.

The initial points to be made merely repeat our findings from the earlier discussion of necessary and sufficient conditions. The first observation is that statements 1 and 5 do not *mean* the same as any of their respective alternatives. That is, to assert a causal connection is not the same as asserting that one event is either a necessary or a sufficient condition for another. The second observation is that statement 1 not only does not mean the same as either 2 or 3 but also does not imply either of these. In asserting 1, we are in no way committed to the assertion of either 2 or 3. This is the basic truth behind the authors' claim that with reason statements there is no implication that "he or other persons had always acted in that way" (p. 52). But it is essential to notice that precisely the same thing can be said in the case of the causal statement 5. When we assert 5 we neither assert nor are committed to the assertion of either 6 or 7. It is possible, of course, that any or all of these general statements 2, 3, 6, and 7 may be true in the particular situations involved, but we are not committed to asserting any of them when we assert the singular reason or the singular causal statements. On the other hand, these general statements might be false. For instance, if a banana peel caused me to slip and fall, this does not necessarily mean that banana peels usually cause either me or other people to fall. Indeed, I may assert confidently in a particular situation that the banana peel caused me to fall, knowing full well that usually when I step on banana peels, I do *not* fall. Likewise, because I succumbed to the $5 bribe on one occasion, perhaps from hunger or a momentary spitefulness, this does not mean that I usually fall for such easy bribes, or that people in general usually can be bribed like this.

Our conclusion, then, is that the authors are correct in claiming that there is a sense in which reason statements are neither explicitly nor implicitly general, but in precisely the same sense this fact is true of causal statements.

b. The authors are likewise correct in their claim that there is a sense in which singular causal statements *do* involve a generalization of some sort. When we assert 5 we certainly do commit ourselves to statement 8, provided we interpret "circumstances" to include the total situation, the environmental and the intrapersonal circumstances. But it is essential to see that the reason statement 1 also involves a generalization of this sort; that is, in asserting 1 we are committed to statement 4, again provided that we interpret "circumstances" in an all-inclusive manner. Hence, we must reject the authors' contention that with the singular reason statement there is *no* implication that "given similar circumstances, he would act again in this way" (p. 52).

The mistake rests with how we interpret "circumstances" in each of the statements. In the case of a reason statement, we usually have in mind the external or environmental circumstances. If this is so, then it is certainly true that if such circumstances were the same I might, nevertheless, have acted differently. Thus, if I were again provided with a $5 bribe, I might well decide not to steal the bread, perhaps because my usually strong sense of guilt about thievery would prevail. Of course, no one would deny this. If other considerations, other reasons had been present, then it is obvious that I might have acted differently. But to say that other reasons *were* present would be precisely to deny that the total circumstances, including both environmental and intrapersonal circumstances, were the same. Likewise with the case of the singular causal statement. When we say that such statements *do* imply a generalization, what we have in mind is that if the total circumstances were the same, then the result would have been the same. But it is nevertheless clear that if, for instance, I had perhaps tensed my body, or alternatively, had relaxed it, then it might have been the case that the same blow would not have caused a bruise.

If the actual mistake is a confusion over alternative interpretations of the term "circumstances," the reasons for making such a mistake go much deeper. Certainly one important factor is some sort of belief that in order for human "free will" to be preserved, it is essential that even if all the circumstances were exactly the same it should still have been possible for me to have done something other than what I did in fact do.

> I remain convinced that moral responsibility requires that a man should be able to choose alternative actions, everything in the universe prior to the act, including his self, being the same (Mabbott, 1956, p. 301).

In this view, statement 1 would *not* commit one to statement 4; that is, the assertion that A was the reason for my doing B, would *not* commit me to the assertion that if all the circumstances were exactly the same I would again have done B. As the above argument makes clear, our own position is directly opposed to this view; however, the issue of determinism is quite obviously too complex and too far removed from our basic concerns to be discussed in this study.

The conclusion seems to be that there is a sense, elucidated above in part a, in which it is true to say that singular reason statements are not covertly general. But in this same sense, it seems clear that singular causal statements likewise do not imply any general statements. On the other hand, there is also a sense, elucidated in the present discussion, in which it is true to say that singular causal statements do imply a general statement. But in this second sense, it is also true that singular reason statements likewise imply such general statements. So far then, there seems no distinction between causes and reasons, at least on these grounds.

4. Causes and Reasons: Comments on an Alternative Formulation

Our examination of Hart and Honoré's distinction between causes and reasons is, as it stands, unsatisfactory in two ways. First, whether or not Hart and Honoré's arguments for the distinction between causes and reasons are correct, it is nevertheless clear that common-sense and ordinary language do in fact recognize some sort of distinction that has not yet been explained. Second, the sense elaborated above in which singular causal and reason statements do imply general statements is rather trivial. What it boils down to is that under exactly the same conditions exactly the same thing would occur. This, by itself, is not very helpful, since in every new situation the problem will be to decide if the conditions are in fact exactly the same or not. It is obvious, then, that a great deal more must be said about the role of general laws in explanations of behavior. This latter problem will be the subject of Chapter 7; in the present section we will attempt to correct the former deficiency by suggesting an alternative view of the distinction between causes and reasons. It must again be pointed out, however, that the basic problem in this chapter is the thesis of the separate domain. Our interest in causes and reasons is limited to the way in which certain analyses of these concepts can give rise to this particular thesis. It should not be thought that either in the previous discussion or in what follows we are dealing adequately with all the complex philosophical issues involved in these important concepts. Neither are we attempting to analyze the psychoanalytic conception of causation as such, but only certain possible misconceptions about it which would lead one to place psychoanalytic explanations in a separate and logically distinct compartment.

a. Causes versus Reasons

How, then, are we to account for the difference between causes and reasons? We have already discussed Hart and Honoré's distinctions and found them inadequate. Yet it is clear from common language that there is some difference between these concepts; it is therefore necessary to attempt an alternative explication. There are, in fact, at least two distinct uses of the term "reason." In the first of these the two terms "cause" and "reason" are used interchangeably. Philosophers may cringe, but this is just the blunt fact, and this use is even recognized by such authorities of usage as the Shorter Oxford Dictionary. There, one definition of "reason" is "a ground or cause of, or for, something." And one definition of "cause" is "that which moves a person to action; ground of action; reason, motive." Both laymen and scientists do indeed often follow this use and employ the terms interchangeably.

There is, however, another use of the term "reason" in which it is not synonymous with "cause." On this use the term is applied to human activities only, and sometimes by analogy, to certain animal behavior. A typical example of this use of reason was given earlier:

1. His offering me $5 if I would do it was the reason I stole the bread.

This statement was contrasted with the typical sort of cause statement:

5. His blow was the cause of the bruise on my arm.

We can now examine these two statements more closely in an attempt to clarify, first, the distinction between causes and reasons and, second, the more fundamental difference between our use of these two concepts on the one hand and the concept of necessary conditions on the other.

It should be noted first of all that in two respects both the above statements make the same assertion that the particular events in question are causally relevant factors. Second, in both cases the cause or reason is being distinguished from other causally relevant factors, other necessary conditions, presumably because it fulfills certain additional criteria, two of which Hart and Honoré mention: abnormality or voluntary human actions. Nevertheless, statement 1, in designating "his offering me $5" as a reason, is asserting about its subject something more than or different from statement 5 which designates "his blow" as a cause. The problem, then, is to elucidate just what this difference is. What precisely is the difference between "his blow" and "his offering me $5"? I think the difference can be seen by examining the causal sequence more closely. In the blow–bruise situation of statement 5, the blow on the arm is a causally relevant factor in the occurrence of the bruise on my arm whether or not I was aware of it at the time. If I choose to call the blow the reason for my bruise, then I am using "reason" as a term synonymous with "cause." On the other hand, in situation 1 the $5 bill held in front of me is a causally relevant factor in the occurrence of my stealing the bread (or, instead, perhaps hitting the person holding it) only if I perceive it, correctly or incorrectly, take some account of it, and act upon that perception. This is, I suggest an important part of what we mean when we choose to distinguish between causes and reasons, namely, that reasons are those causally relevant factors which become causally relevant precisely because they are taken into consideration, or responded to, by the individual. The $5 by itself causes nothing. It becomes a causal factor when I perceive it, correctly or incorrectly, as an inducement to commit some act and then act upon that perception. What action I perform, however, is still left undecided. Thus, my perception of the $5 as a bribe for stealing the bread might be the reason for my going ahead and stealing the bread. On the other hand, it might also be the reason for my striking the individual holding the note. This does not mean, however, that it is necessary for the reason to have been consciously formulated before I acted. Obviously, there are often situations in which the reasons for our actions become conscious and are clearly formulated only in retrospect, or perhaps never at all. Habitual and impulsive actions are typically of this variety. In such cases it is just a fact that one is often able to recollect the factors in response to which the behavior occurred, even though these factors were not consciously expressed at the time.

It might be objected at this point that we are ignoring an important distinction, between the $5 bill and my being aware of the $5 bill. It might be argued that whereas the blow in statement 5 is the cause, it is not the $5 bill itself which is the reason, but my being aware of the $5 bill. Admittedly, there is both in common language and our example this ambiguity; we often speak of X being a reason when we mean that X's effect on us, how we considered or interpreted X, was the reason. However, pointing out this ambiguity does not alter our argument, for it is not a characteristic found exclusively with reasons. In fact, the exact same ambiguity exists in everyday discourse about causes. Thus, we say that the blow caused the bruise, when actually it was our body's reaction to the blow which eventuated in a bruise. This sort of ambiguity is pervasive in our language, and while it can have no effect on how we analyze the cause-reason distinction, it does have other implications to which we shall return in a later discussion (see p. 169).

Our interpretation of reason statements can be clarified by enlarging the blow–bruise example. In our view "his blow" is simply a particular event in a complex behavioral situation; this situation, let us say, consisted in the following sequence of events: Johnny hit the teacher on the teacher's arm, a bruise formed, the teacher sent Johnny to his room. So far, the question of whether the blow was a cause or a reason for any other event has not even arisen. Now suppose we ask for the explanation of the latter two events:

Q1: How did the bruise on the teacher's arm come about?

Q2: How did Johnny's being sent to his room come about (i.e., how did it come about that Johnny was sent to his room)?

These two questions are demands for what we have called explanations in terms of origin. The explanations could be outlined as follows:

A1: Johnny's hitting the teacher was the cause of the bruise on the teacher's arm.

A2: Johnny's hitting the teacher was the reason for his being sent to his room.

In each case the originating event, with the aid of certain implicit common-sense presumptions, accounts for the particular occurrence in question. Johnny's blow, together with our common-sense observations about human skin and the like make the bruise an understandable, no longer incongruous occurrence. Again, Johnny's blow, together with what we know about teachers and schoolroom discipline, etc., makes his being sent to his room understandable. If we choose to distinguish between causes and reasons in these situations (and we need not do so), then it seems that statements A1 and A2 correctly express the usual distinction. Johnny's blow was a causally relevant factor in the formation of the bruise whether or not the teacher had been aware of it. But Johnny's blow was the *reason* for his punishment in the sense that it was in response to this blow, out of consideration of this act, that the teacher issued the punishment he did. Thus, if the teacher had not been aware of who had given the blow, or had decided not to take action upon it, then the blow would not have been a causally relevant factor at all.

This simple example has demonstrated, albeit rather crudely, an important point. Depending upon the sort of incongruity involved, the very same event (i.e., Johnny's blow) can be characterized as *either* a cause or a reason, and this is not because we are using the terms synonymously. It is rather that in different explanatory contexts both terms may be correctly applied to the same occurrence. Thus, when we are concerned to discover the origin of the teacher's bruise, the blow may properly be designated the cause, and when we want to explain Johnny's being punished, the blow may properly be designated the reason. In claiming that the blow was a cause we isolate a voluntary human act and we assert that, roughly, it was a necessary part of the set of sufficient conditions. In claiming that the blow was a reason we assert that the teacher punished Johnny in consideration of, in response to, this occurrence. Reasons, then, are those causally relevant factors which become causally relevant by virtue of the fact that they are taken account of consciously or unconsciously and acted upon by the individual in question. There is, therefore, an important distinction between our concepts of cause and reason; nevertheless, both causes and reasons form a subclass of the class of causally relevant factors.

b. Causes, Reasons, and the Context of Explanation

The distinctions between causes and reasons outlined above are important, but of even more importance is the realization that the really fundamental distinction is not between causes and reasons at all, but rather between our use of these two concepts and our use of all those other terms which fall into the category of "causally relevant factors." It is usually argued that causes are purely physical occurrences, whereas reasons have an "intentional," "social," (or to use our word "contextual") aspect and therefore cannot be designated without reference to intrinsically human concepts such as "intelligence" and the like. In denying this radical difference between causes and reasons, one could argue that reasons do not in fact display this contextual aspect. Our point, however, is precisely the opposite: it is that *both* reasons *and* causes have this same contextual characteristic.

Our contention is that the terms "cause," "reason" (and "motive" and perhaps a few more) occur legitimately *only* in explanatory contexts. There is a sense in which causes and reasons do not "exist in the world" in the way that the elements of human behavior do. The point, however, is not ontological, but logical; it is not intended as an empirical observation but as part of an elucidation of what we mean by explanation. There is a logical difference between causes and reasons on the one hand, and desires, beliefs, fears, etc., on the other, and the difference is that the former concepts have an intrinsic connection with explanation and explanatory contexts. The question of what things are causes or reasons cannot even arise until there is a context of explanation, a situation in which some "incongruity in knowledge" is presumed.

Human behavior results from the interactions of sensations, perceptions, beliefs, attitudes, habits, desires, and the like—all operating within the individual. These "primary" phenomena are observable, and amenable in varying degrees to study and also to modification, both by the individual himself and by others acting upon him. It is such "primary" phenomena we search for in those situations in which there is a "gap in knowledge."

In contrast, causes and reasons are not elements of the same logical type; it makes no sense to inquire after them until there is some sort of incongruity to be explained, some sort of explanatory connections to be discovered. This difference can be brought out very crudely as follows. We do not experience reasons the way we experience feelings. I do not, for instance, perceive a reason the way I perceive a threat, although that threat may *be* the reason for, may explain, my carrying a gun. Likewise, I do not perceive causes the way I perceive events or occurrences. I do not experience a cause the way I experience fear, although fear may *be* the cause of, may explain, my running away. In a particular situation certain of the "primary" phenomena will be designated causes or reasons because we can understand the mechanism by which they explain the event in question. We look for these causes of an individual's behavior among the antecedent conditions and factors acting upon him, but the cause is not another *sort* of antecedent condition over and above the various events and occurrences. We do not come across or discover *both* antecedent events *and* antecedent causes; it is rather that, once the question of explanation arises, we designate, using various criteria, certain of these antecedents as the causes of the behavior in question. Likewise, we look for the reasons for an individual's behavior among his beliefs, emotions, etc. But the reason is not another sort of mental phenomenon as are those "primary" entities. Thus, in the example concerning Johnny and the teacher, insofar as we are concerned with gathering information about and describing the various incidents, the terms "cause" and "reason" were not, and did not need to be, used at all. It was only when the demand for an explanation was made that those terms became appropriate. Likewise, in the full description of an individual's behavior and mental state no mention of causes or reasons will occur. It is rather that in the shift from observation and description to explanation certain feelings, habits, etc., by becoming factors in an explanation thereby become designated causes and reasons. The heart, we should say, does *not* have its reasons, but only its desires and fears, its beliefs and aspirations. It is only when we shift to a context of explanation that we isolate certain of these phenomena as the causes or reasons for the behavior, and which phenomena we designate as causes or reasons will vary both with the facts of the situation and our own interests and purposes in that situation. Thus, the move from descriptions of, and generalizations about situations, to explanations of them in terms of causes and reasons is primarily a logical, not an empirical, step, involving a decision, not a discovery. It represents a reorientation in our thinking and a decision to accept two very special sorts of commitments. Just what these commitments are will become clear in the following section.

c. The "Narrative" and the "Explanatory" Commitments

In the previous section we have argued that the really fundamental distinction to be drawn was between the concepts of cause and reason on the one hand and all those other "primary" entities which go to make up our generalizations about situations and our lists of "necessary conditions" or "causally relevant factors" on the other. It would seem that Hart and Honoré would agree with this point; they admit that something more is involved in "cause" statements than some sort of statistical assertion about the events in question:

> The statement that on this occasion X was the cause of Y differs from the conjunctive statement that X was followed by Y on this occasion and X's are followed by Y's in the majority of cases (1959, p. 45).

The authors emphasize at this point that the truth of general statements, even those stating high probabilities, is not sufficient grounds for asserting a causal connection in any particular case. However, while not sufficient for a causal assertion, the statistical generalization is considered to be a necessary condition by the authors, and this is the basis for their distinction between causes and reasons.

Hart and Honoré state that we use generalizations as evidence for supporting singular reason statements. Thus, to point out that X, for instance, frequently gives in to monetary bribes, is to lend support to the assertion that on one particular occasion the $5 bribe was the reason for his action. With causes, however, the generalization forms a necessary part of our meaning:

> . . . the instances out of which such generalisations [about reasons] are constructed were themselves cases where it was found that an individual had a certain reason for action, and this was known independently of such generalisations. On the other hand, a singular causal statement asserting that one physical event was the cause of another depends on generalisations in a different way: here the latter are not merely *evidence* that in the particular case the events are causally related; they are part of what is meant by causal connexion; and the instances from which these causal generalisations are constructed were not already recognised *apart* from such generalisations as cases of causal connexion but only as cases of succession between events (1959, p. 53).[18]

The point of this quotation seems to be that particular instances of causal connection are recognized only as cases of the succession of events, that we assert a specifically *causal* connection between the events only when we find that such succession is a general phenomenon. In arguing this way the authors place causal connection firmly within the purely empirical realm of "succession between events." That is, a necessary condition for making a causal statement is that we make the scientific discovery that a particular "succession between events" (for instance, Y following X) is in fact a generally occurring sequence. In contrast to this, they argue, reason statements require no such precondition.

The burden of our previous argument, however, is that both cause and reason statements require logical commitments, not empirical discoveries. Statistical assertions about a generally observed succession of events is neither necessary nor sufficient for the designation of *either* a cause or a reason connection. This position can now be clarified through the use of some further examples. In these cases we shall begin with a variety of known antecedent conditions and attempt to delineate the process by which a causal explanation is reached. The first example is an instance of

---

[18] Authors' italics.

lung cancer in a particular hospital patient. Let us suppose that we want an explanation in terms of genesis for this occurrence, an explanation of how the cancer came about.[19]

Among the antecedent characteristics and potentially relevant factors in this patient's case history are the following: low blood pressure, Italian parentage, underweight, knowledge of Sanskrit, cigarette smoking, and extrovert personality tendencies. The first problem is to find the causally relevant factors out of this jumble of antecedents. Of course, not knowing the exact etiology or pathophysiology, we cannot be sure which, if any, of those we have listed are necessary parts of sufficient conditions. We can, however, try one of Hart and Honoré's criteria for causes, namely, abnormal or unusual factors. This rule suggests that reading Sanskrit might perhaps be a cause, but this seems highly unlikely. Although we do not know the exact mechanism, we expect that it will be some sort of physiological one, and that any causally relevant factors should therefore be physiological, or at least have obvious physiological aspects.

The next thing we might try are generalizations based on epidemiological surveys of many cases of lung cancer. These studies will at least tell us what factors consistently appear in patients who develop lung cancer. Of course this sort of net will drag in alot of material that shows correlations only incidentally. Still, among these factors we may find some which are causal factors. Why is this so? Because causal factors will be necessary parts of sets of jointly sufficient conditions. If there is only one such set of conditions, then among those factors which are consistently correlated with lung cancer will be the causal factors. On the other hand, the more sets of sufficient conditions there are, then the less likely it is that necessary factors will show up in epidemiological studies, unless the factors are necessary to more than one set of sufficient conditions. Yet with the case of a disease like lung cancer, we might expect that there are relatively few final pathways, or sets of sufficient conditions, so that any epidemiological generalizations should prove helpful.

In fact, epidemiological studies show (let us assume) that both smoking and extroversion are consistently correlated with lung cancer. The next question is: How do we discover whether either of these is a causally relevant factor? Further studies of the same type will show us whether these conditions are consistently found with lung cancer merely for what Hart and Honoré call "incidental" or "analytic" reasons. For instance, lung cancer patients might have various changes in their pulmonary function such as decreased lung volume or signs of obstruction, but these,

---

[19] The example is imaginary, but it is suggested from proposals made by several psychologists, notably H. J. Eysenck in *Smoking, Health, and Personality* (1965).

quite clearly, would be incidental correlations, simply related to having the disease itself. It might also be found, for example, that lung cancer itself causes individuals to become more extroverted, that this personality trait appeared only after the disease had begun. Perhaps, however, after separating such incidentally correlated factors we would still be left with smoking and extroversion as, almost surely, causally relevant factors. The question then is: Why do we, both in our example and in present-day medicine, still have reservations about definitely calling either of these, and most certainly extroversion, a cause of lung cancer? One point seems clear: Even in the face of generalizations showing positive correlation between the phenomenon and certain causally relevant factors, the assertion of a causal relationship may still be denied.

Not only are generalizations not sufficient; in particular circumstances they may not even be necessary for the assertion of a causal sequence. The next example will bring this out. Consider the following piece of behavior—John's shutting the door. Let us assume that this act was a purposive one, and that we want an explanation in terms of function; that is, we want to find out the considerations, the reasons which were causally relevant factors leading to the execution of this act.

Everyday experience provides a number of generalizations about the sorts of things that are frequent antecedents of such acts. Among these would be: commands to do so by friends or people of authority, fear of burglars, perception of noise, perception of cold drafts, etc. A careful study of the event in question, let us suppose, turns up the following antecedents: trumpet noise outside the door, a cold draught blowing in the door, and the mantle clock stopping. Which of these antecedents might have been the cause or reason for John's shutting the door? Our generalizations suggest that either the noise or the draught are likely possibilities. This being so, we should probably rest content if, when questioned, John admits that his reason was one or even both of these factors. That is, we would say that the noise was the reason for the act, implying that John's perceiving the noise together with his desire for silence were causally relevant factors in the action.

But what if John says that the reason he shut the door was that the mantle clock had stopped? We would probably not be content with this answer. But the reason we would not be content with this answer is *not* that there is no generalization that would have led us to expect such a correlation, although this is true. We do not immediately accept this answer because we cannot see a connection between this reason and the action. There are two alternatives left open to us when we doubt such an explanation: We either attempt to find a more acceptable reason, or we attempt to fill in the steps between the reason given and the actual event.

Thus, we would ask John how shutting the door could possibly be related to the clock's stopping. His defense will not consist in giving some generalization about such things; the possible generalization "Whenever the mantle clock stops, I always shut the door," even if true, leaves us no better off than before, except that we might now have predicted John's action. But this generalization is itself incongruous and needs explanation. Instead, if asked to defend his explanation, John will attempt to "recreate his train of thought." Hart and Honoré put the point in this way:

> If asked to make sure, in giving evidence, that his reasons for acting were as he claims, an honest witness will not be expected to produce generalisations, but to attempt to reconstruct the deliberative situation or his 'state of mind' at the time (1959, p. 52).

John might say, for instance: "Whenever the clock stops it needs to be wound with a special key, but this key is kept hidden in a panel behind the door; therefore, in order to wind the clock I had to shut the door to get the key." If John can spin out such a narrative, then we should be much more likely to accept his answer as being in fact a reason for his action. His answer now seems adequate, although it still might not be true, but it is adequate precisely because it has supplied a narrative framework, a model into which we can now accommodate both the antecedent and the action. And now we need have no qualms about calling the clock's stopping the reason for John's shutting the door.

These last two examples are in some ways opposite to each other. In the case of the lung cancer, we have the generalizations that point to smoking as a causally relevant factor; yet we shy away from definitely designating smoking as a cause of lung cancer. In the second example we lack any generalization connecting the stopping of mantle clocks with the shutting of doors; yet we may confidently say that in this particular situation the clock's stopping was the reason for John's shutting the door. It appears, therefore, that the availability of the relevant generalizations is neither necessary nor sufficient for designating causes or reasons in particular situations. What, then, is necessary; what is lacking in the cancer example?

I think the answer is that in the first example we still lack a conceptual model or framework, a mechanism which can incorporate smoking and cancer into a single understandable process. The most obvious mechanism is that of absorption of a carcinogenic compound by lung tissue from the contaminated atmosphere that is breathed. Unfortunately, most studies with experimental animals have so far failed to substantiate this etiologic process, at least with concentrations of smoke comparable to those attained by smoking. The difficulty might conceivably lie with technical problems in the experimental procedures. Or it might be that species differences make the experimental animals inappropriate subjects for comparison. Our purpose is not to evaluate the evidence for this or some other model of the pathophysiological process; it is only to emphasize that until some such model is confirmed cautious scientists will concede that the evidence is so far only "circumstantial," based upon the consistently observed but conceivably still incidental correlation between two types of phenomena. In the second example by contrast, in giving us an understandable narrative, John supplies us with precisely the conceptual framework which will allow us to accept the mantle clock's stopping as the reason for the behavior in question.

It is essential to note that just as long as we lack a conceptual model of the causal process, the particular phenomena in question remain as independent entities, and this brings us to the fundamental point: To claim that A is the cause of B is precisely to deny that these two entities are any longer to be considered totally independent of each other and to insist, instead, that they are conceived as parts of a single spatial or temporal process. In making this assertion of a causal sequence, we consciously alter our conception of the original two phenomena, no longer viewing them as independent entities which may or may not be constantly correlated in our experience. This explains the inevitable failure of those who, since Hume's time, have searched for the mysterious essence of the "causal connection"; for the step from the constant conjunction or correlation of independent entities to the supposition of a causal sequence does not depend upon a scientific discovery of some further linkage but upon a logical maneuver, a reorientation in our conception of how we look at the phenomena in question. To be sure, this step is not taken arbitrarily or without regard for careful observation and experience. Various experiments may well direct us toward a conceptual framework; in positing that causal framework, however, we commit ourselves to certain logical relationships, not to the truth of any experiential generalizations.

The designation of causes and reasons, therefore, involves a logical commitment to a theoretical structure or framework or narrative in which the phenomena in question are no longer considered independent entities but interrelated parts of a single unified process or sequence of events. We shall call this invoking of a conceptual framework the "narrative commitment" which is involved in the logical procedure of designating causes and reasons. The occurrence of this conceptual reorientation can elucidate an ambiguity mentioned earlier concerning the problem of drawing the line between the cause and the effect in any given process. We can, for simplicity, characterize the issue as that of distinguishing "effects" from "manifestations." The problem is, for instance, to decide whether Lorenz's rat torture fantasy was caused by, was an effect of, his hatred of his father or whether it was a manifestation of that hatred. Insofar as we call various pieces of behavior "manifestations" of some underlying factor, we will often assume that we are not giving an explanation but only *redescribing* that behavior; whereas if we consider some behavior as the effect of an underlying emotion or idea, then we tend to assume that we are giving a straightforward causal explanation. These ambiguities occur most obviously in areas of human behavior, but they occur even in the physical sciences. For instance, does the molecular rearrangement into a crystalline structure cause water to turn to ice? I think we would probably answer affirmatively. However, is the water's turning to ice the *effect* of the molecular rearrangement? We should probably insist that the water's turning to ice *is a part of, is a manifestation of,* the molecular rearrangement rather than an occurrence following upon it. The two things occur simultaneously; yet we would nevertheless designate the molecular rearrangement as the cause. In such a case the "cause" does *not* precede the "effect" in physical time but takes *logical precedence* in our conceptual understanding of the event. The ambiguity results precisely from the fact that in assuming a causal sequence, a single ongoing process, we thereby *deny* that *independent* antecedent and consequent events can be distinguished. Thus, the recognition of a causal sequence represents a definite alteration in our conceptualization of the events in question, from seeing A and B as independent entities sequentially conjoined in time, to understanding them as integrally related parts of a single process. Therefore, it is suggested that this common and very puzzling ambiguity concerning "effects" and "manifestations" is itself further evidence of how far one goes beyond the realm of physical experience when one employs the concepts of cause and reason.

Insofar as our conceptions of A and B alter when we come to consider them a part of a causal sequence or process, then our expectations likewise must alter. We can no longer think of A independently of B, without expecting B. This means, however, that those situations in which A's occurrence is *not* followed by B must be particularly challenging and, indeed, inconsistent, at least on first sight, with our understanding of the process. Thus in considering A and B to be causally related we must simultaneously undertake to explain any further situations in which this causal sequence is interrupted, that is, any situations in which A is not followed by B. Hart and Honoré make this same point in the following way:

> The statement that on this occasion X was the cause of Y differs from the conjunctive statement that X was followed by Y on this occasion and X's are followed by Y's in the great majority of cases. . . . The crucial difference is that, if we assert that X was followed by Y in a given case and Y's are highly probable given X's, we are *not* committed to explaining the cases where X's have not been followed by Y's nor to showing that the given case differs from them (1959, p. 45).

Therefore, in addition to a "narrative commitment" logically involved in the designation of causes and reasons, there is what can be called an "explanatory commitment." This idea will be elaborated in Chapter 7, where we discuss in more detail the role of laws and generalizations in psychoanalytic explanations.

Certainly a great deal more remains to be said about causes and reasons. The purpose of these remarks, however, has been to outline a possible analysis of these concepts which would avoid the rigid dichotomies of movement-action, cause-reason, and physical science–behavioral science. The arguments have so far been philosophical; however, with them in mind we can now return to Paul Lorenz and psychoanalysis.

C. Causes and Reasons in Psychoanalysis

It is one thing to attack the thesis of the separate domain on logical grounds; it is quite another to show that it is contradicted by the actual facts of psychoanalytic explanation. Nevertheless, I think this failure of the separate domain thesis can be demonstrated convincingly, at least with regard to Freud's work. Neither in Freud's theoretical writings nor in his analysis of the Lorenz case does a radical distinction between causes and reasons appear to be employed. In looking through Freud's writings for evidence concerning this issue one finds a total, and some would say shocking, disregard for cause-reason and movement-action distinctions. Of course, this total disregard is certainly not a convincing argument against the separate domain thesis; Freud might simply have been confused on this issue. Indeed, critics of Freud might take this as just another sign that psychoanalysis *is* misguided and mistaken. However, in this chapter it is not criticisms of psychoanalysis which are the subject but the arguments of one group of its defenders; and for those sympathizers who propound the separate domain thesis, the complete mixing of these concepts by Freud must prove very puzzling. For if psychoanalysis offers at least some true statements about human behavior, and is therefore worthy of defense, it is extremely odd that it should nevertheless be so very confused on what is after all a fundamental issue. One would be forced to say that Freud had definite insights into the explanation of human behavior; yet he did not even realize whether he was explaining movements or actions and whether he was explaining them in terms of causes or reasons.

I want to argue first that although he did not draw rigid cause-reason or movement-action distinctions, Freud nevertheless employed a subtle and quite workable analysis of causation. Second, when one looks at the Lorenz case one can see that Freud mixes these terms precisely because in the context of that individual's behavior it would make no sense to separate them. Finally, although Freud does not distinguish between causes and reasons, I want to show that he does draw certain other important distinctions about reasons, rationalizations, and unconscious reasons, and that his use of all these terms fits into the same sort of philosophical analysis outlined in the previous section.

1. Causation in Freud's Theoretical Writings

In 1895 Freud presented an elaborate model of the different varieties of factors that go to make up the etiology of the neuroses. He distinguished among four different terms which together form the "aetiological equation," and which must all be present if the disease entity is to occur. These were: preconditions, specific causes, concurrent causes, and precipitating or releasing causes. Each of these factors is "capable of a quantitative change—that is of increase or decrease," and a certain combined strength of the various causes must be reached before the effect, the disease, occurs (Freud, 1895, p. 135). Freud goes on to characterize these causes in the following way:

> . . . *preconditions* are those in whose absence the effect would never come about, but which are incapable of producing the effect by themselves, no matter in what amount they may be present. For the specific cause is still lacking.
>
> The *specific cause* is the one which is never missing in any case in which the effect takes place. . . .
>
> As *concurrent causes* we may regard such factors as are not necessarily present every time, nor able, whatever their amount, to produce the effect by themselves alone, but which operate alongside of the preconditions and the specific cause in satisfying the aetiological equation (1895, p. 136).[20]

Any of these factors "can in a particular case play the role of precipitating cause"; thus there are in effect only three types of factors, and the one which finally completes the set of sufficient conditions in the particular case can be called the precipitating cause (Freud, 1895, p. 136). In the Lorenz case, for instance, Freud held that the mother's suggestion of marriage to a wealthy cousin was the precipitating cause, the factor which led to the great exacerbation of the patient's illness.

A year later Freud presented a similar model in the context of an assessment of the importance of heredity in neuroses (1896a). In this paper he clarified the distinction between preconditions and specific causes. Preconditions are necessary but "are of a general nature and are equally met with in the aetiology of many other disorders" (1896a, p. 147). In

---

[20] Freud's italics.

contrast, specific causes, although likewise necessary, "are of a limited nature and appear only in the aetiology of the disorder for which they are specific" (p. 147). Freud then went on to clarify this analysis by considering the etiology of hysteria. He admitted that a hereditary neurotic disposition was a precondition, "powerful in every case and even indispensable in most cases" (p. 147). As concurrent causes, Freud listed the "stock agents met with elsewhere: emotional disturbance, physical exhaustion, acute illnesses, intoxications, traumatic accidents, intellectual overwork, etc." (p. 148). The specific cause is a disturbance of "the economics of the nervous system," which has its origin in the patient's "contemporary sexual life or in important events in his past life" (p. 149). There is, moreover, a "regular parallelism" between the type of sexual disturbance, the specific cause, and the type of neurosis developed (p. 149). In this period Freud simply divided these disturbances into two groups and believed that "passive" sexual experiences led to hysteria while "active" experiences led to obsessional neurosis (pp. 152 and 155).

We need not concern ourselves with the actual content of these early speculations but only with the analysis of causation that is here employed. It is surprisingly subtle and draws some of the same distinctions that appear in Hart and Honoré's account. There is first of all the similar assertions that causes are: (1) complex, in the sense of there being a set of causal factors, and (2) multiple, in the sense of there being various possible sets of sufficient conditions. Furthermore, the causal factors, while being equally necessary, nevertheless can show variation in their quantitative strength or importance. Likewise, in Freud's tripartite division of the causally relevant or etiological factors, two of his subdivisions are quite similar to those of Hart and Honoré: conditions which are always necessary, and conditions which may be necessary only in certain situations. Thus, Freud distinguishes conditions which may be necessary to all disease etiologies ("preconditions") and others which, while not always being indispensable, are nevertheless on certain occasions necessary as "concurrent" factors.

In his clear division of necessary factors into conditions and causes Freud again parallels Hart and Honoré in a most important respect. Freud even asks virtually the same question as those authors: "How do we distinguish between a precondition and a specific cause, since both are indispensable [i.e., necessary] and yet neither suffices alone to act as a cause?" (Freud, 1895, p. 136). There is a clear recognition by Freud of the difference between finding the necessary conditions, Hart and Honoré's "causally relevant factors," and finding what Freud calls the "specific causes." One also finds the notion that there may be a host of necessary conditions which nevertheless cannot account for the specific neurosis.

These "concurrent causes," such as physical exhaustion and acute illness, can be factors in any sort of illness, but in addition to these necessary conditions one must discover the specific causes which explain the peculiarities of the individual case, why one type of neurosis rather than another was developed. One criterion for distinguishing causes from conditions which Freud suggests is in fact quite similar to Hart and Honoré's "abnormality," for the specific cause stands in contrast to the other factors because "it is found in no other aetiological equation, or in very few" (Freud, 1895, p. 136).

Freud's analysis of causation, then, is surprisingly similar on more than a half-dozen specific points to at least one philosophical account written over 60 years later.[21] Moreover, it squares well with several commonsense distinctions concerning events in everyday experience. Finally, and most important, it seems to be a model that could function quite well without any radical differentiation between causes and reasons, or movements and actions. To defend this assertion, however, one must return to the case history.

2. Causes and Reasons in the Lorenz Case

It would probably have been most bewildering for Freud had he been questioned about the causes of Paul Lorenz's movements as opposed to the reasons for his actions. Indeed, given his antiphilosophical bias, Freud

---

[21] This similarity is, perhaps, not so surprising as it seems. Hart and Honoré explicitly develop their account of causation as a greatly modified and elaborated version of the one presented by Mill in his *System of Logic*. It is possible that Freud's account, too, is based at least to some extent on Mill. We know that in 1880 Freud translated the twelfth volume of the standard German edition of Mill's writings, then being edited by Theodor Gomperz. This volume contained three late essays by Mill on social problems, including the enfranchisement of women and one essay on Plato (Jones, 1953, pp. 55–56). Freud certainly had also read the *Autobiography* and at least one "philosophical work," and he commented at length on Mill's life and social views in a letter to Martha Bernays, part of which Jones quotes (Jones, 1953, pp. 175–176). This letter is dated by Jones "Nov. 5, 1883," but it appears in full in the *Letters of Sigmund Freud,* edited by Ernst Freud, as Letter 28, dated "Nov. 15, 1883." Freud also knew enough about Mill's thought to be able to comment adversely, in the same letter, about an essay written on him by Georg Brandes. At least one writer, Imre Hermann, has argued, in Hungarian, that Freud's political views were derived from Mill (Jones, 1957, p. 343). It seems at least possible, therefore, that Freud's analysis of causation may also have been derived from Mill. Some writers, however, like David Rapaport, do not mention Mill as a "formative influence" at all, and this writer even insists that the "epistemological implications of psychoanalysis are closest to Kant and most remote from Anglo-Saxon empiricism" (Rapaport, 1960, p. 13). In the absence of definite information, this interesting historical question must remain open.

might have responded quite angrily. Such anger would not signify a denial that there may be important philosophical distinctions to be drawn concerning these concepts. It would simply mean that when one comes to examine an individual patient, these particular distinctions between causes and reasons and movements and actions seem somewhat irrelevant. There are not two sorts of behavior, movements and actions, to be explained in two totally different ways. There is a whole array of behavior ranging from overt acts on single occasions to habitual modes of behaving, to attitudes, beliefs, wishes, etc. To explain this behavior one must take into account a large number of different factors: constitutional factors such as sexual precocity; historical incidents such as the "beating"; and threats and suggestions of other people, such as his mother's plan for marriage. To ask which of all these are causes and which reasons is irrelevant. The important and immensely difficult problems are to discover which factors were actually causally relevant, how important each of them was, and whether the patient's stated motives and feelings were in fact operative.

If Freud does not distinguish sharply between causes and reasons however, he nevertheless draws certain other distinctions, and two of these are of special importance for the present discussion. The first is the distinction between reasons and rationalizations. When Jones introduced the latter term in 1908 into psychoanalysis, it already had, according to the Oxford English Dictionary, a general meaning, among others, of making "conformable to reason." Jones, however, gave the term a peculiarly psychoanalytic twist:

> Everyone feels that, as a rational creature, he must be able to give a connected, logical, and continuous account of himself, his conduct, and opinions, and all his mental processes are unconsciously manipulated and revised to that end. No one will admit that he ever deliberately performed an irrational act, and any act that might appear so is immediately justified by distorting the mental processes concerned and providing a false explanation that has a plausible ring of rationality (1908, p. 6).[22]

It seems safe to say that this new use has reentered ordinary language and has become the most common meaning. The reason-rationalization distinction is roughly equivalent to the distinction between "*the real* reason" and "*his* reason," in those situations where we wish to draw this contrast. Already by 1909, when the Lorenz case was written, "rationalization" had entered the common terminology of psychoanalysis. Like the term "ambivalence," introduced in 1910, the concept of rationalization put a name to a phenomenon that had been recognized earlier. There is excellent evidence

---

[22] Interestingly, this paper was first given, in German, at the First International Psycho-Analytic Congress in April, 1908, where it immediately followed Freud's 5 hour discussion of Lorenz, who was then still under analysis.

for this in the Lorenz case. In the clinical notes, written some six months before Jones' paper was first given, Freud makes a brief comment as a sort of private clarification about the "inevitable misunderstanding of the *Unconscious* by the *Conscious*" (1909b, p. 278).[23] Then, in the published record, written a year after Jones' paper had appeared, Freud uses a similar phrase:

> The patient's consciousness naturally misunderstands [compulsive acts] and puts forward a set of secondary motives to account for them—*rationalizes* them, in short (1909b, p. 192).

Freud even adds a reference to Jones' paper at this point.

One example of how Freud uses this concept should be sufficient for us to grasp the meaning of the distinction between reasons and rationalizations. At the time when the patient was abusing and insulting Freud during the sessions, he would get off the couch and walk around the room. His reason for this, ostensibly, was

> . . . delicacy of feeling: he could not bring himself, he said, to utter such horrible things while he was lying there so comfortably. But soon he himself found a more cogent explanation, namely, that he was avoiding my proximity for fear of my giving him a beating [as his father had done] (1909b, p. 209).

What makes the first reason that the patient gave only a rationalization? It is not that the feeling mentioned could *never* be a cause for the actual behavior; it is simply that in the given situation Freud was convinced that it was not actually a causal factor. Freud asserts that it was not feelings of delicacy, but fear of being beaten that caused Lorenz to walk around the room; it was not considerations of tact and a sense of shame, but memories of the dead father's behavior which led to the patient's cowering and avoidance of Freud. Thus, we can see that rationalizations have the same logical form as reasons, but in the given situation they are not causally relevant factors. To say that X is only a rationalization, then, is to assert that, although it could in other circumstances have been a causally relevant factor, in the given situation it was not in fact an operative consideration in response to which the agent's behavior occurred. Thus, a reason is a "real reason" precisely when it is a causally relevant factor, and it is only a "rationalization" when it is not in fact a causally relevant factor, even though the agent may assert that it was a consideration causing him to act in the way that he did.

This same distinction is implied in Freud's statement that

> . . . [neurotics who] have connected their affects with the wrong causes, will also tell the physician the true causes, without any suspicion that their

---

[23] This entry is dated "Nov. 11," [1907].

self-reproaches have simply become detached from them [the true causes] (1909b, p. 196).

"Wrong causes," then, is a synonym for "rationalizations"; they are simply those potentially causal factors which in the given situation were not in fact causally relevant. Freud's distinction, then, between reasons and rationalizations accords very well with our own elucidation of the concept of reason and offers no support at all for the view that reasons are anything other than causally relevant factors of a special sort.

Another concept that appears in psychoanalytic narratives is the "unconscious reason." It is of course impossible to deal adequately with Freud's conception of "the unconscious" in this study; our purpose in even raising the issue is simply to point out, very briefly, another point at which Freud's understanding of reasons and causes, while being developed quite subtly, nevertheless does not support the thesis of the separate domain. Our remarks are intended to elucidate the concept of an "unconscious reason" solely as it is related to the concept of "reason" which has already been discussed; thus, we shall ignore other somewhat related concepts, such as that of "unconscious motives."

A good example of an unconscious reason in the Lorenz case would be the patient's unconscious hostility toward his father, which Freud emphasizes as such an important cause of much of his abnormal behavior. The problem is what does it mean to assert, say,

1. Lorenz's behavior showed unconscious hostility toward his father.

First, it must be pointed out that there is a descriptive use of such a statement. On this use, to assert 1 is to assert that "Lorenz's behavior is similar to other individuals who are consciously hostile to their fathers." This assertion is only descriptive, however, and makes no explanatory claim. A parallel between appearances of two phenomena is suggested, but there is no claim that the causes of the two phenomena are likewise similar.

There is also a second use, perhaps more common in psychoanalysis, which is meant to be explanatory; that is, "unconscious hostility" is meant to explain in some way certain aspects of Lorenz's behavior. On this second use, then, how must statement 1 be paraphrased? I suggest that at least an important part of what is meant is just that "Hostility toward his father is a causally relevant factor in the patient's behavior, although he could not admit to this." If we wish to accept the whole psychoanalytic account, then we would have to add that the reason the patient cannot be aware of his hostility ("cannot be aware" and "could not admit" as opposed to "is not aware" and "would not admit") is that it is being repressed and that such repression can only be lifted by various technical procedures. The essential point, however, is that the adjective "un-conscious" does not imply that the hostility is of a special sort. Unconscious hostility is not different, as a causal factor, from conscious hostility. If hostility is a cause of, for instance, the patient's "undressing" ritual, then it is a cause whether or not the patient is aware of it. It is certainly important for us to know whether or not the patient is aware of this factor, and Freud, by labeling it "unconscious," tells us that he is not and could not be aware of it. There is, however, nothing mysterious about this ability to do things without being aware of what made us do them, or even our tendency to give false reasons when asked to explain our actions. This use of the term "unconscious," like "rationalization," simply clarifies and extends what is a common-sense observation about human behavior.

It is possible, of course, for the patient to become aware of this hostility, in which case, by definition, it ceases to be "unconscious." This does not, however, mean that it necessarily ceases to be a causal factor or that it changes from a cause to a reason. On the other hand, this awareness itself might well become a causally relevant factor in certain new behavior. Let us say, for instance, that the unconscious hostility is a causal factor in the patient's "undressing" ritual. If he becomes aware of this hostility, then he might well act in an exaggeratedly kind manner in an attempt to prevent the hostility from being expressed. If this occurs, then we could properly say that the hostility was the reason for the cordial behavior, meaning that it was the factor in consideration of which the patient was acting. This situation is a common one; we often take extra precautions to prevent our personal animosities from disrupting various necessary activities and relationships. Indeed, we may become or be made aware not only of our hostility but also of the reasons why this feeling developed. If these reasons are infantile or unrealistic, we may come to see our hostility as unwarranted and act accordingly. On the other hand, if the reasons for the hostility still seem justified, we may then continue our hostile actions but this time knowing full well the reasons for our actions. This is precisely what Freud has in mind when he says that as a result of psycho-analytic treatment, "*repression* is replaced by a *condemning* judgment" (1909c, p. 53).[24] Hostility, for instance, is no longer simply denied, but recognized and then either consciously acted upon or rejected.

If this rough outline of the concept of "unconscious reason" is at all correct, then we can see this concept's relationship to those of cause and reason discussed earlier. To say "X is the unconscious reason for P's doing Y" is *similar* to saying "X is the reason for P's doing Y" in that both statements assert that X is a causally relevant factor in Y's occurrence.

---

[24] Freud's italics.

The first statement is *unlike* the second in that only the second makes the further claim that "X was a causally relevant factor by virtue of the fact that P was aware of it." However, if the unconscious reason statement is unlike the conscious reason statement in this important way, then why is the word "reason" used at all? I think there are two good justifications for this extension of the concept. In the first place, there is the justification by analogy. The X's we tend to designate as unconscious reasons are just the sort of X's which, in other cases, are reasons of the usual variety. Thus, by labeling Lorenz's hostility, which caused so much of his behavior, an "unconscious reason," we emphasize that this is the sort of factor which in other cases could be a conscious reason for behavior. Second, by this label we emphasize the possibility that through various procedures Lorenz may come to be aware of this factor, in which case that new awareness itself may perhaps become a causally relevant factor, a reason for altered and improved behavior.

Obviously, a great deal more needs to be said about how psychoanalysts use the concept "unconscious reason." We have discussed only two important uses, but there may be a number of others. Unfortunately, even these two uses are sometimes not clearly distinguished in psychoanalytic writing. It is also obvious that our own discussion has provided only a sketch, that it would require further elaboration to be convincing. The outline we have presented, however, should be sufficient to show that both in Freud's early theoretical writings and in his analysis of the Lorenz case there is no suggestion at all of any "radical difference" between causes and reasons, nor is there any hint that psychoanalysis operates according to principles entirely separate from those used in the other sciences.

D. "Overdetermination" and the Separate Domain Thesis

In Sections A and B we discussed two specific forms of the separate domain thesis, and we tried to argue that its application to explanations of human behavior was misguided. In Section C we returned to Freud's own writings and attempted to show that no evidence at all could be found for the so-called radical division between causes and reasons, between explanations in the physical sciences and explanations of human behavior. It is, I think, true to say that until fairly recently psychoanalysts themselves have never defended their procedures by taking up and defending in a systematic fashion this viewpoint. The thesis of the separate domain was for the most part an "outsider's" defense. It is all the more unfortunate, therefore, that now, when at least some philosophers seem to be moving away from these positions, certain analysts have begun to adopt these old arguments. Insofar as this development suggests that psychoanalysts are beginning to take philosophers seriously and to read their commentaries on the field, it betokens in general a change for the better. The problem remains, however, that on this particular issue the arguments are no more convincing in the hands of psychoanalysts than they were in those of the philosophers. There is, moreover, the added fact that in taking up these positions analysts have sometimes claimed historical justification from Freud's writings and in so doing have distorted his original concepts. Our examination of the separate domain thesis would therefore not be complete without some discussion of this new development.

From our point of view some of the most interesting arguments have centered upon Freud's concept of "overdetermination," and perhaps the most explicit and extended presentation is in Harry Guntrip's *Personality Structure and Human Interaction* (1961). Before we can examine Guntrip's argument, we shall have to outline Freud's use of the concept of "overdetermination." In the *Studies on Hysteria* Freud writes:

> Almost invariably when I have investigated the determinants of such [hysterical] conditions what I have come upon has not been a *single* traumatic cause but a group of similar ones (1893, p. 173).[25]

Somewhat later, Freud expands on this point and uses the word *"überdeterminiert"* for the first time. He emphasizes

> . . . the principal feature in the aetiology of the neuroses—that their genesis is as a rule overdetermined, that several factors must come together to produce this result . . . (1893, p. 263).

> We do not usually find a *single* hysterical symptom, but a number of them, partly independent of one another and partly linked together. We must not expect to meet with a *single* traumatic memory and a *single* pathogenic idea as its nucleus; we must be prepared for *successions* of partial traumas and *concatenations* of pathogenic trains of thought (pp. 287–288).[26]

In 1895 Freud once again defined the term: "As a rule the neuroses are *overdetermined;* that is to say, several factors operate together in their aetiology" (1895, p. 131).[27] From this time on the concept recurs often in Freud's writings, without any alteration, and further quotations are unnecessary. The basic idea is quite simple, and it has been touched upon in the previous sections: There is never a single cause, but a whole set of factors which only together are causally sufficient. The point was of course not new in philosophy (Mill, for instance, had stated it explicitly); nor was it new to psychology, and Freud was aware of this. In 1901 he

---

[25] Freud's italics.
[26] Freud's italics.
[27] Freud's italics.

stated that he was following Wundt's "principle of the complication of causes" (1901, p. 61). Not only is this principle not very original, it is also, I suggest, not very important in terms of its ramifications for science. Moreover, it is certainly not applicable exclusively to explanations of human behavior. It is interesting, therefore, that overdetermination has been repeatedly "rediscovered" and hit upon by many different analysts as being an essential and differentiating concept of psychoanalytic theory.

In Guntrip's discussion of the status of psychoanalysis as a science, he quotes extensively and approvingly from Hutten's "On Explanation in Psychology and Physics" (1956). Hutten explains overdetermination as the idea that

> . . . there exists more than one set of antecedent conditions, or causes, and each set *alone* is capable of explaining how it [the effect] occurs. . . . This disagrees with the ordinary causal explanation as we know it from physics (p. 73).[28]

It must be pointed out for the record that this is *not* what Freud means by overdetermination, at least in the quotations given above. Freud refers to the fact that "several factors must come together" to cause the particular occurrence. This is not the same as asserting that there exists more than one such group of factors, and each of these sets alone could produce the result. Nevertheless, in interpreting overdetermination in this second way, Hutten remains true to Freud's thought, if not to his definition, since, as we have seen, Freud clearly held that the causes of behavior were *both* complex (overdetermined) and multiple (in the sense of there being alternate sets of sufficient conditions). Hutten then goes on to point out that in psychoanalysis we often do not speak

> . . . about causal laws but about the *aetiology* of a symptom or illness. Similarly, instead of description and prediction, we have *diagnosis* and *prognosis*. . . . Unlike mass points human beings have a history . . . (p. 76).[29]

Hutten argues that in behavioral explanations we refer to biological and social predisposing conditions and that such reference "introduces immediately the so-called plurality of causes—in contrast to the causal scheme of physics" (p. 77).[30]

> Human actions are affected by cultural, social, economic, physical and other factors. . . . Classical physics is taken as a standard when it is said that a scientific theory must explain a given phenomenon in one way only; but this is not really true even there, and certainly not in modern physics. . . .

---

[28] Quoted by Guntrip (1961, p. 152).
[29] Quoted by Guntrip (1961, p. 153).
[30] Quoted by Guntrip (1961, p. 153).

In psychology the situation is not as simple as in physics, where we have a single set of fixed *static* (initial and boundary) conditions and *constant* forces (p. 83).[31]

I think only a few brief and rather categorical comments are warranted, since our focus is not on Hutten but on Guntrip. It seems obvious from even these few quotations that there is here being invoked only the very roughest caricature of physics. First, it is just not true that the idea that there can exist "more than one set of antecedent conditions, or causes, . . . disagrees with the ordinary causal explanation as we know it from physics." Indeed, it was the example of the physical sciences which suggested to Mill, and later to Freud, the possibility of multiple causation. Second, it seems equally clear that few physicists would be willing to accept as it stands the statement that in physics "we have a single set of fixed *static* (initial and boundary) conditions and *constant* forces." This would certainly have to be modified and interpreted in a very special way, and in so doing the contrast with psychology would be removed. Finally, it should be noted that a great deal of unwarranted weight is placed on the terms "etiology," "diagnosis," and "prognosis." This is the language preeminently of medicine and pathophysiology, not psychology; by themselves these terms carry no logical implications but only serve to underline the complexity of the subject matter. In discussing the etiology of disease we *are* discussing a causal, genetic explanation; in offering a prognosis we *are* making a prediction; logically, the terms are quite on a par.

Guntrip accepts this straw man conception of physics and then goes even further for his own conclusion:

The upshot is that the terms of physical science and the physical cause-and-effect type of explanation are not relevant or suitable to psychic phenomena. Psychoanalysis provides a new type of model for personality as a complex of various psychic levels and structures that enables the phenomena of personal living—i.e. those of conscious and unconscious conflict—to be explained on the basis of over-determination and plurality of causes, 'cause' being no longer understood in the physical sense (1961, p. 155).

Here, then, is an explicit statement of the separate domain thesis emphasizing the essentially overdetermined aspect of human behavior. Let us disregard the fact that the argument is based upon a very misleading conception of physics and physical science, and let us also avoid the very important question of just how the concept "cause" is to be understood, if not "in the physical sense," since the author unfortunately does not elaborate on this point. The question then is simply: what would it mean to say that some particular piece of behavior is overdetermined; what, for instance, would it mean to assert that "Dr. Jones' pleasure in his practice of surgery is overdetermined"?

---

[31] Quoted by Guntrip (1961, p. 154).

First of all, one might simply be making an empirical observation, namely, that in general there are a variety of sets of factors which can lead different individuals to an interest and pleasure in surgery. In precisely the same way one might observe that in general a variety of sets of conditions can cause a tire blowout, namely, overinflation, a nail puncture, etc. So far there can be no argument, but there is likewise no reason on this account to distinguish between human behavior and tire behavior.

It is more likely, however, that we mean our assertion to be applied specifically to the one situation or individual under consideration; that is, we mean Dr. Jones' interest in surgery, which he claims to be based on a love of humanity, is in fact overdetermined. This would actually be at least a very crude example of a fairly typical sort of psychoanalytic statement, and two interpretations of it are possible. We might mean that for this particular individual at least two factors were operative—love of humanity and, for instance, sadistic love of inflicting injury—either of which by itself, let us say, would have been sufficient to engender an interest in surgery. In the same way, a person might swallow strychnine and an overdose of barbiturate, in which case there would be two factors operative in the suicide either of which would have been sufficient to cause death. In this case, however, the death resulted from a combination of both factors. Such a statement is medically accurate and I think logically unimpeachable. Just so, the doctor's interest in surgery might have resulted from a combination of two factors. We might, however, go further and interpret our assertion in such a way as to cast doubt upon the one, usually conscious, factor and place either an absolute or relative priority upon the second, usually unconscious, factor. Thus, we might be implying that love of humanity would not by itself have led Dr. Jones to an interest in surgery, that the "really important" factor was the unconscious sadistic motivation.

Thus, in asserting that "Dr. Jones' love of surgery is overdetermined" we might be asserting any of the following:

1. This behavioral characteristic is the sort of thing which has been found to have a variety of different causes in different individuals.
2. There is in addition to Jones' love of humanity another good and sufficient reason which he had for being a surgeon, namely, sadism.
3. Love of humanity is only Jones' rationalization for his choice of professions; the real reason was his sadism.

We may simply be pointing out the variety of possible motivations which can lead different individuals to make a certain choice of career. Or we may be making a definite assertion about a particular individual, emphasizing the complexity of his motivations. Or we may even be casting aspersions upon his avowed reasons and suggesting other, unrecognized motivations.

Any of the above interpretations might be true in a particular situation; the danger of misinterpretation, however, particularly when the original statement is not fully elucidated, is evident. In each case, the assertion is reasonable, arguable, and potentially verifiable. To say that the assertion is *arguable,* however, is to imply and insist that it *be argued,* that it be scientifically evaluated according to any relevant evidence. The concept of overdetermination, then, on any of its several interpretations does not lead away from ordinary scientific methods but right back to them. I suggest, therefore, that the concept of overdetermination, far from being an essential feature of the psychoanalytic approach, is one that might well be dropped entirely without loss. It is constantly open to misinterpretation; moreover, it has recently become the foundation of yet another attempt to divorce psychoanalysis and the study of human behavior from the natural sciences. Such an attempt, we have seen, is both historically unjustified on the basis of Freud's original formulation and philosophically untenable.

In this chapter we have examined three different forms of a common defense of psychoanalysis—the thesis that psychoanalysis is a radically different sort of discipline separate from all other sciences. This position has been criticized on both philosophical grounds and also by examination of Freud's writings. We have also tried to outline alternative analyses of movement and action, causes and reasons, and overdetermination that would not necessitate the division of the sciences into two separate domains. This sort of separation would be a "bad" way of "saving" psychoanalysis from the pressure of facing up to the rigorous standards developed in the natural sciences. To accept such relegation to a separate domain would be to trade the vitality and growth of a living discipline for the security, but sterility, of an exhibit case in the museum of the history of medicine.

In the following two chapters the opposite or converse point of view will be taken, emphasizing not the radical differences but the similarities between psychoanalysis and other scientific fields, and we shall look at the ways in which it can actually meet the standards set by those disciplines.

Chapter 6/THE PSYCHOANALYTIC NARRATIVE

A. EXPLANATION AND DESCRIPTION

We have seen that Freud's explanation in the Lorenz case does not fit into a "separate domain" of actions and reasons. Nevertheless, it is rather special and peculiar, so peculiar in fact that it has sometimes been questioned whether it is an explanation at all—whether Freud has given us an account that, if true, would be an adequate explanation of Paul Lorenz's behavior, or only a new description of that behavior, albeit a strikingly original one. In Chapter 2 we discussed this distinction between explanation and description in very general terms; we now must deal with the point in reference to the specific case under consideration.

Several authors have suggested that a major portion, if indeed not all, of Freud's achievement lies in his brilliant "redescription" of many aspects of human behavior. We have G. E. Moore's account of Wittgenstein's lectures in 1932 and 1933, in which this point and certain other criticisms of Freud were put forth.

> . . . there are so many cases [in Freud's writings] in which one can ask how far what he says is a 'hypothesis' and how far merely a good way of representing a fact—a question as to which [Wittgenstein] said Freud himself is constantly unclear. He said, for instance, that Freud encouraged a confusion between getting to know the *cause* of your laughter and getting to know the *reason* why you laugh, because what he [Freud] says sounds as if it were science, when in fact it is only a 'wonderful representation.' This last point he also expressed by saying 'It is all excellent similes, e.g. the comparison of a dream to a rebus' . . . what is most striking about [Freud] is 'the enormous field of psychical facts which he arranges' (1955, p. 316).

The same point occurs in Wittgenstein's remark about Darwin's mistake in:

> . . . thinking that 'because our ancestors, when angry, wanted to bite' is a sufficient explanation of why we show our teeth when angry. [Wittgenstein] said you might say that what is satisfactory in Darwin is not such 'hypotheses,' but his 'putting the facts in a system'—helping us to make a 'synopsis' of them (p. 316).

A similar point is made by Alasdair MacIntyre in his study *The Uncon-scious* (1958) when he argues that certain sorts of putative explanations offered by Freud, namely, those involving "the unconscious," must in fact be interpreted either as causal explanations *not* involving an entity, the unconscious, or as descriptions of purposive activity. It is this latter alterna-tive with which MacIntyre is more concerned. "For an essential part of Freud's achievement lies not in his explanations of abnormal behavior but in his redescription of such behavior (p. 61).[1] Thus, MacIntyre, like Wittgenstein in the quotation from Moore, lays great emphasis on the cause-reason distinction, an issue we have dealt with in the previous chapter. At this juncture, however, we are concerned with the suggestion that Freud, for the most part, offered new descriptions or arrangements rather than putative explanations.

It is quite likely that a concentration on certain of Freud's more theoretical and systematic works might lead one to just this view, namely, that he is primarily offering new and sometimes brilliant descriptions of common pieces of behavior such as dreams, jokes, and slips of the tongue. In such works as *The Psychopathology of Everyday Life* (1901) a multi-tude of illustrative examples are put forward to demonstrate certain theoretical principles with no regard for preserving the clinical context out of which each item arose. For purposes of exposition this procedure may be best; yet it inevitably accentuates the arbitrary quality of Freud's in-terpretations and suggests that they may be brilliant, but often unfounded, guesses. Whatever evidential support for these new interpretations there might have been lies buried in the unpublished and perhaps even un-recorded case histories. It is important, therefore, to note that Wittgenstein's basic text for the lectures Moore describes apparently was *Jokes and their Relation to the Unconscious* (1955, p. 316). Likewise MacIntyre makes use of *The Interpretation of Dreams*. This supports the point made in the first chapter that the use of such anecdotal material and broad theoretical principles as is contained in such works might well be somewhat deceptive. If, however, one studies a single case history as we have done, the impres-sion is altogether different. What might well seem arbitrary comments out of context may become, in the light of all we know about the patient, care-fully reasoned explanations of his behavior.

Freud certainly believed he was explaining behavior in the Lorenz case. We have only to see the repeated use of the word "explanation" in conjunc-tion with such adjectives as "good and bad," "profound," "partial," "com-plete and incomplete." Of course, neither Freud's conviction that he was explaining, nor his sincere desire to explain behavior is at all decisive; he

---

[1] The thesis is stated explicitly on p. 72 of that book.

might simply have been confused. But our point is that he was not confused in this way. It is of course true that Freud did redescribe certain of the patient's actions. But the point is that by doing so he *was* attempting to explain them. The discussion of description and explanation in Chapter 2 is relevant here. In given contexts to offer a new description may in fact be to offer an explanation. The distinction between these two procedures is not always a sharp one, and in any event is dependent upon the context, the situation in which it occurs.

Yet it is not enough simply to reiterate the point that new description may be explanatory; this much is easily conceded. Thus, MacIntyre recognizes that "illuminating description may count as a kind of explanation" (1958, p. 79). We go further by insisting that Freud's account is *primarily* explanatory; it is indeed just what we should desire from a psychiatrist or any other person who would attempt to explain Paul Lorenz's behavior. Freud, like us, recognized incongruities in his patient's actions and attitudes. Many items seemed inconsistent with what we know of human behavior in general and what we were told by the patient about himself. Freud tried to reconcile these inconsistencies. In the sense of drawing connections of various types between events, attitudes, etc., Freud certainly was offering possible explanations to us. He found the origins of various attitudes (e.g., hostility to the father) in childhood experiences. He traced unusual pieces of behavior (e.g., the stone moving incident) back to their motivating desires or fears. He showed how certain actions (e.g., compulsive dieting) functioned within the patient's mental economy. He explained the significance of dreams and rituals (e.g., the prayer formula).

That Freud offered different types of explanations is undeniable, and we shall examine some of these below. But it seems perverse to insist that only certain of these varieties are bona fide explanations. Thus, for instance, MacIntyre claims that in the case of dreams "Freud was decoding rather than explaining" (1958, p. 76). Certainly, to explain the meaning of a dream is different from explaining the origin of the dream or its function. But whoever would deny this? As long as we recognize that different contexts may give rise to different types of explanations, there seems no need to go further by denying that one can explain the meaning of a dream and to substitute the peculiar term "decoding." We have common speech on our side and no valid objections to maintaining the relationships embodied in it.

Our contention, then, is that the Paul Lorenz case provides a good example of a psychoanalytic explanation that would be, if true, a more or less adequate explanation of the patient's behavior. That it may also offer a "wonderful representation" or "brilliant redescription" is an interesting but secondary observation. This does not mean that we are at all clear at this stage as to just what *are* the logical properties in virtue of which the explanation is judged to be adequate. The point is simply that some such account of the type Freud has presented is just what we have in mind, and should rightly insist upon, when we ask for an explanation of an individual's behavior. Any explanation, whether psychoanalytic, behavioral, neurological, or some other sort, must answer the same questions Freud does; e.g., why does the patient develop this particular ritual; why does the patient act in this particular way? Therefore, we must pursue our analysis of the logic of behavioral explanations by studying just such an explanation that, if true, would be adequate rather than developing *a priori* criteria and then trying to decide if a given explanation fits them.

B. THE PSYCHOANALYTIC NARRATIVE

Having agreed that Freud's account is a putative explanation of his patient's behavior, we can now go on to inquire as to its general characteristics. First, we can ask: What is its subject matter; what is the principal focus of interest for the analyst in this case? If we were to choose a single word to characterize the subject matter, there could probably be none more appropriate than "individual." But just as the question "What is the subject matter?" is not as simple-minded as it may appear, so, too, our answer is not as obvious as it seems and will require some elaboration.

In the first place let us note that Freud's explanation concerns the patient *as an individual patient,* and indeed as an individual human being. Freud and ourselves as latter-day observers are confronted by a single sick individual whose life story presents a variety of incongruities—events and attitudes demanding to be explained, to be brought within the framework of understandable human behavior. The subject, however, is not a class of particular psychiatric symptoms—prayer rituals, say, or beliefs in the prophetic quality of dreams and the like. Nor is the subject a class of people—those judged to be suffering from an obsessional illness. It is, rather, a single person whose life includes features ranging from the mundane and common sensical to the outlandish and bizarre, and we must attempt to comprehend it in its entirety. Freud, like the historian, is interested in a particular course of events, namely, an individual's history. And far from disregarding those aspects which fail to conform to the typical patterns or classes of disturbed behavior, the opposite is nearer the truth. It is precisely the peculiarities, the "individuality" of that behavior which appears to be incongruous and calls for an explanation.

This is not to say that Freud does not use generalizations about obsessional neurotics as a group of psychologically disturbed people. We shall see in Chapter 7 just how very important is this aspect of Freud's explanation. Nor are we implying that there is no general theory of human behavior behind this explanation of one sick individual's behavior. There is, as we have seen, a large and complex theory, and it was one of Freud's purposes in publishing the case to demonstrate the application of this psychoanalytic theory in a particular patient's therapy. Nevertheless, our point remains that there is a logical gap between both the psychoanalytic theory and previous clinical experience on the one hand and the individual patient on the other.[2] Freud confronts us with a single individual, and we are asked first to evaluate his explanation of that particular individual alone. Only if and insofar as this explanation seems plausible does he go on to draw general conclusions. Freud does not argue that because his general theory is correct, then its application to this particular individual must likewise be correct. Nor does he argue directly from other clinical experiences to the present case. It is rather that if the explanation of the patient's illness seems correct, then it may be possible to extrapolate from it to theories of a more general relevance or to other patients with similar histories. This direction to Freud's thinking is made explicit in his introduction to the published case and can be inferred from his form of presentation: two sections, the first consisting of case history and the second, labeled in later editions "Theoretical," consisting of a discussion of obsessional neuroses in general.

There is a second aspect to the "individual" nature of the subject matter of psychoanalytic explanation. On the one hand, the emphasis is on the patient as an individual, with peculiarities of history and disposition that distinguish him from other somewhat similar cases and that necessitate particular explanations. But, on the other hand, there is a sense in which the subject matter is not individual behavior at all, that is, not *individual bits* of behavior. Freud's subject is Paul Lorenz, a person suffering from an obsessional neurosis. The particular events or incidents in the patient's life are, however, of secondary importance. Naturally, an immense number of incidents, attitudes, and beliefs emerge during 11 months of psychoanalysis. Many are incongruous, demanding explanation, and all offer insight into the patient's general personality structure. In the course of giving the full psychoanalytic explanation a number of such particular bits of behavior are explained, some more satisfactorily, others less. But just as the argument is from the explanation of the individual's behavior

---

[2] Obviously, we are at this point merely asserting what seems to us to be an important observation. In Chapter 7 this view will be discussed in detail. This logical gap, it should be noted, is not the same as that spoken of as existing between theory and therapy.

to the general theory, so too, it is from the over-all explanation of the whole life history to the explanation of particular incidents.

It is our contention that the core of the psychoanalytic explanation presented lies in a general, over-all account of the patient's life history and "life style," the peculiar modes and patterns of behavior which mark that history.[3] The analyst's explanation is what we shall now call a "psycho-analytic narrative."[4] Basically, Freud has created a single extended account of Paul Lorenz's past history and present circumstances. He has isolated certain general mechanisms (e.g., hostility toward his father, conflict over choice of love object) and has used them as main threads to weave together a multitude of biographical detail into a fairly unified narrative within which a great deal of previously unexplainable material takes on comprehensible form. Psychoanalysis supplies a context, a narrative about an individual patient within which isolated pieces of his behavior come to be understood, fitted together, and organized into a comprehensible whole. The explanation of, say, a particular dream or a transient compulsive idea is based upon and subservient to some framework of general principles within which the whole life history of the individual is organized and made meaningful. This is another reason, therefore, why any analysis of psycho-analytic explanations that proceeds from piecemeal, anecdotal material is bound to be misleading, for it is just this narrative property, which we take to be essential, that will be ignored. This accounts for our going into such detail over a single case history, for it is only in this way that we could bring out the psychoanalytic narrative that is the core of Freud's explanation.

Freud gives us a story ranging over the whole life history of Paul Lorenz, from his parents through birth, childhood, adolescence, right up to the onset of illness and extending into the period of analysis. There is, essentially, but a single long and exceedingly complicated narrative to fit the single long and exceedingly complicated life history. Within that narrative, as we shall see in the following sections, one can isolate various types of explanations accounting in different ways for particular bits of behavior; but it would be a grave distortion to see the narrative as simply the summation of these separate explanations, for this would be to reverse the order of procedure.

---

[3] The phrase "life style" is used advisedly, knowing that it was popularized by Alfred Adler; nevertheless, it seems an appropriate term for our own use.

[4] The use of this word as a philosophical term in discussions of explanation in psychoanalysis is not new. Brian Farrell employed it in "Can Psychoanalysis Be Refuted" (1961a) and in later writings. More recently W. B. Gallie in *Philosophy and the Historical Understanding* (1964) has developed a detailed analysis of historical explanation in terms of a narrative, stressing many points that we, too, have urged in our discussion of context.

. . . to relate [the explanation of a single symptom] in detail would occupy the whole period of this lecture. The chain of associations always has more than two links; and the traumatic scenes do not form a simple row, like a string of pearls, but ramify and are interconnected like genealogical trees, so that in any new experience two or more earlier ones come into operation as memories. In short, giving an account of the resolution of a single symptom would in fact amount to the task of relating an entire case history (Freud, 1896c, pp. 196–197).

It is simply not accurate to suggest that Freud explains particular pieces of behavior and then abstracts from them, or adds them together to form a general narrative. Instead, after listening to the patient he gradually, bumblingly, puts forth certain ideas, altering them as new material emerges[5]: Perhaps the trauma of seeing a rat by the grave under conditions of heightened feeling. . . . Perhaps being the first-born boy in a family of girls. . . . Perhaps the inherited strength of sexual drive coupled to his father's forcefulness led to incomplete resolution of childhood jealousy and hostility. . . . Out of such musings a single over-all narrative is eventually built up that covers the patient's whole history and within which his peculiar attitudes and actions become understandable.

The logic of psychoanalytic explanations, then, resolves itself into the logic of psychoanalytic narratives, and this fact will have important ramifications when we turn to discuss traditional philosophical problems such as the testability of explanations. We have, of course, only begun to elaborate our sense of the term "narrative" and its implications, but certain ambiguities will, perhaps, be removed as our analysis proceeds.

C. Explaining and Understanding

Let us immediately clear up a possible confusion concerning a criticism which would argue that what we are suggesting by the concept of a narrative is somehow very different from what should be a truly scientific approach to behavior. This is the objection raised by certain psychologists, notably Professor Eysenck, who discusses the issue in *Uses and Abuses of Psychology* (1953).[6] He claims that there is a profound distinction

---

[5] Just how gradual and how bumbling is apparent primarily in the clinical notes; in the published record mistakes and blind alley hypotheses are less prominent. This is still another benefit of having Freud's notes for study.

[6] This understanding-explaining dichotomy is an old issue of German psychology, and it is fitting that Heinz Hartmann some 40 years ago answered this same criticism that psychoanalysis is only an "understanding" discipline. His 1927 paper "Understanding and Explanation" has recently been translated and appears for the first time in English in *Essays on Ego Psychology* (1964).

between "a common-sense psychology which tries to *understand* human beings, and a psychology which tries to *explain* their conduct on a scientific basis" (p. 222). It turns out that psychoanalysis attempts the former, and "that consequently it is essentially non-scientific and to be judged in terms of belief and faith, rather than in terms of proof and verification" (p. 226). Of course, our insistence on the narrative aspect of psychoanalytic explanations might be mistaken for just such an affirmation of psychoanalysis as an "understanding" discipline; hence, it is important that we clarify this issue.

Eysenck's argument suffers in that the two terms of his dichotomy— "explanation" and "understanding"—are never made precise, and from the various metaphors and examples used it seems clear that several different claims are here conflated. First, Eysenck speaks of two kinds of psychology, and two sorts of approach to any phenomena; he contrasts them by reference to Eddington's famous example—the sensible table which is a part of our everyday environment and the scientific table which is made up of electrons, etc.[7] Insofar as this implies that what one takes to be the subject matter for any inquiry depends upon one's interests, then the point is well taken, but actually understated. We need not repeat the discussion of Chapter 2 but merely emphasize the conclusions. There are surely many more than two tables—the man in the street's, the artist's, the carpenter's, the chemist's, and, most recently, that subatomic one of physicists which apparently leaves electrons and protons far behind. Yet it is certainly not the case that only the physicist, as opposed to the chemist or the carpenter, can make scientific statements about tables, albeit the way of characterizing their subject is different in each case. Science is possible not only when one particular frame of reference is employed. Nor, conversely, are there an indefinite number of ways of doing science simply because there are an indefinite number of ways of organizing phenomena. Indeed, if Eysenck were to pursue his metaphor, it would prove very embarrassing. For just where is behavioral psychology to be placed in his dichotomy, considered in contrast to, say, neurology? Clearly it is with the sensible tables and the sensible human beings. Yet on that account scientific explanation in psychology should be just as impossible as it is with psychoanalysis, a conclusion at odds with Eysenck's own views.

A second idea of Eysenck's seems to be that we *understand* in terms of common-sense concepts, but that we *explain* in terms of laws employing the "exact, precisely defined, clear-cut concepts of the scientist" (1953, p. 225). Then, from this contrast between "common sense" and "scientific" it is an easy, but unwarranted, jump to "subjective intuition" versus "objec-

---

[7] This example occurs in *The Nature of the Physical World* (1928, pp. xiii–xv).

tive experimentation" and the equating of understanding with the former. There are two objections to these dichotomies. First, the degree to which explanatory concepts differ from those of everyday experience is absolutely no criterion at all of either their scientific utility or their explanatory power. Indeed, if it were, psychoanalysis, contrary to what Eysenck thinks, would on this ground alone be a highly respectable science, for its terminology can be second to none in both complexity and remoteness from common-sense experience. The sad fact, however, is that the history of science is strewn with ingenious systems of laws and concepts that were neither true nor "scientific." What is true is that precision in definition and some sort of testability are certainly essential, without which there can be neither understanding nor explanation of behavior. But these characteristics can be found or built into common-sense concepts just as they may be absent from artificial "scientific" jargon.

The second objection concerns Eysenck's criticism of the use of intuition, self-observation, and one's own experience of life situations. It is one thing to rely exclusively upon such sources of information; it is quite another to use them for suggesting new insights. It is a species of the genetic fallacy to criticize hypotheses, as Eysenck would seem to do, simply on the basis of their origin either in commonplace or unusual, atypical situations. The usefulness of the scientific method is that hunches gained in ways however disreputable can be put to the test without reference to their shady origins. Common sense and everyday experience certainly do not provide the only, or even the last, word for judging hypotheses concerning human behavior, but they may well provide the first.

Another metaphor of Eysenck's suggests a third basic confusion.

> . . . psychological insight and understanding by themselves have nothing whatsoever to do with psychology as a science, just as little as facility in dealing with physical 'things' is an essential asset for the physical scientist . . . physicists of the highest standing are frequently incapable of adjusting the carburetor in their cars . . . (1953, pp. 224–225).

The contrast in this statement is not, as Eysenck believes, between understanding and explaining, but between understanding and explaining, on the one hand, and controlling and changing on the other. The man who can explain how a carburetor works may not have the knack of adjusting one, just as the man who can explain human behavior may nevertheless lack clinical therapeutic talent. No one with any experience of either garage mechanics or psychiatrists can doubt this. But this fact is quite different from and lends no support to the distinction between understanding and explanation. It is not that the therapist understands while the psychologist explains. It is rather that the therapist may be able to control and change without any understanding at all.

The final distinction in Eysenck's argument seems to be between understanding particular individuals and explaining human conduct as a whole. It is certainly true that these are separate pursuits, but it is wrong to think that only one of these is scientific. In fact, psychology is, at least partially, the science of individuals. And with regard to individuals the whole understanding-explaining distinction breaks down. It does not even make sense to say that one understands John's behavior, but that one cannot explain it, except in the derivative sense of "commiserating" or "empathizing" with him. And this is perhaps the most important source of whatever plausibility Eysenck's distinction may have, for there may be a tendency to confuse understanding in the sense of "empathizing" with scientific understanding in the sense of "explaining." These two usages are very different, and Eysenck's warning on this point is well taken. Yet it must be emphasized that we are using "understanding" precisely in the common usage in which it makes no sense to say that one understands but cannot explain.

Being able to understand and explain an individual's behavior is a valuable goal. Being able to understand and explain human behavior in general is another, different but equally valuable goal, and both these goals are approachable through scientific investigation.[8] Psychoanalysis may well be unscientific in certain other ways, and we have no intention of denying many of Eysenck's criticisms that he presents elsewhere, but it is not unscientific just because it attempts to understand and explain an individual's behavior for its own sake without reference to human nature in general. Nor is it an unscientific species of "understanding" simply because its explanations are essentially unified narratives about individuals.

D. THE COMPLEXITY OF A PSYCHOANALYTIC NARRATIVE

In Chapter 2 we attempted to distinguish five types of explanations which could occur in various contexts. What was bluntly asserted at that point concerning the richness and variety of explanations of human behavior can now be demonstrated within the actual example we are studying. Our purpose is in fact twofold—first, to emphasize the complexity of a psychoanalytic explanation and, second, to underline the necessity of viewing such explanations as functioning within individual, single narratives. For the existence of different sorts of explanations does not contradict our position; rather, it makes necessary the analysis of psychoanalytic explanations as single narratives encompassing within themselves a variety of

---

[8] The view that an explanation of individual behavior depends upon and commits one to some general statements about human behavior will be taken up in the next chapter.

different explanations of particular events. As the examples will demonstrate, Freud's explanation of, say, a particular obsessional idea must always be understood within the framework of the over-all narrative.

In a section of his published report entitled "Some Obsessional Ideas and their Explanation," Freud provides us with a good statement of the varied types of explanations he is interested in finding.

> Obsessional ideas, as is well known, have an appearance of being either without motive or without meaning, just as dreams have. The first problem is how to give them a sense and a status in the subject's mental life, so as to make them comprehensible and even obvious. . . . The solution is effected by bringing the obsessional ideas into temporal relationship with the patient's experiences, that is to say, by enquiring when a particular obsessional idea made its first appearance and in what external circumstances it is apt to recur. . . . We can easily convince ourselves that, when once the interconnections between an obsessional idea and the patient's experiences have been discovered, there will be no difficulty in obtaining access to whatever else may be puzzling or worth knowing in the pathological structure we are dealing with—its meaning, the mechanism of its origin, and its derivation from the preponderant motive forces of the patient's mind (1909b, pp. 186–187).[9]

We could hardly ask for a better recapitulation of the types of explanation discussed in Chapter 2. Thus, Freud says that we must first discover in what circumstances the behavior in question is apt to occur; this is what we described as the limited sense of explanation in terms of prediction— uncovering certain rule-of-thumb generalizations that make the behavior "expectable" in certain situations. Following this we can pursue each of the other types of explanation, "whatever else may be puzzling or worth knowing in the pathological structure." There is "the mechanism of its origin"—explanation in terms of origin. Second, the "derivation from the preponderant motive forces," "the interconnections between an obsessional idea and the patient's experiences"—explanation in terms of genesis.[10]

---

[9] Similar statements concerning the variety of explanations to be sought occur in other places, too. One excellent example, written just before the Lorenz analysis was begun, occurs in "Obsessive Actions and Religious Practices" (1907, p. 120).

[10] Freud's terminology did not, of course, remain constant throughout his career. Moreover, he sometimes used different terms to express the same or similar points. In the present instance there is a good example of this. The distinction between explanations in terms of origin and genesis mentioned in passing in the passage quoted was more carefully discussed by Freud in an earlier paper, "The Aetiology of Hysteria" (1896c). There he speaks of explaining the cause of hysterical symptoms by reference to an infantile sexual incident, and the separate problem (which he admits is not yet fully understood) of explaining the "mechanism" whereby this incident (or the unconscious memory of it) has "the abnormal effect of leading a psychical process like defence to a pathological result . . ." (1896c, pp. 213–214). This seems a clear indication of Freud's recognition of the distinction between dis-

Third, the "status in the subject's mental life"—explanation in terms of function. And finally, the "sense" or "meaning" of the behavior—explanation in terms of significance.

In this section we shall demonstrate examples of each of our first four types taken from Freud's case. It will be remembered that the fifth category, explanations in terms of prediction, differed in various ways from the other four. Because of its peculiarities, and because the issue of prediction is a central one, a discussion of this type of explanation as employed by Freud will be put off until Chapter 7.

1. Explanation in Terms of Origin

The term "origin" or "source" is used frequently by Freud to distinguish particular types of problems or incongruities which must be explained. For example, after reaching the conclusion that the patient harbors a great deal of latent hostility directed at his father, Freud goes on to state:

> To be sure, the hatred must have a source, and to discover that source was certainly a problem; his own statements pointed to the time when he was afraid that his parents guessed his thoughts (1909b, p. 181).

Again, speaking of the same problem:

> This wish (to get rid of his father as being an interference) must have originated at a time when circumstances had been very different—at a time, perhaps, when he had not loved his father more than the person whom he desired sensually, or when he was incapable of making a clear decision (1909b, p. 183).

Further references to origin or source could be quoted.[11]

We have already observed that Freud emphasized unresolved hostility directed at the father as the underlying cause of the patient's neurosis.

> We may regard the repression of his infantile hatred of his father as the event which brought his whole subsequent career under the dominion of the neurosis (1909b, p. 238).

Here, the idea of explaining the neurosis in terms of its origin is quite unmistakable.

But it is not just within the over-all narrative that origins are sought. We can also find examples of particular pieces of behavior being explained in terms of their origin. For instance, the patient always had a tremendous fear of physical violence, of being beaten. On the other hand, he had a

---

covering the origin of a neurosis and discovering how, from that origin, the actual symptoms came to be formed.

[11] See, for instance, pp. 186 and 189. Also, one section of the paper is partially entitled "The Origins of Compulsion and Doubt" (p. 237).

great loathing for such cowardice as he would from time to time display; "in [certain of his fantasies] he recognized the quality of *cowardice* which was so particularly horrible to him" (1909b, p. 185). After the important beating incident emerged, both Freud and the patient believed that the origin of his cowardice had been found:

> The patient believed that the scene made a permanent impression upon himself as well as upon his father. His father, he said, never beat him again; and he also attributed to this experience a part of the change which came over his own character. From that time forward he was a coward—out of fear of the violence of his own rage (1909b, pp. 205–206).

In this peculiar incident Freud saw an origin of both the fear of expressing emotions—the cowardice itself—and the hatred of this particular trait— the suppressed rage at having to hold back emotions for fear of bringing down anger or parental rejection.

2. Explanation in Terms of Genesis

We have already mentioned Freud's use of the phrase "the interconnections between an obsessional idea and the patient's experiences" (1909b, pp. 186–187). Elsewhere he speaks of various factors that may play a part in "the genesis of neurosis" (1909b, p. 247). Many of the explanations given by Freud would fall into this category; we shall give only two short examples.

At one time during their courtship Gisela was seriously ill in bed, and the patient had the wish that she might remain like that forever. Freud suggests two motives accounting for this wish: the hostility and antagonism felt because of Gisela's first rejection of the patient's marriage proposal, and the desire "to know that she was powerless against his designs" (1909b, p. 194). Such motives could certainly account for, or lead to, the expression of the patient's wish.

Not only wishes or beliefs are often explained in terms of their genesis, but overt actions also. Consider the example mentioned for a different purpose in a previous chapter concerning the period during the analysis when the patient began heaping abuse on Freud:

> While he talked like this, he would get up from the sofa and roam about the room,—a habit which he explained at first as being due to delicacy of feeling: he could not bring himself, he said, to utter such horrible things while he was lying there so comfortably. But soon he himself found a more cogent explanation, namely, that he was avoiding my proximity for fear of my giving him a beating (1909b, p. 209).

Freud goes on to point out that in such incidents we see the development of the first phase of the patient's transference, where Freud became the patient's father:

> If he stayed on the sofa he behaved like some one in desperate terror trying to save himself from castigations of terrific violence. . . . He recalled that his father had had a passionate temper, and sometimes in his violence had not known where to stop (1909b, p. 209).

Thus the patient was reenacting with Freud an old pattern of relationship to his father; and it was these old feelings, once directed to the father, now generalized to Freud that led to, accounted for, explained, the genesis of the peculiar behavior of running around the analyst's office.

3. Explanation in Terms of Function

A great amount of energy is expended in psychoanalysis in attempting to clarify the function of particular bits of behavior within a patient's mental life. This function usually falls within the so-called economic aspect of psychoanalytic explanations, the examination of behavior in terms of its function in the release of various forces and in its maintenance of what might now be called "psychological homeostasis."[12] But even before this concept was developed, at the time the Lorenz case was published, we can see that considerations of behavior's function within the patient's psychological structure play an important part. In addition to this special form of functional explanation there is also the more typical case of explaining actions by giving the goals to which they are believed to be the means, that is, by typical explanations in terms of purpose. Both of these varieties can be found in the present case.

We remember that the patient, after having been religious as a child, gradually became a free thinker by the time he was a young man. However, after the onset of his serious disturbances when his aunt died, an obsessional belief in the next world developed together with a fear that in that next world various terrible things would happen to his dead father. Freud offers this explanation:

> The strange extension of his obsessional fears to the 'next world' was nothing else than a compensation for these death-wishes which he had felt against his father. It was introduced eighteen months after his father had died, at a time when there had been a revival of his sorrow at the loss, and it was designed—in defiance of reality, and in deference to the wish which had previously been showing itself in fantasies of every kind—to undo the fact of his father's death. We have had occasion in several places to translate the phrase "in the next world" by the words "if my father were still alive" (1909b, pp. 235–236).

Freud conceives of an original hostility giving rise to a strong sense of guilt, and this guilt, in order to be expiated, in turn giving rise to the

---

[12] The "economic" conception of psychological functions is developed most fully by Freud in the important paper "The Unconscious" (1915c).

fantasy that the father is not really dead, or is really living on in the next world. The belief in the next world, then, Freud explains functionally as a balancing compensation for the original wish for the father's death. The behavior is placed within a system of psychological forces and shown to be in certain relationships to other components of that system.

Our second example concerns Freud's explanation of the onset of illness as being precipitated by the suggestion from his mother that the patient marry one of her wealthy nieces and thereby insure a successful business future for himself:

> The proof that this view was correct lies in the fact that the chief result of his illness was an obstinate incapacity for work, which allowed him to postpone the completion of his education for years. But the results of such an illness are never unintentional; what appears to be the *consequence* of the illness is in reality the *cause* or *motive* of falling ill (1909b, p. 199).

Freud proposes that the crippling obsessions of the patient fulfilled a function, served a purpose for him by forcing the postponement of any decision on his marital and professional futures. Here, then, is the second type of function explanation, in which the behavior is placed within a means-to-end system.

4. Explanation in Terms of Significance

This fourth variety of explanation needs no introduction in regard to psychoanalysis. Indeed, it is quite notorious, and some people even seem to believe that Freud's major contribution was to discover the unconscious significance of dreams and the like. In fact, however, as we have seen the full-scale psychoanalytic narrative is a very complex affair containing explanations of a variety of types. Nevertheless, explanations in terms of significance do form a numerous and important group. These explanations can be given for various actions in addition to the more often encountered interpretations of dreams.

Once on a holiday with Gisela, in the summer of 1903, the patient developed the idea that he was too fat (*dick* in German). He began a series of compulsive activities aimed at losing weight. These included dieting, strenuous exercise in the hot sun, cold plunges, etc.

> Our patient could think of no explanation of this senseless obsessional behaviour until it suddenly occurred to him that at that time his lady . . . had been in the company of an English cousin, who was very attentive to her and of whom the patient had been very jealous. This cousin's name was Richard, and, according to the usual practice in England, he was known as *Dick*. Our patient, then, had wanted to kill this Dick; he had been far more jealous of him and enraged with him than he could admit to himself, and

that was why he had imposed on himself this course of slimming by way of a punishment (1909b, pp. 188–189).

In this instance, Freud gives us a combination of explanations in terms of function and significance. First, there is the hostility and jealousy directed against Gisela's cousin. This is symbolically represented by the awareness that there is too much fat (*dick*) around, and the desire to get rid of that fat, i.e., to diet. As in the case of the compulsion to slash his throat, hostility originally directed against another (Gisela's grandmother or cousin Richard) is not allowed conscious expression because of the ancient childhood pattern of repressing anger. Instead, the feeling is directed against the patient himself. This serves the double functions of releasing the emotion and punishing himself for having that emotion. However, as Freud points out, the original direction of the hostility always seems to come out eventually, if only in a distorted form. Thus, the patient ran for a razor, then realized that he must first kill the grandmother. Likewise the impulse to diet only incompletely disguised the thought that there was "too much Dick (fat)."

A number of dreams of the patient are also explained symbolically by Freud. Several of these have been deleted from our presentation, but one example may be specially noted.

> [The patient] dreamt that *he saw my daughter in front of him; she had two patches of dung instead of eyes.* No one who understands the language of dreams will find much difficulty in translating this one: it declared that *he was marrying my daughter not for her 'beaux yeux' but for her money* (1909b, p. 200).[13]

Lorenz had earlier told Freud that the cousin whom his mother wanted him to marry was in fact renowned for her beautiful eyes. Thus, Freud is here interpreting dung as a derogatory symbol of money or "filthy lucre" and the idea of having money for eyes as relating Freud's daughter to the wealthy girl relative.

Another example of this type concerns the unusual formula word *"Glejsamen"* that the patient used in his compulsive prayers. The patient explained this word as being made up from the first letters of the first words of several short prayers with an "Amen" added on. Freud, however, observed that the formula was in fact an anagram of the name of the patient's cousin, Gisela (in the original German), connected to the word *"samen"* (German for "semen"), with the *"s"* serving as a bridge to each part.[14] Freud suggests that with this word the patient symbolically "united

---

[13] Freud's italics.

[14] There is a textual inconsistency here, and Mr. James Strachey, the General Editor of the Standard Edition, has been kind enough to check Freud's original notes to clarify the problem. The following information is based on correspondence with

his '*Samen*' with the body of his beloved, i.e., putting it bluntly, had masturbated with her image" (1909b, p. 281). The patient had never noticed this extraordinary rearrangement and hidden meaning; yet once having had it pointed out, he was quick to accept this alternative explanation of the meaning of his formula.

These last two examples represent a typical variety of explanation of small bits of behavior in terms of their latent meaning, a type we have included within the category of explanations in terms of significance.

All of the above examples have been given to emphasize two important and related points which we have referred to under the title of the complexity of psychoanalytic narratives. The first is that psychoanalytic explanations are extraordinarily complex in the sense of doing several things at once. A psychoanalyst is called upon to answer a wide range of questions about human behavior, and his explanations may be of very different types. It is obviously true, however, that a good psychoanalyst will attempt all these tasks at once—to explain the origins, functions, significance, etc., of his patient's behavior. It is likewise true that a good psychoanalytic explanation will include explanations of all these various types and that these may in practice be difficult to separate. Nevertheless, these observations in no way cancel or even minimize the importance of our contention that a psychoanalytic explanation attempts to answer several different sorts of questions and to perform a variety of tasks. Any oversimplified analysis of such explanations in terms of a single model is therefore sure to be extremely misleading.

Our second point is that psychoanalytic explanations must be examined in their context, that is, within the over-all framework that is implicitly or explicitly invoked. The point is strikingly reinforced by the last two examples given above, where Freud explains the patient's dream concerning Freud's daughter, and where he explains a peculiar formula used by the patient in his compulsive prayers. In both cases Freud's explanation taken out of context, for instance as an example of psychoanalytic dream interpretation, would seem extremely arbitrary, far-fetched, and biased—

---

him. The magic word occurs in three different spellings in the S.E. text (1909b): *Glejisamen,* p. 280; *Gleijsamen,* p. 291; and *Glejsamen,* p. 294. The "*i*" on p. 291 is a misprint; the original notes show the same spelling as on p. 294, *Glejsamen.* The spelling on p. 280, however, is reproduced correctly. This inconsistency is never entirely explained and raises some interesting questions about Freud's thought processes at this point. The issues are too involved and speculative to be published here. Perhaps, however, the problem is solved by considering the fact that in the Viennese German of that period the "*i*" and "*j*" were considered vowel and consonant aspects of the same letter.

at best, a "brilliant analogy." Whatever cogency and force these explanations may possess is acquired only through our close acquaintance with the whole case history of the patient and the whole psychoanalytic narrative Freud weaves about him. Yet once we do know that past history and have some idea as to the conflicts and forces Freud posits as underlying his behavior in general, then the interpretation of, say, the formula *"Glejsamen"* as being an anagram of the name of the patient's cousin may well strike us as being shrewd, immediately understandable, and probably correct. This fact supports our contention that the ultimate basis of a psychoanalytic explanation is a long narrative account applicable to the individual as a whole rather than isolated explanations of particular bits of behavior.

It is important that we keep both these aspects of complexity in mind as our analysis progresses: (1) that the psychoanalytic narrative attempts to do several things at once, and (2) that any explanation of a particular piece of behavior must always be studied within its context, as a part of a larger, unified narrative. If these points can be remembered we should not be tempted to strive too hard for a unitary analysis or to cut off too many loose ends in our zeal for a simplified model or formulation.

Chapter 7/A CONTEXTUAL ANALYSIS
OF PSYCHOANALYTIC EXPLANATION

In Chapter 6 we pointed out certain general features of Freud's explanation in the Lorenz case and introduced the concept of a narrative. In this chapter we shall continue this analysis by examining Freud's narrative in greater detail and particularly the various explanations of specific pieces of behavior which occur within it. Our goal is to discuss, first, whether one commonly adopted analysis of explanations is adequate for a psychoanalytic narrative; second, the possibility of some alternative analysis; and, third, the extent to which such explanatory narratives are open to systematic evaluation.

A. GENERALIZATIONS, LAWS, AND THE HYPOTHETICAL-DEDUCTIVE MODEL

1. Generalizations in the Lorenz Case

When we attempt to analyze the sort of explanation we are dealing with in the Lorenz case, one of the first questions we have in mind is whether it makes use of empirical generalizations. It has sometimes been maintained, as we have discussed in Chapter 3, that explanations of human behavior, in contrast to those in the physical sciences, contain no generalizations. But at least in the case of the present example this view is quite mistaken: Freud includes numerous empirical generalizations based upon his own and others' observations of normal and pathological behavior. At least 18 examples occur of what are undoubtedly meant to be taken as empirical generalizations developed out of clinical experience. It will be sufficient for us to quote only a few[1]:

---

[1] Other examples occur on the following pages of the Standard Edition text (1909b): pp. 164, 165 (another, not that quoted above), 192 (two examples), 225, 227, 228, 229, 233, 236, 241, 243, 244, and 247.

> To find a chronic obsessional neurosis beginning like this in early childhood, with lascivious wishes of this sort connected with uncanny apprehensions and an inclination to the performance of defensive acts, is no new thing to me. I have come across it in a number of other cases. It is absolutely typical, although probably not the only possible type (1909b, p. 165).

> In the first place, experience shows that an obsessional command (or whatever it may be), which in waking life is known only in a truncated and distorted form . . . may have its actual text brought to light in a dream. . . . Secondly, in the course of the analytic examination of a case history, one becomes convinced that if a number of obsessions succeed one another they are often—even though their wording is not identical—ultimately one and the same (1909b, p. 223).

> If we consider a number of analyses of obsessional neurotics we shall find it impossible to escape the impression that a relation between love and hatred such as we have found in our present patient is among the most frequent, the most marked, and probably, therefore, the most important characteristics of obsessional neurosis (1909b, p. 239).

In each of these generalizations the reference to clinical experience is explicit; in others, although it may be implicit, there is no doubt that an empirical, experiential basis is intended. The truth of such statements is immaterial at this point; our purpose is simply to point out that it is just not true to say that all psychoanalytic explanations fail to make use of empirical generalizations.

On the other hand, there are also statements the logical status of which is not at all clear. For instance:

> For obsessional acts tend to approximate more and more—and the longer the disorder lasts the more evident does this become—to infantile sexual acts of a masturbatory character (1909b, p. 244).

Such a statement is given in the form of an empirical generalization; yet there is a certain ambiguity connected with it that seems to prevent its direct application to everyday experience. It is not simply that the phrase "tend to approximate" is vague; this sort of looseness could be tightened up. It is rather that the particular feature obsessional acts are supposed to show, namely, "masturbatory character," seems rather more closely bound up to a theory than other features mentioned in statements of a clearly empirical nature. This expression is presumably meant to serve as a technical concept capable of being applied to some examples of behavior that are not *overt* cases of masturbation. But unless and until some psychoanalyst tells us what is to count as (i.e., what are the criteria of application for the theoretical concept) "masturbatory character," we are unable to evaluate this generalization. We have no intention of attempting such a reformulation; our purpose is only to point out that this difficulty, so often discussed, does in fact exist, at least with reference to certain statements in Freud's explanation. But the problem does introduce a new order of complexity into our discussion—the role of theory in psychoanalytic explanations.

Against the charge that psychoanalysis does not make use of empirical generalizations we have pointed out that when one actually examines a case study a great number can be found. But this use of generalizations has its negative side as well, for another common criticism is that psycho-analytic explanations are not in fact *explanatory* at all, provide no theo-retical framework, but offer only a collection of generalizations, rules of thumb gleaned from clinical observation. Psychoanalysis might be said to provide a "natural history of neurosis," perhaps, but nothing more. These two criticisms seem conflicting and paradoxical, but they are not. The first claims a lack of empirical generalizations. The second points out that empirical generalizations by themselves are not really explanatory, but that something more is essential.

Perhaps this latter view is too extreme. As we saw in Chapter 2, there are contexts in which simply showing that a particular event or property is to be expected according to some set of generalizations is enough to warrant the term "explanation." It is true, however, that insofar as an explanation consists solely of generalizations we are apt to regard it as a very low level form indeed. It would fit only our category of explanation in terms of prediction. There is, however, a second usage of the term "explanatory" in which it contrasts with "predictive," and it is this usage which is employed in the criticism that psychoanalytic explanations are not explanatory but provide only empirical generalizations. In the following discussion this new usage will be adopted in contrast to the one in Chapter 2, where it was recognized that in some situations explanations are simply "explanations in terms of prediction." It will be easier to follow this new usage rather than each time adding the qualification that we mean explanation "in terms other than prediction."

What, then, can be said against the criticism that psychoanalytic expla-nations rely only upon empirical generalizations as opposed to theoretical statements and so do not really explain in some important sense? This contention is most assuredly not true of the psychoanalytic explanation under consideration. As we have seen there is, for better or for worse, an immense and complex body of theory that impinges upon Freud's explana-tory narrative at virtually every stage. Our first point, then, is that a psychoanalytic narrative does contain straightforward empirical generaliza-tions, and our second point is that it also contains high level theoretical statements as well. The real problem is to discover just how these theoretical statements relate to the actual explanatory narrative which Freud presents in the Lorenz case.

2. The Hypothetical-Deductive Model

We shall begin by examining one suggestion concerning this relationship between theory and explanations, the one proposed by the hypothetical-deductive or deductive-nomological analysis of explanation (hereafter called the H-D or "covering law" model). Statements of this model have been made by various authors. We shall concentrate on two, Professors Karl Popper and Carl Hempel, with the obvious understanding that each of these writers has a somewhat different analysis and that certain formulations of the one might not be acceptable to the other.

Popper summarizes the model thus:

> I suggest that to give a causal explanation of a certain *specific event* means deducing a statement describing this event from two kinds of premises: from some *universal laws,* and from some singular or specific statements which we may call the *specific initial conditions.* . . . Thus we have two different constituents, two different kinds of statements which together yield a complete causal explanation: (1) *Universal statements of the character of natural laws;* and (2) *specific statements pertaining to the special case in question, called the 'initial conditions'* (Popper, 1957a, pp. 122–123).[2]

Hempel suggests the following schema for H-D explanations:

> $L_1, L_2, \ldots, L_r$
> $C_1, C_2, \ldots, C_k$
> E
> Here, $L_1, L_2, \ldots, L_r$ are general laws and $C_1, C_2, \ldots, C_k$ are statements of particular occurrences, facts, or events; jointly, these premises form the explanans. The conclusion E is the explanandum statement . . . (Hempel, 1962, p. 100).

It must be understood that the H-D model has been proposed, at least by the writers we are considering, as being primarily applicable to the physical sciences rather than to explanations of human behavior (however, see Hempel, 1965). In this discussion, then, we are simply attempting to determine whether or not such an analysis might be applicable to psychoanalytic explanations. Moreover, we shall at this point concentrate on certain general features of the H-D theory; then, later in this chapter we shall examine the extent to which this analysis can be applied in a specific example, that is, to Freud's explanation in the Lorenz case. To avoid confusion two separate contentions of this theory will be examined in turn: the need for generalizations used in the H-D model to be unconditional or lawlike, and the reciprocal nature of explanation and prediction.

---

[2] Popper's italics.

3. Laws and Generalizations

In Chapter 3 the thesis was discussed that there are no laws in the sense of empirical generalizations true of human behavior and that therefore a science of human behavior must be theoretically impossible. In arguing against this view we distinguished between unconditional generalizations and those limited by various sorts of conditions. It will pay to list these varieties once again:

G1. AB is the case.
G2. At times T_1 . . . T_n, AB is the case.
G3. Under conditions C_1 . . . C_k, AB is the case.
G4. For individuals P_1 . . . P_j, AB is the case.
G5. AB is the case in $p\%$ of cases.
G6. At times T_1 . . . T_n, under conditions C_1 . . . C_k, for individuals P_1 . . . P_j, AB is the case in $p\%$ of cases.

We argued that it seems quite possible for true generalizations of at least the G6 form to be found concerning human behavior. In this chapter we have pointed out Freud's use of several supposedly true empirical generalizations which could be analyzed roughly according to these schemata. Although the point may be conceded that very limited generalizations might occur in psychoanalytic explanations, it could still be argued that only unconditional, in the sense of nonprobablistic, generalizations can function in deductive scientific explanations. Such a view draws a distinction between natural laws and rule-of-thumb generalizations or trends and holds that only the former are appropriate for explanations fitting the H-D model. Hempel affirms that only laws or lawlike propositions (sentences of the law form whose truth is unknown) can properly be used in the H-D type of explanation, although he explicitly avoids characterizing just what would distinguish between these two types—laws and generalizations (Hempel, 1962, p. 102, Note 7). Popper, however, argues explicitly for the law-trend distinction and takes universality, absence of probabilistic conditions, as a defining characteristic of laws.

> In spite of the impossibility of making sure of their universal validity, we do not add in our formulation of natural laws a condition saying that they are asserted only for the period for which they have been observed to hold, or perhaps only within 'the present cosmological period.' . . . If we were to admit laws that are themselves subject to change, change could never be explained by laws (Popper, 1957a, p. 103).

> A statement asserting the existence of a trend is existential, not universal. A universal law, on the other hand, does not assert existence; . . . it asserts the impossibility of something or other. . . . The practical significance of this logical situation is considerable: while we may base scientific predictions

on laws, we cannot (as every cautious statistician knows) base them merely on the existence of trends. A trend (we may again take population growth as an example) which has persisted for hundreds or even thousands of years may change within a decade, or even more rapidly than that (p. 115).

Let us consider the argument in two stages. First there is the contention that a criterion exists such that we can distinguish between statements which are merely statements of trends or nonlawlike generalizations and those which are explanatory laws. Take Popper's example of population growth. Considered by itself a statement such as "Total world population increases geometrically every two hundred years" may simply be an *ad hoc* generalization stating a trend during the past thousand years, or it may be a confirmed law, summarizing a definite biological mechanism; but logic alone will not tell us which, only science. Populations of pneumococci on an agar plate, for instance, *do* increase geometrically within certain limits, and this is not just a rule of thumb. On the contrary, there is a good scientific explanation why this should be so.

Hempel's discussion is even more instructive. He gives as an example of a nonlawlike (i.e., nonexplanatory) general statement: "All objects ever placed on this table weigh less than one pound" (Hempel, 1962, p. 124, Note 28). He argues that this statement, even if true, would never be adduced to support subjunctive or counterfactual conditional statements such as: "If you had placed a one volume edition of Shakespeare on the table, it would have weighed less than one pound." Of course, in normal circumstances Hempel would be quite right; the original statement would certainly not be adduced to explain, for instance, why a particular book weighed less than one pound. But the point is that we usually do assume that the normal circumstances are in fact present, and it is this which convinces us that the statement is not explanatory. By itself, however, this statement is no different in kind from others that are lawlike in normal situations.

We can, moreover, conceive of contexts in which statements similar to Hempel's might well be explanatory. Consider the case where we have a self-adjusting balance set to maintain any weight placed upon the pan at the level of the one pound reading on the calibration scale. What if we now say "All objects ever placed on this balance register one pound." This might be meant simply as a summary of past experience, to be paraphrased as "In the past all objects ever placed on this balance have registered one pound." But it might also be used as a lawlike statement to explain to a bewildered onlooker why a heavy Shakespeare edition registers only one pound. And, indeed, the statement *is* explanatory in this situation; that is, it can be elaborated into a very reasonable account of just how this phenomenon occurs by demonstrating the facts about this peculiar balance and how its mechanism works. Moreover, we could use the statement to predict the counterfactual conditional: "If you had placed the Shorter Oxford Dictionary on the balance, it would have registered one pound." Thus, even in such very odd cases we can never decide whether or not a statement is explanatory by examining it alone. The question is settled only by understanding the context in which the statement is made and whether it in fact is a shorthand statement, covering, for instance, an explanatory narrative of the kind suggested in the balance example.

There is, then, a very real and basic difficulty about attempting to separate laws and generalizations without any reference to the context in which they occur. But now let us take our argument to the second stage. Suppose we are able to decide whether particular statements are unconditional laws. What of the contention that only such law statements can be used in H-D schemas for prediction? This view is very puzzling. It certainly *seems* that generalizations of even the very limited G6 variety can be used to make predictions; that is, they can fit into the H-D model very well:

1. In middle class Viennese families in the late nineteenth century, 85% of the children were cared for most intensively and received their earliest sexual enlightenment from nursemaids.
2. Paul Lorenz was a child of a middle class Viennese family, raised in the late nineteenth century.

3. Therefore, there is an 85% chance that Paul Lorenz will be found to have been cared for most intensively and received his earliest sexual enlightenment from nursemaids.

In this example the prediction 3, based upon the generalization 1 and the statement of initial conditions 2, seems quite valid; i.e., it is a properly drawn conclusion although of course not necessarily true. It seems clear that predictions such as the one above can properly be based upon generalizations involving various sorts of limiting conditions. If Popper's emphasis on unconditional generalizations is interpreted to mean that only such statements can be used in making predictions, it is simply wrong and can be flatly rejected. Even on the strict H-D model of prediction, there is no logical reason for employing only unconditional G1 generalizations. One must not confuse limitations of range with logical limitations. The more conditions added, the more restricted the range of applicability, but this does not mean that within that range, under those conditions, the prediction is any the less proper.

The truth of both the generalization and the relevant statements of initial conditions is sufficient to guarantee the truth of our prediction. The falsity of the generalization, however, does not necessarily mean that the prediction will be false; i.e., Paul Lorenz might have had certain sexual experiences with his nursemaid even though the majority of Viennese children at that time did not. But both these points are irrelevant. We are only interested in the question: If we *assume* the truth of some generalization such as "Under conditions C_1, C_2, AB is the case" and if we *assume* the truth of a statement of initial conditions such as "C_1, C_2 are the case," then are we *justified* in making the prediction: "AB is the case"?[3] The answer to this question is surely "Yes." If we *assume* the truth of a generalization, then we are logically justified in using it within an H-D schema to make a prediction, and this remains the case whether or not either the generalization or the prediction turn out on further study to be true. Popper would surely not insist that predictions are valid only when generalizations are *known* to be true. To do so would be to ignore the whole "hypothetical" aspect of the H-D model. The confusion seems to be between what *justifies* a prediction's being made and what *guarantees* its truth. We hypothesize or assume that certain statements are true, and we can as readily hypothesize conditional or unconditional generalizations and justifiably employ them in H-D schemas to make valid predictions.

Surely, however, there is more to it than this. If it is so obvious that conditional generalizations can be used in an H-D schema for prediction, then there must be some other reason for Popper's and Hempel's insistence on a distinction between nonlawlike conditional generalizations and unconditional laws, of which only the latter may be used in scientific explanations. The answer seems to lie in the psychological observation that we do feel a sense of arbitrariness about certain sorts of generalizations, such as:

4. In July, in England, whenever cows in a field lie down, rain follows in 2 hours.

Such statements, no matter how useful for prediction, seem like arbitrary rules of thumb, and we need in some way to separate them from those other statements which can properly be called explanatory in a sense other than predictive. Yet whatever explanatory quality we feel to be missing,

---

[3] It is important to understand that this question is entirely separate from: Are we ever *justified* in assuming or asserting "If C_1, C_2, then AB is the case," given that we have observed this sequence in the past? This question is the basis of the classical problem of induction, a subject we shall not touch upon at all. It seems clear that whatever problem there is will arise equally with either conditional or unconditional generalizations that are stated in the "timeless present" tense:

"AB is always the case."

"If $C_1 \ldots C_k$, then AB is always the case."

Therefore, whatever solution is adopted for the problem of induction will be applicable to both varieties.

it is likewise absent from a new generalization which lacks the original limiting conditions:

> 4a. It is always and everywhere the case that if cows lie down, rain follows within 2 hours.

The arbitrariness we felt with 4 remains unmitigated in 4a, when the limiting conditions are discarded.

There is, in short, nothing mysterious, or especially commendable, in the move from

> at intervals T_1 . . . T_n, AB is the case

to

> at intervals T_1 . . . T_∞ (i.e., at all times), AB is the case.

The distinction between arbitrary generalizations and explanatory laws is not based upon the presence or absence of limiting conditions. The insistence on the unconditionality of explanatory generalizations represents an attempt to supply a criterion for making this distinction based upon the mistaken view that the source of this "arbitrariness" lies in the fact that the generalizations are conditional. In fact, however, the arbitrary quality has a quite different origin, which we can now examine.

Let us begin by distinguishing between two possible ways of using conditional generalizations. Consider the following generalization:

> 5. In even-numbered years the cost of living rises by over 3%.

We might use such a generalization merely as a predictive rule, with the temporal limitation per se governing its application. In so doing we would be saying that a change in the time period to an odd-numbered year is *by itself* sufficient to render the generalization inapplicable. Surely, with this use we have a very arbitrary sort of generalization which in most normal situations could not be explanatory in any but the predictive sense. Whatever the truth of the rule as a matter of fact, and however useful it might be for making predictions, we would not consider it a part of the explanation of, for instance, why the cost of living in 1968 rose by 3.7%. We might call this the "absolute" use of conditional generalizations.[4] It is certainly this sort of "absolute" use Popper is attacking when he says:

> If we were to admit laws that are themselves subject to change, change could never be explained by laws. It would be the admission that change is simply miraculous . . . the *ad hoc* hypothesis that the laws have changed would "explain" everything (Popper, 1957a, p. 103).

It would, however, be wrong to believe that all or even most conditional

---

[4] For an example of this use of the term "absolute" see Popper (1957a, p. 153).

generalizations are used in this way. Consider the situation of Freud attempting to explain to a layman Paul Lorenz's feelings of hostility toward his father. He might well have said at one point something like:

> 6. Young boys between the ages of three and five pass through a period of intense rivalry with and hostility toward their fathers over the attentions of their mothers . . .

Clearly, statement 6 does not by itself explain why Paul Lorenz showed hostility at four years of age. It is not the (perhaps) true fact that all boys pass through such a period that *explains* why one particular boy should do so. Statement 6 only gives us grounds for *expecting* that Paul Lorenz should manifest the attitude.

It would, however, be quite perverse to interpret statement 6 in the absolute sense of implying that the child's feelings result *simply* from his being, say, four years old. Surely the psychoanalyst would be using this statement in quite a different way. What a psychoanalyst would be saying in statement 6 is that at some period of life, delimited temporally, certain conditions are operative, perhaps in the case of virtually all individuals, which have the result that a boy develops a specific constellation of attitudes toward his father. There is of course nothing mystical about being four years old which causes hostility; it is rather that the influences which do tend to have this result are usually present around this age. If statement 6 is meant to explain why Paul Lorenz is hostile, it would do so not because being four years old is a cause of hostility; it is rather that the statement is used to imply a whole set of causal conditions, in fact, the whole narrative about the oedipal situation, rivalry with the father, etc. For this reason this second use of generalizations could be called the "implicative" use, insofar as the actual statement is used as a sort of shorthand to imply a whole set of unmentioned causal conditions.

This implicative use of generalizations has a further very important feature. In many scientific disciplines, especially psychiatry, there may often occur generalizations involving rather arbitrary limitations such as that AB is the case for "unmarried women over 40," or for "children raised without fathers," or for "eldest boys in families where other siblings are girls." Usually these limitations are meant to be interpreted as implicative, shorthand notations for other, unmentioned causal factors, *even though such factors may not yet be known.* In such cases there is only the implied *conviction* that causal factors can be discovered to account for the peculiarities of behavior which characterize the groups singled out by the rather arbitrary categories employed.

An interesting example of these two uses of generalizations, the absolute and the implicative, occurs in an early paper of Freud (1896c). He states that his clinical experience had shown that hysterical symptoms regularly begin no earlier than the age of eight, while the traumatic sexual experiences invariably date back much earlier. Freud then goes on to emphasize that there must be a causal mechanism accounting for this "boundary-line," and he suggests that it is "very probably connected with developmental processes in the sexual system" (1896c, p. 212). Thus, Freud explicitly opts for an implicative use of the generalization even though at the time he had no knowledge of the causal mechanism, but only a conviction that such a mechanism could be found to explain this empirical, seemingly arbitrary observation about hysterical symptoms.

This distinction between two possible ways of using generalizations seems applicable in several ways; for example, it provides an easy way to deal with arguments such as: "Human nature changes through time, and hence generalizations about behavior are impossible to find." Take the generalization "In the seventeenth century, AB was true of human behavior." If the temporal limitation is being used implicatively, then to say that AB was true only in the seventeenth century is to assert that the causal conditions which are held to account for the phenomenon of AB's presence were in fact operative only during that century. This is an important, potentially verifiable observation, but it is different from the question of whether the underlying causal generalization is true. That generalization implies that when certain causal conditions are present such and such is the case, but it says nothing at all about those other situations, or other periods, in which the relevant conditions do not obtain. The generalization is simply inapplicable in those circumstances, or those centuries, but this does not necessarily mean it is false.

Alternatively, we may use this temporal limitation in an absolute way, implying that the passage of time per se, rather than the presence or absence of other causal conditions, makes people behave differently. This would be equivalent to saying that it was just the fact that it was the seventeenth century which made AB true. But this contention is very dubious, and implies a peculiar, almost mystical view of the universe. Thus, the thesis that human nature changes through time is either irrelevant to the question of the possibility of finding generalizations about behavior or very dubious and unsubstantiated.

Our main reason, however, for discussing various ways of using generalizations is to point out an important source of the feeling of arbitrariness that accompanies many supposed general statements. Supporters of the H-D model have been aware of this characteristic, but they have located its source in the wrong place. It is not the fact that a generalization is limited by various sorts of conditions which makes it arbitrary for, as we have seen, the removal of these limitations does not necessarily remove this quality. The arbitrariness is in fact the result of using the generalizations in an absolute way. We have argued, however, that generalizations need not be so used and that in the behavioral sciences, including psychoanalysis, generalizations about human behavior are most often used implicatively, and it is this use which removes any sense of arbitrariness.

4. The Reciprocal Nature of Prediction and Explanation

In the previous section we have discussed one basic tenet of the H-D thesis, the universality or lawlike nature of scientific generalizations, but there is another which must also be examined. It is part of the H-D model that prediction and explanation must be reciprocal procedures. Popper makes this point in the following way:

> . . . the use of a theory for *predicting* some specific event is just another aspect of its use for *explaining* such an event. And since we test a theory by comparing the events predicted with those actually observed, our analysis also shows how theories can be *tested*. Whether we use a theory for the purpose of explanation, of prediction, or of testing, depends upon our interest; it depends upon the question which statements we consider as given or unproblematic, and which statements we consider to stand in need of further criticism, and of testing (1957a, p. 124).[5]

Hempel makes the same point:

> In a deductive-nomological explanation of a particular past event, the explanans logically implies the occurrence of the explanandum event; hence we may say of the explanatory argument that it could also have served as a predictive one in the sense that it could have been used to predict the explanandum event if the laws and particular circumstances adduced in its explanans had been taken into account at a suitable earlier time. (This remark does not hold, however, when all the laws invoked in the explanans are laws of coexistence and all the particular statements adduced in the explanans pertain to events that are simultaneous with the explanandum event.) (Hempel, 1962, p. 113.)

In other words the view is that to explain event E, we give the laws and statements of initial conditions from which E can be deduced; to predict event E, we use the same laws and statements of initial conditions to deduce E. In the case of explanation, we have the event's occurrence, and we search for the relevant laws; in the case of prediction, we have the laws and use them in conjunction with statements of initial conditions to deduce the event's occurrence.

In Chapter 2 it was pointed out that a prediction is nothing more than a statement about some state of affairs or event which is asserted to hold

---

[5] Popper's italics.

true at some time or place, or under conditions other than those describing the circumstances or conditions during which the prediction is put forth. We also argued in Chapter 2 that explanations function in different ways than descriptions. This fact alone should make us suspicious of any thesis which insists that prediction, a form of description, could be equivalent to explanation. An examination of a few examples confirms this suspicion.

Let us look at a prediction based upon a generalization mentioned earlier.

7. In July, in England, whenever cows in a field are lying down, it rains within 2 hours.
8. It is July, we are in England, and the cows are lying down.

9. It will rain within 2 hours.

Here, a rule-of-thumb generalization and a statement of initial conditions together form the basis for a prediction, and as a model of that prediction the H-D schema seems adequate. But now let us approach from the other direction. Given that it does rain in the above situation, suppose we were to make the demand: "Explain why it rained." Only if we interpret this request as "Explain how I might have expected or predicted rain" would we be at all willing to accept the generalization about cows as being explanatory. In any other of the more usual usages of the word "explanation," this rule of thumb would not be considered in the least explanatory, and this would continue to be the case no matter how many times predictions based upon it turned out to be true. Knowing what we do about our world, the statement of a correlation between cows lying down and rain, no matter how generally that correlation is said to hold, can never explain why it *did* rain on a particular occasion. In this respect statement 7 is different from statements such as the one given in Hempel's balance example where, as we saw in the previous section, in certain situations that statement could be explanatory. Statement 7 can only tell us we should *expect* rain in certain circumstances, and in the deduction above it is being used only for prediction. This is not to say that one could not imagine a universe in which such an observation about cows would *explain* why it rained on a particular occasion, but it would be a world in which "cows" would be very different beasts from those we know, and perhaps meteorology a different body of knowledge. Indeed, the very effort required by such imagining underlines the fact that in our world statement 7 would not be explanatory.

In contrast, consider the following prediction:

7a. Whenever cows forage in a field, the grass will be cropped to a height of about 2 inches.

8a. The cows are foraging in this field.

9a. The grass will be cropped to a height of about 2 inches.

Logically, this schema is quite on par with the previous one; yet now, when we ask "Explain why the grass is cropped to a height of about 2 inches," we will quite likely accept 7a along with certain other statements as being an adequate explanation. Once we are told that cows have been grazing in the field and that they tend to crop grass to such a height, our finding is explained, fitted in with other known facts. Thus, the H-D analysis fits both our examples indiscriminately, insofar as they are examples of prediction; yet it is incapable of distinguishing 7a, which could be explanatory, from 7 which could not.

Typically, sample applications of the H-D model of explanation concern the physical sciences or else are constructed out of simple events of everyday experience like the cow examples above, but the shortcomings of this analysis become even more apparent when one turns to examples taken from human behavior. Professor John Hospers (1953, p. 187), for instance, offers the following as a deductive explanation of "why I went shopping this morning":

a. People act so as to fulfill their purposes unless prevented by external circumstances.

b. My purpose was to go shopping this morning, and I was not prevented by external circumstances.

c. Therefore, I went shopping this morning.

As an example of an explanation of a particular piece of human behavior, it is so extraordinary as to be almost beyond comment. We need only remember that this "explanation" was to be given in answer to the question "Why did you go shopping this morning?" In fact, a situation can hardly be conceived in which a person might actually respond with the explanation Hospers gives. It is most probably the case that the questioner desires an explanation in terms of function or purpose. In asking "why did you go shopping?" he presumes you had a purpose and wants to find out what that purpose was. To answer "I went shopping because my purpose was to go shopping" is simply to repeat what the questioner presumed. Only theoretical rigidity could account for one's insisting on the explanation in fact proposed. It seems clear that what is needed in such discussions is closer examination of what really goes on in actual attempts to explain human behavior, both normal and abnormal, such as the account Freud gives us of Paul Lorenz's behavior.

When we look again at that account it is evident that Freud certainly was in no doubt about the difference between prediction and explanation and made this distinction explicit. As he stated in the quotation (Chapter 6, Section D) about the various tasks the psychoanalyst sets himself, the first job is to discover the conditions under which the peculiar, incongruous behavior occurs, that is, to develop rules for predicting. Then the next job is to look for the explanatory "interconnections"—the factors causing that behavior, its function within the patient's mental economy, and its significance for the patient. In other places this same distinction recurs. For instance, at the end of the Lorenz history Freud adds a short speculative remark, unconnected with the actual explanation of the case, about the sense of smell and its possible relevance to neurosis. He points out that the patient was a *renifleur,* someone who took unusual pleasure in odors and, at least as a child, had an abnormal sensitivity to them. He adds:

> I have met with the same characteristic in other neurotics, both in hysterical and in obsessional patients, and I have come to recognize that a tendency to taking pleasure in smell, which has become extinct since childhood, may play a part in the genesis of neurosis (1909b, p. 247).

Here Freud states a predictable phenomenon he has noted about neurotic patients, and in the following discussion he goes on to theorize about the possible explanation of this finding. Again, when Freud is discussing the general mental characteristics of his patients, he draws attention to the patient's superstitiousness and his need to find support for his beliefs from the unusual coincidences of daily life.

> I have come across a similar need in many other obsessional patients and have suspected its presence in many more besides. It seems to me easily explicable in view of the psychological characteristics of the obsessional neurosis . . . (1909b, p. 231).

He then goes on to explain this predictable characteristic in terms of the general principles he has outlined: that is, finding significance in coincidences is a projection or externalization of the unconscious feeling of a connection between one's repressed emotions and one's compulsive ideas. In these two examples, then, Freud states predictably useful generalizations or rules of thumb about certain types of neurotic individuals; then, he goes on to attempt to explain these peculiar findings. Thus, there seems no doubt whatever that Freud was quite aware, often painfully so, of the gap between being able to predict certain typical features of his patients' behavior and being able to explain their origin, genesis, psychological function, and significance.

We can now return to our examination of the H-D model of explanation and see how far we have progressed. It seems that three important
conclusions have emerged concerning this position. The first is that the
H-D model does provide an adequate analysis of prediction. A set of
generalizations and statements of initial conditions together are sufficient
for the deduction of predictions; this is true enough. But a second point
seems equally true—that this model can use laws and generalizations, both
conditional and unconditional, indiscriminately, at least as far as prediction is concerned. The contention that predictions can only be based on
unconditional generalizations seems untenable. To these two observations
is added a third, thereby creating the present difficulty. This third point is
that generalizations, by themselves, may have no explanatory power even
though they may properly be used to provide a basis for prediction. In
terms of our discussion in Chapter 2 we can say that generalizations may
provide a basis only for explanations in terms of prediction but not for
any of the other varieties of explanation. The conclusion would therefore
seem to be that the H-D model alone cannot provide an adequate analysis
of explanation.

A problem arises, however, if one is for other reasons committed to
this model. Covering law theorists have taken the predictive type of explanation and set it as the foundation of scientific explanation as a whole.
This procedure is quite understandable. Certainly one important goal of
science is control over the human environment, both internal and external,
physical and social. Where control looms large as a goal, one would
expect that the most frequent question would be: How could one have
predicted this occurrence? That is, a concern for explanations in terms of
prediction might well be paramount. It is, then, not altogether accidental
that philosophers who approach scientific explanation through physics
should be most impressed by the centrality of questions of control and
predictability. Given this starting point it is not surprising that the H-D
model, which does seem to fit explanations in terms of prediction, should
be proposed as an adequate analysis of explanations of all sorts. The
problem is that in other fields the focus is most often on the understanding
and explanation of what has already occurred rather than the prediction
and control of future events. Psychoanalysis is one of the prime examples
of such a "retrospective science." Of course it does seem that if we are in
a position to explain an event, then we should likewise have been able to
predict it—*had the same knowledge been available prior to the event's
occurrence.* This is the basic observation upon which it is mistakenly
asserted that prediction and explanation are reciprocal procedures. However, the importance of this observation is reduced with regard to human

behavior because we often do not know the relevant facts beforehand. The commission of certain acts is sometimes just the evidence we need to know that certain other factors are or were operative. This means that in practice, although we may be able to explain the act in retrospect, we could not have predicted it.

We have argued on general grounds that the H-D model could not be an adequate analysis of explanations in psychoanalysis. Indeed, it seems as if a similar insight about explanation in the physical sciences is implicit even in the writings of Popper and Hempel. On the one hand, there is the insistence that the H-D model provides a sufficient analysis of scientific explanation; on the other hand, there is the admission that this model, while adequate for prediction, must be modified in some way in order to be correct for explanations. For Hempel, only "laws" are to be used, although these are not explicitly characterized. For Popper, only "unconditional generalizations" or "natural laws" are proper, terms which sometimes seem to be used interchangeably.

In Chapter 3 we used the term "law" as an equivalent to "empirical generalization." However, for Hempel and Popper this term is to be contrasted with generalization, and we can now follow this usage in which a law is, very roughly, a statement with a capacity for explanation. Our point, then, is precisely that by itself the H-D model functions equally well for prediction with rule-of-thumb generalizations or with explanatory laws. To allow any further limitations on its use is to sneak in at the back door what one has banished from the front, and to admit that the model is after all not adequate for explanation unless modified in certain ways. And what sort of modifications would be necessary? It is our contention that the dichotomies of "law-generalization" and of "unconditional–conditional generalizations" both raise contextual considerations of a type similar to that for which we are arguing. We certainly do not deny that there is a difference between using statements for prediction alone and using them for explanation. But it is neither the grammatical feature of the presence or absence of conditions nor the logical feature of fitting into an H-D schema for predictive purposes that can decide whether or not a particular statement is potentially explanatory. We must look elsewhere for that feature of general statements which makes them more than simple rule-of-thumb generalizations and conveys the explanatory power of laws. Indeed, it seems impossible to distinguish between the two on the basis of the statements alone. There is no characteristic of logic or of grammar through which explanatory power is assured. Rather, the answer must always be found in the situation within which the statement is made, the context within which the statement functions, and the way in which it is used.

B. PSYCHOANALYTIC NARRATIVES AS EXPLANATIONS

1. Predictive Generalizations and Explanatory Statements

In the previous section it was admitted that there is a difference between using statements as generalizations and using them as explanations, and we distinguished between an absolute and an implicative use of general statements. Nevertheless, it is clear that an implicative use by itself, although avoiding arbitrariness, is not sufficient to confer explanatory power; the mere *conviction* that there are causal conditions upon which the generalization rests is not enough. Something more is required, and just what this characteristic is will emerge from a closer examination of the contexts in which general statements are used for explanatory purposes. Consider the following statement:

> 10. Paul Lorenz has a deep hatred of his father of which he is not aware.

Let us assume, to avoid a separate issue, that we have workable criteria for recognizing this emotion in particular situations; for instance, scores on a series of tests or even the judgment of chosen psychoanalytic observers as to what motivations are present. As a general statement about the patient, statement 10 can be intended either as a rule of thumb enabling us to predict certain typical behavioral responses, or as some sort of explanatory law about him. In the previous section it was stated that one could only decide between these two possibilities by examining the context in which the statement is used, and we can now attempt to pin down just how this task is to be accomplished.

Used as a generalization, statement 10 is an assertion which describes the patient by ascribing a certain characteristic to him. On the basis of this dispositional generalization various pieces of behavior could be predicted including, for instance, that the patient would be very relieved when the father finally dies. Yet, it turned out that when the father did in fact die, the patient was not jubilant but so disturbed that he could not accept this fact for nearly two years. The essential question is how the psychoanalyst deals with this incongruous fact when it comes to light in the course of the analysis. If, as we are supposing, he is using statement 10 as a rule-of-thumb generalization, his response is quite simple. He either gives up the rule completely or, more probably, inserts some sort of qualifying phrase such as "usually" or "sometimes" or "under certain conditions tended to. . . ." Alternatively, if he considers statement 10 only as a summary of his past clinical experience with the patient, then he need do nothing at all. That is, if statement 10 simply means that in the past the patient's behavior showed definite evidence of his hating his father, then the truth of this summary of past experience is unaffected by a new piece of information about his present behavior. The analyst may just accept it as another interesting addition to the body of knowledge about the patient.

On the other hand, it is possible that a psychoanalyst would use statement 10 implicatively, as a part of an explanation of the patient's fear that the rat torture would happen to his father in the next world. For some reason, probably on the basis of his clinical experience with the patient, various ideas would have emerged concerning the causal relationships between certain early life situations and their resulting personality characteristics. As a result of this, the analyst has developed what we have called in Chapter 5 a "narrative commitment" to certain explanatory principles. Exactly the same statement 10 might be used, but it would now have to be interpreted as presupposing *some such* causal narrative as the following, which is a sketch of the one Freud employs:

> 10a. Paul Lorenz was sexually precocious and had a strong, domineering father who did not allow adequate expression to his son's feelings of rivalry and hostility during the very early years of childhood. Owing to their strength, the family situation, and the child's immaturity, these feelings could find no suitable outlet but were repressed. As the child grew up any conscious admission of this lingering hostility became intolerable, and instead fears about his father's death, especially in situations where the child's sexual desires were aroused, were expressed. But these fears were in fact only a conscious reaction-formation to the persisting unconscious hatred and wish for his father's death.

We can ignore the obvious incompleteness and inaccuracies of this summary. The important point is to see that it is a narrative of this sort which forms the implied basis for a psychoanalyst's making the original statement 10 in those situations where he uses that statement as part of an explanation instead of as a predictive or descriptive generalization.

It is just because this narrative commitment might remain unstated that we can be in doubt, until we examine the context, as to whether a statement is being used as a generalization or an explanation. Statement 10 itself might remain unchanged in the two situations. It is rather the psychoanalyst who changes. What began, perhaps in the early stages of an analysis, as a rule of thumb for predicting certain basic responses of the patient has become the conviction that this particular characteristic—hatred of father—is an aspect and manifestation of an early developmental process. In stating 10 now, the psychoanalyst intends to commit himself to a whole causal narrative accounting for certain aspects of the patient's behavior.

There is a second aspect to the analyst's explanatory use of statement 10 which can be brought out by asking the same question as before: How does the analyst deal with apparently incongruous pieces of behavior such as, in our example, the fact that the patient was not jubilant and relieved but terribly depressed after he accepted his father's death. Clearly, the analyst's response must be quite different from before; he is no longer allowed to shrug his shoulders and qualify his generalization, or worse, simply to accept this new information as an interesting addition to the case record. If the analyst intends his statement to be explanatory in other situations, then besides being committed to some causal narrative he also makes what we have called an "explanatory commitment"; that is, in putting forward his account he is also committing himself to explaining within that same narrative any additional and any apparently contradictory pieces of behavior that may emerge on further inquiry into Lorenz's history. For instance, the patient is said to have felt a deep hostility toward his father. Then how does one account for the intimate, apparently loving relationship with him during later childhood? And why should the patient have felt such remorse at the father's death if he hated him? It is items like these which present at least a *prima facie* incongruity; they seem to be inconsistent with the narrative given. If possible they must be accounted for by extending the narrative in various ways or perhaps by introducing certain new concepts such as reaction-formation. In fact, this is just what Freud does; he extends his narrative to account for such behavior by introducing the idea of a sense of guilt: So strongly was the original hostility repressed that the patient could not accept the death of his father even in circumstances where he was completely blameless. Instead, the death appeared as a retribution for his unconscious hostility, and, indeed, as evidence of the potency of his hostile wish. Hence, rather than relief, the death triggered off a terrible sense of guilt and a period of "pathological mourning."

We need not accept this explanation, but the point is that if Freud intends a statement like 10 to be explanatory, then he must be prepared to explain any behavior that appears incongruous with that explanation. Thus, if the statement that Lorenz had a deep hatred of his father is given to explain, for instance, the strange ritual of going to the door late at night and exhibiting his penis, then Freud is obliged to explain other pieces of behavior which do not seem to be consistent with the narrative presupposed by that statement. If such an explanation proves impossible, then it must be recognized that certain incongruities remain, and to that extent the narrative account of the developmental process is unsatisfactory or at the very least incomplete.

It should now be apparent that our argument is applicable to a similar distinction between descriptions and explanations. As we pointed out in Chapter 2, the same statement can be either descriptive or explanatory; the difference depends on how the statement is used. Just as with predictive generalizations, in using statements for description alone we avoid the same two commitments—a narrative and an explanatory commitment. Consider the following statement:

11. Paul Lorenz undertook a rigorous regimen of dieting because he was masochistic.

It has often been pointed out[6] that psychoanalysts frequently mistake description for explanation, and a statement like 11 shows how this can easily be done, for by itself it could be either descriptive or explanatory. To describe a person as masochistic is to claim that he tends to do certain things which normal people consider to be painful, distasteful, self-effacing, humiliating, etc. One such activity could be rigorous dieting. Thus, in stating 11 one might simply be making a descriptive assertion. Of course, it is true that on this interpretation statement 11 is somewhat ambiguous or misleading, and one might object that the analyst should instead say:

11a. In undertaking a rigorous regimen of dieting Paul Lorenz was acting masochistically.

Here the descriptive usage is more apparent; nevertheless, the point is that laymen and even psychoanalysts sometimes use 11 and 11a synonymously, in which case the following statements are quite consistent with both 11 and 11a:

12. Paul Lorenz wished Gisela to remain ill forever because he was sadistic.
12a. In wishing Gisela to remain ill forever, Paul Lorenz was acting sadistically.

If one is only describing behavior, then it is obvious that the same individual can, on different occasions, be described as behaving differently or even in opposed and contrasting manners.

On the other hand, a psychoanalyst might wish to *explain* Lorenz's dieting on the basis of masochism. He might use the same statement 11, but now as a part of an explanation. If it is so used, it is because the analyst has developed some sort of theory about the factors causing Lorenz's behavior. If masochism is one of these factors, then those occa-

---

[6] See, for instance, Lawrence Kubie's contribution to *Psychoanalysis as Science* (1952), where an example similar to our own is mentioned.

sions where Lorenz could be described as acting *sadistically* present the analyst with a *prima facie* incongruity demanding an explanation. We are not, of course, implying that any feeling must be present at all times, or that during any period in which it is present it must be manifest in all situations. Nevertheless, we intend our narrative to be generally applicable to a wide variety of behavior. Therefore in those specific instances in which our account seems to fail we are committed to having an additional specific explanation. It is, therefore, not an empty witticism which claims that an expert is a person who can predict what will happen and then explain to us why it did not. If we state that Lorenz hates his father, then we must explain how it was that in certain important situations he did not act in ways compatible, at least ostensibly, with that emotion.

Thus, statements 11 and 12 are consistent with each other as descriptions, but if they are used as explanations, then the analyst is obligated to show how it is possible that these apparently opposing factors—masochism and sadism—can be present simultaneously. If the analyst insists that his statements 11 and 12 are explanatory, yet refuses to or cannot show how they are consistent with each other, then it is difficult to see what he means.[7] To assert both 11 and 12 without any further elaboration would seem to be equivalent to the descriptive statement:

13. Paul Lorenz sometimes acted masochistically and sometimes acted sadistically.

If this is all the analyst means, then there is no argument; but if he believes his statements to be explanatory, then it is beholden upon him to show how they are compatible. He might, for instance, explain that although Lorenz is basically masochistic because of a feeling of guilt for harboring hostile wishes or because of certain other factors, nevertheless, this guilt is at times successfully sidetracked by rationalizations which allow him to express his hostility without being aware that his action is in fact hostile.

The real division, therefore, does not lie between description and explanation or prediction, but rather between description and prediction on the one hand and explanation on the other. Thus, the difference between using statements as descriptions or predictive generalizations and using them as explanations rests upon the same two sorts of narrative and explanatory commitments. Obviously, however, we are not contending that this shift from a predictive use to an explanatory use need ever have been clearly formulated by the psychoanalyst, or that it occurred in some

---

[7] This idea of inconsistency in explanatory statements is important and we shall return to it at greater length in the last section of this chapter.

"Eureka" moment. In most cases such growing commitment to a set of explanatory principles extended over a long period of time and may well have been, for the most part, unconscious. But the point is that eventually, perhaps (but not necessarily) on the basis of new observations, a narrative relating the various behavioral phenomena comes to be adopted. What began as a rule of thumb about the patient is now understood as sum- marizing a whole explanatory narrative accounting for the origins, mean- ings, and functions of his behavior. In summary, then, a generalization becomes explanatory when we give it a certain interpretation and use it in certain ways. First, we use it in a strictly conditional and implicative way as a shorthand for some general narrative about the subject in question. And, second, we assume responsibility for accounting for any "negative data" which appear to be inconsistent with that narrative.

2. Psychoanalytic Narratives as Explanations

In the previous section we discussed certain general characteristics that mark the use of statements for explanation as opposed to the use of state- ments for prediction or description. The next problem, then, is to examine to what extent the statements composing psychoanalytic explanations possess these characteristics. Then, since we have argued that the H-D analysis is inadequate, it is essential to see what alternative can be pro- posed. In order to do this we shall have to examine in detail particular portions of Freud's explanation. In the previous chapter we pointed out the complexities of the psychoanalytic narrative as a whole. We shall therefore choose an example from the narrative which itself mirrors this complexity in the sense that different types of explanations occur for this one piece of behavior. Luckily, a very good example can be found, namely, Freud's explanation of Lorenz's miserliness, a trait which was discussed previously in our exposition.

Since this trait was, presumably, a long-standing personality charac- teristic, perhaps the first question to be asked is how it developed, what factors can account for it; that is, we shall want an explanation of the genesis of this trait. In addition, because it lasted unabated into adulthood and perhaps even became accentuated, we might suspect that it served some sort of function for the patient, or had some peculiar significance for him; hence, we should also be interested in possible explanations of func- tion or significance, if any can be found.

Freud did in fact find various factors to account for this trait, some primarily concerned with the original sources of it, and others concerned with the reasons for the miserliness remaining and becoming even more prominent in adulthood. Although these factors were combined in a single explanation, we can examine them separately at first, before going on to consider the whole comprehensive explanation of the trait.

The first factor concerns the patient's relationship with his father. There is good evidence that the patient's father was a spendthrift, or at least that the patient perceived him in this way. We know, for instance, that the father was a gambler, especially before his marriage, and that once while in charge of army funds he had lost these funds gambling and thereby would have been caught in a serious offense had a friend not bailed him out. The patient himself admitted that this incident provoked in him a sense of guilt for his father and shame for this failing. There was even the suggestion that the father might have married for money, not having the strength of mind to save enough of his army earnings to be able to marry the poor butcher's daughter who was his first love. Even after marriage the father was very free and generous with money, and for this reason it was the mother who ran the household. Indeed, the father secretly paid the rent of certain well-liked lodgers the family took in who were unable to meet the payments.

A second factor is the patient's hatred of his father and his determination not to be like him. This, of course, is one of the most important causal factors in a great deal of the patient's behavior. *Why* Lorenz hated his father is not our present concern, but *that* he did there can be little doubt. There is a great deal of evidence to support this assertion, quite apart from the fact that as the analysis progressed the patient came to admit to this hatred openly, after working through a period in which Freud, identified with the father, was the subject for much abuse. The evidence also suggests strongly that this hatred was related to the fact that the father obstructed the patient's expression of sexual feelings, or at least that the patient saw his father in this obstructive role. Among the evidence for this hatred and its connection with sexuality, there are the following points: (1) the patient's fear of his father's beating him, subsequent to the "beating" incident; (2) the incident of being thrown out of his parents' bed for wetting it; (3) the wish at about age 12 that if only his father were dead, then a particular little girl would be kind to him; (4) the fear that if he masturbates something bad will happen to his father; (5) the fact that father had, before his death, opposed the relationship with Gisela; (6) the fact that masturbation began shortly after the father's death; (7) the connection of masturbation to incidents where commands or prohibitions are broken; (8) the ritual of taking out his penis and exhibiting it to the spirit of the dead father who would come to the door at midnight; and (9) the thought "this is glorious; one might murder one's father for this" on the occasion of intercourse. All of these bits and pieces were evidence for Freud that the patient hated his father, and that this hatred was connected with the father's assuming, at least in the patient's eyes, the role of an obstructor of sexual gratification.

Other factors involved in the explanation of miserliness concerned Gisela. In spite of conscious ambivalent feelings about her, especially when she was absent or when she would spurn him, there seemed no doubt to Freud that Lorenz was deeply in love with the girl. Again, aside from the patient's own testimony on this point, there was a wealth of behavioral evidence. There was the hostility he had expressed toward Gisela's grandmother during a period when the woman's illness posed an obstacle to the girl's being with Lorenz. Moreover, he was intensely jealous of other suitors, or even other male friends of Gisela, such as the cousin Richard who accompanied them on the summer holiday in 1903. Then, too, the patient suffered terrible pangs of guilt whenever he would have some other affair or sexual encounter. And, of course, the patient had actually proposed marriage at least twice to Gisela.

The relationship with Gisela received additional support by becoming symbolically related to the patient's family situation. Both the father and mother were actively against this liaison, and the mother, after the father's death, tried to bring about a financially more secure marriage to a wealthy relation. Other relatives also tried to use their influence to bring about this match. In such a scheme the patient would be repeating his father's own marriage choice. Therefore, being true to Gisela came to signify an open break with his parents, especially his father, and the establishment of his own independence. This conflict was symbolized, according to Freud, in the patient's dream of Freud's daughter having dung for eyes, a dream discussed in Chapter 6.

In this brief summary we have ranged over a wide area of behavior in an attempt to get at the factors accounting for the patient's miserliness, and it must be emphasized that this *is* only a summary. A great deal of other evidence could be mustered to add additional support for Freud's argument. But now let us see how Freud put these factors together to explain the miserliness. One of the problems with a long psychoanalytic narrative is that individual pieces of behavior are usually discussed only in passing, while the emphasis is on the over-all account. It was for this reason that miserliness was picked, first, because it is an isolated trait, and, second, because in this case Freud does offer a neat capsule summary of his explanation:

> His miserliness is now explained. He was convinced, from a remark which his mother let fall to the effect that her connection with Rubensky was worth more than a dowry, that his father had married her and abandoned his love [the butcher's daughter] for his material advantage. This, together with his recollection of his father's financial embarrassment during his

military service, made him detest the poverty which drives people into such crimes. . . . He economized, therefore, so as not to have to betray his love (1909b, p. 297).

Here we see the basic factors outlined above all brought together. Because of the father's loose attitude toward money, the patient already had a motive for going to the opposite pole of miserliness, since he unconsciously hated the father and tried to be unlike him. After reaching maturity, however, miserliness had an important function in the patient's immediate life situation and hence the trait was reinforced. Given his father's disapproval of the Gisela affair, and his mother's insistence upon an alternative marriage into a wealthy family, the patient felt great pressure to insure his financial independence so that he need not be forced by circumstances to abandon Gisela. Thus, he was afraid to loan his money, or even to trust himself with his inheritance, but left it to be held by his mother. Moreover, in maintaining the relationship with Gisela the patient was actively disobeying the dead father's instructions and disregarding the example he had set by his own earlier marriage. Miserliness, therefore, fulfilled an important function as a means to a goal which was desired in its own right by the patient, and which signified his triumph over his father's will.

The complexity of psychoanalytic explanations comes out clearly in such an example; even the explanation of a single isolated character trait requires familiarity with a great deal of biographical information. The explanation also attempts to combine the answer to various questions as to the origin, function, and significance of the particular behavior. Freud's remark, quoted in the last chapter, now seems quite convincing: that the explanation of "a single symptom would in fact amount to the task of relating an entire case history."

A great deal can be said about this explanation of a single behavioral trait. We shall divide the following discussion into three parts, each addressed to a single question: (1) What observations relevant to the problems under examination can be made about this explanation itself? (2) What is the relationship between this explanation and the H-D model of explanation? (3) What is the relationship between this explanation and the general theory of human behavior Freud employed at the time?

3. The Properties of the Psychoanalytic Explanation of a Particular Symptom

With regard to the first question, several observations can be made. It must be remembered that Freud's account quoted above is only a summary of a wealth of biographical information. Nevertheless, this explanation can be still further reduced; that is, it seems that Freud's account implies, or involves a commitment to, statements such as the following:

1. Lorenz perceives his father as a spendthrift.
2. Lorenz unconsciously hates his father and tries to be unlike him.
3. Lorenz loves Gisela in the face of family disapproval and in spite of her being a poor girl.
4. Lorenz sees his relationship with Gisela as signifying an act of rebellion against his father and as establishing his independence from his family's aspirations for him.

A portion of the evidence for each of these statements was presented earlier. Together these statements amount to at least a part of what we have previously called the "narrative commitment." It can be clearly seen that these general statements are *not* "theoretical" in the sense of being a part of a theory of human behavior, nor are they "general" in the sense of referring to human behavior in general. They are specific empirical assertions about a single individual and his life situation. They are "general" only in the sense of being generally applicable to that individual and not referring to any specific activities or pieces of behavior, and they form part of a "commitment" only in the sense that often, as in this example, they are never made explicit in the actual explanation itself. These statements assert the basic themes around which the explanation of the particular trait is elaborated.

The second observation to be made about Freud's explanation is that it involves what we called in the previous section an "explanatory commitment." Freud's whole account, and specifically the general statements given above, are not generalizations to be used simply for predictive purposes but are meant to be explanatory statements. Freud does not just state as a matter of fact observation that Lorenz tended to act as if he hated his father; he claims that he *did* hate his father, that this state of affairs or disposition caused him to act in certain characteristic ways, and that in those situations where the opposite seems true, where affectionate behavior toward his father occurred, there were good additional reasons for this. The assertion of a simple descriptive generalization about an observed tendency is quite compatible with the observation of other pieces of behavior not exhibiting that tendency. But once such a tendency is invoked as an explanatory factor, then it can be challenged by apparently conflicting incidents or events from the patient's history. We discussed such a challenge earlier in this chapter with the example of the patient's sadness and guilt after his father's death, which seems on the face of it to contradict Freud's assertion that hatred of his father was an important causal factor in the patient's behavior. In the same way Freud's explanation of Lorenz's miserliness relies on certain basic general statements that must be considered challengeable, capable of being confirmed or refuted by careful examination of the patient's behavior.

The third observation is that Freud certainly believes his account to be a more or less adequate explanation of the patient's miserliness. The question is: Why does Freud consider it to be explanatory; and, if we accept his account, on what grounds do we consider it to be a good explanation? Our earlier analysis of explanations in terms of incongruities now becomes useful, for it seems clear that the patient's miserliness presents us with an incongruity; that is, we cannot understand how this peculiar trait came to develop in the educated and intelligent son of a fairly well-to-do family; we cannot tie it up with various events or influences in the patient's past. It is just this sort of incongruity which Freud's explanation resolves. His narrative explains how this trait developed from certain factors in the family situation, and how upon reaching adulthood it came to be reinforced by fulfilling a definite function; it served as a means to a goal which had particular significance for the patient, namely, providing financial security in order to preserve the relationship with Gisela, thereby asserting his independence from his parents. Thus, Freud provides a narrative the basis of which is a set of general statements about the individual which suggest the factors accounting for the development of the trait in question, how it functioned as a means to certain goals, and what those goals signified.

This explanation may, of course, be criticized on various grounds concerning the behavior in question and the facts of the patient's history. Nevertheless, it is not enough, for instance, to show that the father was not in fact a spendthrift; the vital factor was that the patient is said to have seen him as such and acted upon this perception however mistaken. If, however, this perception was not based on reality, then we should want to ask Freud how it was that the patient should characteristically make this error; and this would demand a separate explanation. On the other hand, we may attempt to put some other interpretation on the same biographical information, thereby presenting a new explanation. Thus, we may look for new evidence about the patient's behavior to disprove the explanation, or we may take the same evidence, reorganize it, and construct another narrative. But the sort of explanation we shall eventually want to get is precisely the sort that Freud in fact gives us. He tells us how Lorenz perceived his life situation, and how he acted upon that perception, given the desires and goals that he had. Moreover, Freud also tells us how it is that Lorenz came to have those goals, and how it is that he came to interpret his life situation in the way he did. This is, I suggest, just what we would demand of any explanation to be given for behavior similar to that of Paul Lorenz.

4. The Psychoanalytic Narrative and the Hypothetical-Deductive Model

The second question to be asked about Freud's explanation of Lorenz's miserliness is this: What is its relationship to the H-D model? In Section A we discussed this model in general terms and criticized it on grounds quite apart from any considerations of actual case material. Yet however valid those arguments might be, the most important test of the model must nevertheless be its application in actual case examples. Moreover, any alternative analysis such as the one now being developed must receive at least negative support if the model originally proposed is found to be inadequate in these cases. Thus, it is necessary to make a detailed study of the extent to which the H-D model applies to an actual extended psychoanalytic explanation. At this point we can distinguish two separate contentions: (1) that the H-D model provides an adequate analysis of the process of psychoanalytic explanation, and (2) that the H-D model provides an adequate analysis of the statements and assertions composing a psychoanalytic explanation. These two contentions are independent, and it is necessary to examine them separately.

The first thesis is certainly the more radical, and it appears much harder to support when one comes to examine actual material. The problem can be stated bluntly in the question: Does the process of explanation consist of the deduction of statements describing the behavior from general assertions, either about human nature in general or the particular individual concerned? The answer "No" seems evident, on the basis of what has been observed of Freud's procedure in the Lorenz case. The process of psychoanalytic explanation is not one of deduction but construction. Psychoanalytic explanations begin with an individual case history, and the real job of explanation occurs through ordering the mass of biographical material and attempting to organize it into a coherent whole. This is accomplished by constructing some sort of narrative account containing as much of the material as possible. Thus, with the present case, the real explanation of the patient's miserliness occurred in the course of working through the mass of discrete pieces of evidence until some sort of pattern emerged which brought this trait into line with what we know about the patient's total behavior and with what we know through common sense about human behavior in general. For we must remember that the particular trait is not incongruous per se, but only incongruous in terms of what else we know about the patient and what we know of human beings in general. The psychoanalytic narrative resolves both these sorts of incongruity through the construction of a single coherent explanation connecting the various pieces of behavior into an understandable narrative.

Most writers would probably concede this point, that the H-D model is inadequate as an analysis of the process of psychoanalytic explanation, that it is not deduction but something rather like construction which takes place. Yet the second contention might still be insisted upon, that the H-D analysis provides a good model or summary of the actual explanation proposed. Indeed, the fact that we were able to reduce Freud's explanation to a small set of assertions about the patient may well encourage one to attempt to apply this deductive model, if not to the process of constructing the explanation, at least to the finished production itself. Unfortunately, this task is more difficult than it appears.

The four general statements asserted earlier about Lorenz (Section B,3) can in fact be used to form three different partial explanations of the patient's miserliness: explanations of genesis, function, and significance. Let us first consider the genetic explanation; reduced to its bare essentials, it is this:

1. Lorenz hates his father and wishes to be unlike him, according to the way in which he, Lorenz, perceives him.
2. Lorenz perceives his father as being a spendthrift.
3. Therefore, Lorenz desires to be a miser, i.e., a "nonspendthrift."

For convenience we can drop the references to Lorenz's perception, since they make no difference to the logic of the argument, and we can adopt some obvious symbols to schematize the statements:

1. L. desires to be a member of class "unlike-F."
2. Members of class "unlike-F" have property "non-S."
3. L. desires to have property "non-S."

Of course, this is terribly artificial, but this fact can be ignored for the moment, since our concern is only with the argument's logic. Clearly, statement 3 does not follow deductively from statements 1 and 2; some additional premises are necessary. In fact, it appears that this argument can be made deductively valid in at least two possible ways: by adding a general law about human behavior or by further specification of the particular assertions about Lorenz. By adding a general law we can construct the following argument:

L1. All persons who desire to be members of a class are persons who desire to have all the properties of members of that class.
1. L. desires to be a member of class unlike-F.
2. Members of class unlike-F have property non-S.
3. L. desires to have property non-S.

This argument is not yet valid, but it can be expanded into a valid deduction in the following way:

    L1. All persons who desire to be members of a class are persons who desire to have all the properties of members of that class.
     1. All persons who desire to be members of class unlike-F are persons who desire to be members of a class.

---

     2. Therefore, all persons who desire to be members of class unlike-F are persons who desire to have all the properties of members of that class (i.e., unlike-F).

     2. All persons who desire to be members of class unlike-F are persons who desire to have all the properties of members of that class (i.e., unlike-F).
     3. All persons who desire to have all the properties of members of that class (i.e., unlike-F) are persons who desire to have property non-S.

---

     4. Therefore, all persons who desire to be members of class unlike-F are persons who desire to have property non-S.

     4. All persons who desire to be members of class unlike-F are persons who desire to have property non-S.
     5. L. is a person who desires to be a member of class unlike-F.

---

     6. Therefore, L. is a person who desires to have property non-S.

This expanded argument is now very close to a standard, formally valid deduction. The problem, however, with this deduction is that although it may well be logically valid, it is quite obviously psychologically false; that is, law L1 is simply not true. One can, for instance, desire to be a millionaire without necessarily desiring to pay 75% income tax, a property which might characterize members of this class.

In the deduction presented above we have made the original argument logically valid by introducing a general law, but another alternative remains. It is possible to make the argument valid by making our assertions about the individual concerned even more specific. For instance, in terms of the millionaire example, it does not follow that because one desires to be a millionaire one desires to pay 75% income tax. But if we amend this assertion by specifying the particular desire even further, then we can make the argument valid: If one desires to be "like a millionaire in respect of the amount of taxes paid," then it follows that one desires to have the property of "paying 75% income tax," since, let us suppose, to be like a millionaire in this respect *is* precisely to pay 75% taxes. In this way an empirical correlation—between "like a millionaire in respect of the amount of taxes paid" and "paying 75% income tax"—is made into a definitional equivalence; that is, the two phrases are now considered to be alternative characterizations of the same property. In the language of class calculus one could say that the two classes defined by these phrases are no longer simply extensionally, but intensionally equivalent.

In this same way the genetic explanation of Lorenz's miserliness could be made deductively valid. Let us look again at the original logically invalid argument in its schematized form:

1. L. desires to be a member of class unlike-F.
2. Members of class unlike-F have property non-S.
3. L. desires to have property non-S.

Rather than introducing a general law, let us now use the second method to make the argument valid—further specification of the assertions:

4. L. desires to be a member of class "unlike-F in respect of money dealings."
5. To be unlike-F in respect of money dealings is equivalent to being non-S.
6. L. desires to be non-S.

This argument is not yet valid, but it can be expanded into a valid deduction in the following way:

1. All persons who desire to be members of a class are persons who desire to be members of any class to which that class is intensionally equivalent.
2. All persons who desire to be members of class unlike-F in respect of money dealings are persons who desire to be members of a class.

---

3. Therefore, all persons who desire to be members of class unlike-F in respect of money dealings are persons who desire to be members of any class to which that class is intensionally equivalent.

3. All persons who desire to be members of class unlike-F in respect of money dealings are persons who desire to be members of any class to which that class (namely, unlike-F in respect of money dealings) is intensionally equivalent.

4. All persons who desire to be members of any class to which that class (namely, unlike-F in respect of money dealings) is intensionally equivalent are persons who desire to be members of class non-S.

---

5. Therefore, all persons who desire to be members of class unlike-F in respect of money dealings are persons who desire to be members of class non-S.

5. All persons who desire to be members of class unlike-F in respect of money dealings are persons who desire to be members of class non-S.
6. All persons who desire to be members of class non-S are persons who desire to have property non-S.

7. Therefore, all persons who desire to be members of class unlike-F in respect of money dealings are persons who desire to have property non-S.

7. All persons who desire to be members of class unlike-F in respect of money dealings are persons who desire to have property non-S.
8. L. is a person who desires to be a member of class unlike-F in respect of money dealings.

9. Therefore, L. is a person who desires to have property non-S.

This expanded argument is now very close to a logically valid deduction. The first deduction, given earlier, was based upon a law that would necessitate, for instance, that if one desired to be a millionaire, one necessarily desired to pay 75% income tax. That deduction was unsatisfactory because such a law was clearly false. The second deduction, presented above, does not contain an empirically false general law; instead, it is based upon a simple logical rule that would necessitate, for instance, that if one desired "to be like a millionaire in respect of paying taxes" then one necessarily desired "to pay 75% income taxes"—for the reason that these are, *ex hypothesi,* considered alternative formulations or specifications of the same property. In the same way, the phrase "unlike-F in respect of money dealings" is to be considered a rough caricature of some sort of alternative specification, involving person F, of the property "nonspendthriftness."

However, this second method of making the original argument deductively valid is also unsatisfactory, for the explanation has now been trivialized in at least two ways. The deduction is valid because we have made the original assertion about Lorenz more specific; we have changed the original observation that Lorenz desires to be unlike his father into the more specific assertion that Lorenz desires to be unlike his father in one specific respect, namely, in respect of the father's spendthriftness. Statement 8 in the deduction above makes this explicit; it says that Lorenz desires to be unlike his father insofar as his father is a spendthrift. But this assertion is really nothing else than another way of saying that Lorenz desires to be a nonspendthrift, i.e., a miser, which is the conclusion of the argument. The supposed explanation is therefore no more than a restatement of the original fact which was to be explained. This fact that deductions yield nothing new but only what is already contained in the premises is of course a logical point only. It does suggest, however, that to the extent that an explanation does posit something new, to that extent it will not fit a deductive model.

This deduction is also trivial in a second respect, since it cannot now be used to explain any additional pieces of behavior. The original explanation was significant and explanatory, in part at least, precisely because it could account for a variety of traits or pieces of behavior. Freud's narrative about Lorenz's hatred of his father and his desire to be unlike him leads us to expect, albeit not with certainty, that a variety of other things would be true. We are led to expect, for instance, that Lorenz would show signs of rebelliousness or that he would be happy when his father died. Some of these expectations, as we have seen, were not fulfilled, but this did not necessarily disprove Freud's explanation; instead, the narrative required elaboration and extension to account for these additional findings. In the deduction above, starting from a logical rule and a very specific assertion about the patient, it does indeed follow that we can predict with certainty the occurrence of the particular trait involved, nonspendthriftness. But this is simply because, in one sense, we have just restated the original fact which was to be explained and added nothing to it. Moreover, the deduction, although predicting miserliness with certainty, offers no further expectations of any sort about Lorenz's behavior, let alone completely certain expectations. Freud's original narrative, in contrast, while not offering deductive certainty about miserliness, had a more general applicability and was, therefore, not trivial as is this deductive reformulation.

It seems, then, that Freud's genetic explanation of Lorenz's miserliness can be made to conform to the H-D model only by introducing a psychologically false law, or else by making it trivial and removing whatever explanatory quality it originally possessed. These same arguments could be repeated with the other two parts of Freud's original narrative—the explanation in terms of function and that in terms of significance. To avoid needless repetition, we need only present the analogous schemas. First, let us consider Freud's account of Lorenz's miserliness in terms of the function of this trait. As we have seen in the previous section, Freud argued that Lorenz was miserly "so as not to have to betray his love." The miserliness served the patient as a means to gain the financial security that would insure his being able to protect his relationship with Gisela. Very roughly, we can schematize Freud's basic argument in this way:

1. Lorenz loves Gisela and desires the financial security which would insure that he could remain faithful to her.

2. Miserliness is a means to financial security.
3. Lorenz desires to be a miser.

Considering only the logic of this argument it is clear that the conclusion does not follow deductively from statements 1 and 2. Nevertheless, we could add a general law to this argument:

L2. All persons who desire a given end are persons who desire any means to that end.
  1. L. is a person who desires end financial security.
  2. Miserliness is a means to that end.
  3. L. is a person who desires to be a miser.

The argument is still not valid, yet it seems that it could now be expanded, as we did before, into a formal deduction. However, L2, is psychologically false, so we can try the second alternative of making the argument more specific:

4. All persons who desire some particular state of affairs are persons who desire any state of affairs which is logically equivalent to that state of affairs.
5. L. is a person who desires "to save money by being parsimonious in order to obtain financial security."
6. "To save money by being parsimonious in order to obtain financial security" is equivalent to "to be a miser."
7. L. is a person who desires to be a miser.

This argument could likewise be expanded into a valid deduction, but the effect would be to trivialize Freud's original explanation.

Finally, with Freud's explanation in terms of significance, the same points can be made. Briefly, Freud argues that the patient's love for Gisela is reinforced by his desire to rebel against his parents. In maintaining this relationship he was symbolically freeing himself from his parents' influence and acting contrary to what his father had done when he had given up a poor girl to marry the patient's mother. The miserliness, therefore, served as a means to achieving a symbolic separation from his parents. The first part of this argument can be schematized in this way:

1. Lorenz desires to rebel against his parents.
2. The affair with Gisela signifies an act of rebellion against his parents.
3. Lorenz desires to maintain the affair with Gisela.

The first method of making the argument valid would be to add a general law:

L3. All persons who desire any act or state of affairs are persons who desire any act or state of affairs which symbolizes or signifies that act or state of affairs.
1. L. is a person who desires an act of rebellion against parents.
2. The affair with Gisela signifies an act of rebellion against parents.
3. L. is a person who desires to maintain the affair with Gisela.

Alternatively, the original argument can be made deductively valid by specifying more precisely the way in which Lorenz desires to rebel:

4. All persons who desire to maintain some state of affairs are persons who desire to maintain any state of affairs which is logically equivalent to that state of affairs.
5. L. is a person who desires to "rebel against his parents in his dealings with Gisela."
6. To "rebel against his parents in his dealings with Gisela" is equivalent to "maintaining the affair with Gisela."
7. L. is a person who desires to maintain the affair with Gisela.

Again, it seems that both these arguments could be expanded into a deductively valid form.

What can be concluded from all these schematic exercises in the syllogism? Compared with the actual explanation Freud gave of the patient's miserliness, which we presented in the previous section, one point is obvious: all of these schemas, both the valid and the invalid, appear grossly artificial, distorted, and inadequate. Part of this distortion, no doubt, is because of our own insufficient care in attempting to present H-D analyses of the original material, but this is probably not the whole fault. It certainly seems that one is here faced with a species of the general difficulty of attempting to fit philosophical models to complex pieces of verbal behavior which arise in various sorts of situations. To the extent that this inevitable distortion becomes appreciable, the value of the proposed model may well be diminished. But quite apart from this obvious limitation, the attempt to fit the explanation of miserliness into a deductive framework has raised other problems. It appears from our examples that the explanations can be made deductively valid only by resorting to one of two unacceptable modifications. We can on the one hand add a general law such as laws L1, L2, and L3. The problem with these, however, is that they are all quite clearly false as statements about human behavior. Alternatively, we can make the original explanation deductively valid by making the premises more specific. This procedure, however, seemed to trivialize the argument; deductive certainty was gained only by sacrificing the explanatory quality of the original narrative. It appears, therefore, as if our hopes of applying this model were unfounded. Although Freud's explanation of Lorenz's miserliness can be outlined in a few brief assertions, even then it cannot be made to conform to the H-D model without encountering the difficulties discussed above.

In Section A we criticized the H-D model on general grounds. Now we have shown in a particular example that this model cannot be applied without either committing one to laws which are psychologically false or else trivializing the original explanation. The argument could rest at this point, but there is an obvious objection to our procedure that could be raised. What we have so far demonstrated is only that two alternative ways of fitting the explanation of Lorenz's miserliness to the H-D model are unsatisfactory, but there is the possibility that further manipulation and reformulation might succeed in making the explanation deductively valid without either introducing a false law or trivializing it. Indeed, it is conceivable that some such reformulation would also be much less artificial and distorting than the examples discussed above. Rather than argue this hypothetical objection, the point can be conceded that we have not shown conclusively that the H-D model cannot be fitted to the explanation of the patient's miserliness. What has been shown is that any method at all is likely to be artificial, and, also, that two possible sorts of reformulation are unsatisfactory. Yet even if some further reformulation could avoid these obstacles, another set of problems remains, which we can now examine. The point of these new criticisms is that even if the H-D model could be fitted to a psychoanalytic explanation in some way, it would still be a *misleading* analysis of that explanation.

To begin with, there are two related faults of the H-D model as an analysis of Freud's explanation. The first is that it puts the emphasis in the wrong place and draws attention to the wrong statements. While it is true that the four general statements given earlier represent a part of the basic commitment of Freud's explanation, it is *not* true that they are the essence or heart of that explanation. The actual explanation is a long and involved narrative tying together a great number of biographical factors into a coherent account. The four general statements are at best only summaries of the wealth of biographical information which went into the actual narrative. Taken by themselves, however, they appear as rather arbitrary assertions, totally lacking in explanatory power, and this suggests the second, more important fault of the H-D model: It mistakes the source of the explanatory quality that we associate with the psychoanalytic narrative. If we consider that the miserliness has been explained by Freud, it is certainly not because we can deduce it from the four general statements. If we have been convinced, it is because we have followed Freud through a complicated narrative which has attempted to organize a wealth of biographical data into some understandable whole. But this narrative is in no meaningful sense equivalent to a few stark assertions arranged into a rather artificial schema. By itself, none of the deductions presented above would be anything more than a predictive schema. In making Freud's explanation deductively valid, the H-D model takes predictive certainty as equivalent to, or at least a criterion of, explanatory power. This is, as we have seen at the beginning of this chapter, a quite mistaken notion. Indeed, as the schemas presented above suggest, insofar as the original argument is reformulated to make it deductively valid the explanation is trivialized. Miserliness, for instance, might now be predicted with certainty, but the explanation no longer has any general applicability to the rest of the patient's behavior. The explanatory power of Freud's discussion resides in the narrative itself or else is nonexistent. Generalizations abstracted from that matrix will of course appear arbitrary and unconvincing. But the sense of conviction is restored not by supplying an artificial logical schema, but by returning those statements to their original explanatory narrative.

There is still a fourth way in which the H-D analysis provides a misleading model of an actual psychoanalytic explanation. What if it were possible to give three different valid deductions of the sort outlined to cover the three aspects of Freud's explanation? *Ex hypothesi,* these three deductions would each be logically valid, and each would yield the statement that Lorenz desired to be a miser. This would mean, according to the H-D analysis, that any of these deductions would be by itself a sufficient explanation of the trait in question. Since they present valid deductions from presumably true assertions about the patient, there is no way to choose between them. At best, if we accept that the general statements are true, we can say that there are three equally sufficient explanations of the trait. This is a possibility, but it seems clear from the actual case record that Freud made no such claim. As his own statement quoted earlier shows, he considered his explanation of the miserliness to be a single narrative account which made reference to several different factors. Thus, according to his account the hatred of the father, the need for money to insure his love relationship with Gisela, and the desire to rebel against his parents were all important factors. Obviously, it is possible to form some idea about the relative strength of these factors, and Freud himself did so; but the question whether any of them was sufficient by itself can probably never be conclusively answered, and in any case it is an unnecessary problem. Once we have ascertained which factors were operative, and how important each of them was, there is no further necessity to raise problems about hypothetical situations.

In conclusion, then, we can say that the H-D thesis is completely inadequate as an analysis of the actual process of psychoanalytic explanation. Regarding its relationship to the explanation itself, however, our conclusions are somewhat less strong. We have argued that any attempt to make Freud's explanation of the patient's miserliness deductively valid is bound to be somewhat artificial and distorting. Moreover, two possible ways in which this reformulation might be done were shown to be unsatisfactory because they either commit one to laws that are psychologically false, or because they trivialize the original argument. Nevertheless, even if these objections could be met by some sort of further manipulation or reformulation, we have argued that the result would still be misleading for at least four different reasons: (1) it would focus attention on the wrong part of the explanation, (2) it would substitute predictive certainty for explanatory power as a criterion of adequacy, (3) it would mistake the source of that explanatory power, and (4) it would divide the original explanation into several separate deductions, each apparently sufficient to explain the trait in question. In short, then, the H-D analysis could at best provide nothing more than a rather misleading sketch or outline summary of the actual psychoanalytic explanation of a particular piece of behavior.

5. The Psychoanalytic Narrative and General Theories of Human Behavior

The third question we can ask about Freud's explanation of Lorenz's miserliness is: What is its relationship to theoretical generalizations about human behavior? One important fact already established is that the narrative itself does not involve generalizations about human nature but instead makes certain empirical assertions about the particular individual in question. Nevertheless, even if the explanation does not actually assert statements about human behavior as a whole, it might still be that the explanation commits one to some such general assertions. Indeed, if we return to the deductive schemas presented above, it does seem that certain very general assertions about human behavior are necessary and have not been made explicit. For instance, Freud argued that because Lorenz hated his father, he desired to be unlike him, and therefore desired to be a miser. But in order to get from this desire to the actual miserly behavior, we need some sort of general law such as:

P1. People who have certain desires tend to act upon them.

Likewise, Freud argued that being a miser served a specific purpose, namely, the gaining of money in order to protect the patient's relationship with Gisela. To get from this intention, however, to the actual behavior we need another general law such as:

P2. People tend to act in such a way as to fulfill their intentions, unless prevented by circumstances from doing so.

This statement is similar to the one Hospers gave in his example quoted earlier in this chapter (Section A,4). Clearly, all such statements are no more than platitudes; and like so many platitudes about human behavior, it is uncertain whether they are meant as empirical observations or part of the definitions of various terms. In fact, it is usual to find that such platitudes are sometimes used as defining criteria for deciding, for instance, if someone is in love or really has a purpose in mind; and on other occasions they are used as empirical generalizations about how people act in certain situations or under certain conditions.

Rather than get involved in this side issue, let us simply accept these statements as platitudes with both empirical and definitional uses. The question then is: Does the psychoanalytic explanation of Lorenz's miserliness commit one to such statements? The answer is "Yes," but only in a weak sense, for it is not the case that the explanation as it stands would be any the less explanatory without them. Here again the H-D model proves misleading, for while these platitudes may be necessary in order that the general assertions or principles about Lorenz be logically sufficient to imply the miserly behavior, it is quite clear that in themselves these platitudes add nothing to the explanatory strength of the psychoanalytic narrative. In fact they form a part of the presumption of knowledge that enters into the explanatory context itself. As argued in Chapter 2, it is only because some such platitudes are a part of our knowledge in the first place that the patient's behavior appears incongruous and in need of a special explanation. These platitudes, then, are not implied by the psychoanalytic narrative but presumed by it.

However, when the problem arises of an explanation's relationship to generalizations, what are usually meant are not platitudes which belong to everyone's body of common-sense knowledge but specialized, high level statements which form a part of a general theory of human behavior. Thus, the question should be: What is the relationship between Freud's explanation of miserliness and his general theory of human behavior? The H-D analysis asserts that the deductive model is appropriate and suggests that the particular explanation is deduced from laws of a general theory of human behavior. Here is yet another place at which this analysis leads us astray, for we have seen that even if the H-D model could fit the explanation as an outline or sketch, it is not general laws of human behavior but assertions about the particular individual which would form the premises of that explanation.

It is certainly true, however, that one could put forth a deductive schema based upon Freud's general theory from which it would follow, for instance, that the patient had a love–hate conflict. Let us assume for the sake of argument that "obsessional neurosis" is a purely descriptive term to be applied when a certain number of symptoms from some set are found in any individual. This set would include prayer rituals, counting phenomena, compulsive hand-washing, and various sorts of commands and prohibitions. According to these criteria Lorenz would be labeled an obsessional neurotic. Let us also assume that certain general observations about obsessional patients have been made and form part of a theory about this illness. In fact, as we saw earlier in this chapter, Freud used a number of such generalizations in his case record, two of which were, roughly, that these patients showed a love–hate conflict and premature sexual development. We could therefore set out the following deduction:

1. All obsessional patients show love–hate conflict and premature sexual development.
2. Paul Lorenz is an obsessional patient.

---

3. Paul Lorenz shows (will be found to show) a love–hate conflict and premature sexual development.

Here is a deductive schema using, let us grant, a theoretical generalization that Freud himself asserts in the case record and a true statement of an initial empirical finding; from these two statements it follows that the patient would show two traits which he in fact did show. The question then is: Is this deductive schema an explanation of the presence of these traits? I think the answer is certainly "No." The situation is similar to an example given earlier in this chapter: The fact that all four-year-old boys hate their fathers does not *explain* why one particular boy should do so. The general point made then now recurs in this example from Freud's case: The deductive schema is neither necessary nor sufficient to guarantee explanatory power. This deduction about Lorenz does not *explain* the behavioral characteristics in question but at most allows us to predict, to expect, them. For an adequate explanation we should still have to examine the actual biographical material and construct a coherent narrative about that particular life history which would show the origin, development, and function of these characteristics.

Our point must not be misinterpreted, however. In Chapter 4 we outlined Freud's basic theory within which he was operating at the time of the Lorenz case. There is no doubt whatever that this theory influenced Freud when he came to analyze Lorenz, and again when he came to write up that case. However, as we stated in the first chapter, the very real problem of determining the extent of this influence is not being touched upon; we are all along accepting Freud's description of the patient as being undistorted by his theoretical ideas. Our point is simply that the explanation in an individual case does not make any commitments to general theoretical statements but only to assertions about the individual patient; the explanation is not deduced from a general theory of human behavior in conjunction with statements of initial conditions. The role of the general theory, including both empirical generalizations and higher level theoretical statements, can be characterized as *directive* in the sense of pointing out to the analyst the areas that should be investigated and the sorts of factors likely to be found operative. It seems clear, for instance, that if Freud did not believe (1) that the roots of neurosis lay in the period of development during the years three to six, and (2) that there is a stage in which a child is in rivalry with the opposite parent—if he had not believed such theoretical generalizations, then he would probably not have put forth the construction which led the patient to remember the "beating" incident. Nevertheless, the fact that his theory directed him to this important event does not mean that when he uses this event as part of an explanation he is logically obliged to invoke the theory.

If the psychoanalytic explanation is not deducible from a general theory of human behavior in conjunction with statements of initial conditions, then clearly the truth of that general theory is not sufficient to guarantee the truth of the explanation of a particular case. Conversely, the truth of a particular explanation does not guarantee the truth of the general theory which directed the analyst to that explanation. Yet it is obvious that the truth of the explanation in a particular case should provide at least *some* evidence for the truth of the general theory, and the truth of the general theory should lend at least *some* weight to any explanation it suggested. Just how this interaction is to be described will emerge in the following section when we turn to our final problem: the evaluation of psychoanalytic narratives.

C. The Evaluation of Psychoanalytic Narratives

It must not be thought that because psychoanalytic explanations are not reducible to a few straightforward laws, evaluation and judgment of them are therefore impossible. Our emphasis on the narrative aspect of psychoanalytic explanations does, however, have important implications for this problem. In the first place we would argue that the simple either–or criterion of logical validity is inadequate. The concept of logical validity seems appropriate only to deductive schemas. It does make sense to say that a prediction necessarily follows from certain general statements, and also that certain sets of statements are logically sufficient to make a prediction. Predictions, then, can be valid or invalid, that is, properly deduced or not. On the other hand, when we turn to explanations we find additional parameters of appraisal. We speak of explanations that are more or less adequate, incomplete, partial, shallow, deep, and a variety of other terms besides. Yet none of these terms seems applicable to deductions. What, for instance, would a partial or shallow deduction look like? One of the useful features of a contextual account of explanations is that it allows for the ranking of explanations along a whole spectrum of adequacy. Because there is an unavoidable contextual aspect to explanations that is absent from predictions based upon the H-D model, we must substitute for the simple two-valued standard of logical validity a more flexible set of criteria. For this reason, then, we speak of evaluation, rather than verification or proof.

It must be emphasized that evaluation *is* possible. There is nothing in what we have so far argued which would preclude this or offer any support for some sort of relativism or subjectivism. Specifically, our insistence upon the narrative aspect of psychoanalytic explanations does not imply that they must be accepted or rejected as a whole. Psychoanalytic narratives are not simply totally true or totally false. It is quite obvious to anyone who actually reads case studies that such a belief is far too great a simplification. The most diehard analyst would not refuse to admit that some particular narrative, although true in its general outlines, nevertheless might have certain errors. Nor, I think, would the severest critic of Freud refuse to admit that a psychoanalytic explanation, however misguided as a general theory, nevertheless, occasionally offers some striking insights about particular facets of a patient's behavior. The Lorenz case seems quite typical in this respect. On certain points, such as the unconscious hostility directed toward the father, Freud seems to be pointing to something of great importance for an understanding of the patient's behavior. In various other ways the narrative may appear more dubious. But all this is perfectly appropriate for an explanation which is, as we have continually pointed out, of a very complex nature.

Let us grant, then, that evaluation of psychoanalytic narratives is possible, even though this evaluation is different from and more difficult than the checking of deductions according to logical criteria alone. The next question is obvious: By what criteria are psychoanalytic narratives to be evaluated? It must be admitted that we are here facing an immense and largely uncharted area, and if a simple map exists, I certainly do not have it. Indeed, the problems of evidence and testability that will be raised in the following discussion are extremely complex and could well be the subject of another study. For these reasons, then, what will be said is very tentative and programmatic.

Up to this point the argument has centered upon a single psychoanalytic narrative. Having seen how that narrative works, we are now going on to suggest certain criteria by which that narrative could be evaluated. We are not, however, concerned with the question of how the Lorenz narrative in fact measures up to these standards. Our problem is to develop criteria which could be generally applicable, rather than to decide upon the adequacy of any particular psychoanalytic explanation. Obviously, implicit in the whole book is the belief that the Lorenz narrative is not anomalous but fairly characteristic of psychoanalytic explanations in general; and if this is true, then the standards that are applicable to it should, with only slight modification, be generally useful.

In Chapter 2 we discussed the criterion of *appropriateness* of explanations, with reference to the presumptions of explanation that were outlined at that point. Having now examined one psychoanalytic narrative in detail we can move on to the two other sets of criteria mentioned there. The first, criteria of *adequacy,* offer standards whereby we can attempt to answer the question: Would this narrative, if its assertions could be confirmed, be acceptable as a more or less "adequate" explanation? We will attempt to elucidate just what is meant by "adequate" when used in this way. Then, given that an explanation is appropriate and adequate, a third question presents itself: Is this narrative confirmed? In order to answer this question we shall want still another set of criteria, criteria of truth or *accuracy.* Each of these last two sets will be outlined separately, but it must be remembered that we are only offering possible suggestions, not a definitive or complete set of criteria. Moreover it is quite true that in the actual practice of psychoanalysis these sets are often not distinguished. Analysts are frequently unclear as to the different ways in which various sorts of evidence support their explanations. Often, standards of adequacy are mistaken for standards of accuracy. This is an important issue, of course, but it relates only to the practice of psychoanalysis, and hence, at this point, falls outside the range of our interest.

1. Criteria of Adequacy

The first criterion of adequacy is the self-consistency of the general statements to which the narrative is committed. We ask for an explanation because we find ourselves confronted by incongruities in a particular individual's behavior. Insofar as the narrative offered generated new incongruities it would be inadequate and the need for further explanation would remain. Hence, an adequate explanation must employ general statements about the individual which are consistent with each other.

This criterion, however, is more complicated than it appears. That conflicting drives, conflicting needs, and conflicting emotions may be simultaneously present in an individual is of course one of the basic truths of human experience. Any narrative that recognized such conflicting factors would not thereby be inconsistent; indeed, unless it gave proper weight to such complexities we would probably say it was untrue. Clearly, then, the inconsistency must be of a deeper, more fundamental sort. It would, let us say, appear *prima facie* inconsistent if a psychoanalytic narrative about a single patient posited an unresolved positive oedipal conflict and residual paternal hostility to explain certain neurotic symptoms, and at the same time a homosexual or negative or reversed oedipal conflict (for a boy, love of father and rivalry with mother) to explain other symptoms. We would be puzzled if an analyst had to employ both these principles in an explanation of a single individual's behavior.

At this point, no doubt, two standard objections could be raised. The first can be called the "outsider's" criticism, namely, that psychoanalysis uses constructs such as "oedipus complex" which are so loosely formulated that one can never be quite sure what statements employing them would or would not be inconsistent with each other.[8] This objection is valid, and examples of such difficulties can be found both in Freud's writings and in that of present-day theorists. Perhaps the above example using positive and negative oedipus complexes is just such a case where it is not clear whether it would be inconsistent to assert the two statements about a single individual.

The second objection to our particular example of an inconsistency is at the same time a defense of psychoanalysis against the first criticism that the discipline's concepts are not clearly defined. This is the "insider's" general point that the ambiguities of psychoanalytic formulations are necessitated by the complexities of the subject matter itself. As a general defense, however, this argument seems quite inadequate in that it is based on the faulty notion that concepts must in some sense mirror the material they concern. Conceptual clarity, however, is consistent with, and indeed essential for the proper explanation of the contradictions and incon-

---

[8] Our example, the "oedipus complex," is in fact one of the standard concepts about which this criticism is concerned. A number of statements of this objection occur in the symposium *Psychoanalysis, Scientific Method, and Philosophy,* edited by Sidney Hook (1959), and especially in Professor Hook's own contribution. The "insider's" objection, outlined below, can also be found in the analysts' contributions to this symposium, especially that of Dr. Arlow.

sistencies of human behavior. The ambiguity of the subject matter in no way implies that the theoretical analysis must likewise be ambiguous.

Nevertheless, although the argument is unsound as a general position, it may well be a valid specific criticism of our particular example; that is, an analyst might say that in fact he had seen just such a case where there was an unresolved positive oedipal conflict along with a negative or homosexual oedipal conflict. Of course, this might simply be meant as a descriptive assertion, that a particular individual showed hostility and rivalry with regard to both parents. If this is true, then these conflicting emotions themselves require some further explanation, and the assertion that the person had both a positive and a negative oedipal conflict would now be only descriptive, not explanatory. If it were meant to be explanatory, however, the analyst must show us how these two basic constructs are not in fact inconsistent with each other, and if he can do this, then we must withdraw our example.

These two objections, then, do not refute our assertion that one criterion of adequacy is self-consistency. The first, the "outsider's" objection, argues that it is often difficult or even impossible to apply this standard to actual psychoanalytic narratives. If this is true, then it is an unfortunate commentary on psychoanalytic theory, but surely it is no argument against the logical propriety of attempting to apply such a criterion. The second, "insider's" objection as a general point simply emphasizes the necessity for using the criterion subtly, giving full consideration to the complexities of human behavior. As a specific criticism it can at most demonstrate that our example of an inconsistency is a bad one, not that the criterion itself is unworkable.

This conclusion as to the utility of the criterion of inconsistency is, of course, what one would expect; for it certainly seems that a psychoanalytic explanation must involve some sort of assertions about the individual patient which would be inconsistent with other assertions one would make if the patient's behavior were different. It may, of course, be very difficult to state this criterion of inconsistency explicitly. Nevertheless, some sort of inconsistency must be possible, for if all narratives were consistent with each other, it is hard to understand how any of them could be explanatory.

A second criterion of adequacy, given that the proposed narrative is at least self-consistent, is coherence—the accommodation of the individual's behavior into a coherent whole. This criterion is in fact simply the converse of our analysis of explanations as dealing essentially with incongruities. For one important way to evaluate any proposed explanatory narrative is to see how many of the original incongruities can now be accounted for within the one over-all framework. Insofar as certain aspects of the individual's behavior remain incongruous, we judge the explanation to be inadequate.

Related to this second criterion of coherence is a third, that of comprehensiveness. It may well be that a particular account simply fails to cover various portions of the case history of an individual, and insofar as this occurs we would say the explanation is incomplete or partial. It must be emphasized that this criterion applies only to the sort of explanations exemplified by Freud's explanation of the Lorenz case. It is obviously true that in everyday experience we ask for the explanation of particular actions and events, and these phenomena can often be given an adequate explanation without any long involved narrative going back to early childhood. Nevertheless, most psychoanalytic explanations do aim at comprehensiveness, not in the sense of accounting for every event or piece of behavior, but at least every incongruent and puzzling circumstance. It is quite enough that other events or characteristics not specifically accounted for be at least consistent with the analyst's narrative.

Taken together the three standards mentioned—self-consistency, coherence, and comprehensiveness—make up at least an important part of what we mean by judging an explanation of human behavior to be adequate. It must be remembered, however, that we are dealing with a spectrum of adequacy, a whole range along which we can place explanations. Moreover, just because we speak of partial and more or less complete explanations, we should not go on to the mistaken view that there is one absolutely complete explanation. To search for explanations that are more complete is quite feasible. But to demand a totally complete explanation is to demand the attainment of a logical standard for something which is essentially context-dependent. Such context-dependency makes total completeness logically impossible, for there is an indefinite number of ways to approach any subject matter, and an indefinite number of ways in which aspects of that subject matter may be incongruous.

Not only does context-dependence make completeness impossible, it likewise allows for several explanations being equally adequate. As long as we stick to the criteria of consistency, coherence, and comprehensiveness, it seems that several different narratives might rank equally. The comparison with historical narratives is instructive here. Just as different explanations in history offer new perspectives and viewpoints, so too do the various sorts of psychoanalytic explanations. We speak of Marxist historians and capitalist historians in much the same way as Jungian analysts and Freudian analysts. Each group may produce evocative and perceptive, but radically different, views of the same subject matter that are each self-consistent, coherent, and comprehensive. It might even be said that psychoanalysis, particularly in its clinical and therapeutic setting, functions essentially in this way, by presenting new and varied perspectives to patients of their own behavior, rather than by telling them the true causes of that behavior.

In raising this issue of the function of psychoanalytic explanations, an important truth is made explicit, namely, that the goal of therapeutic efficacy is entirely distinct from the goal of the discovery of the true causes of human behavior. This is not necessarily to deny that the same psychoanalytic methods are capable of achieving both these goals; yet the possibility must be kept in mind that the techniques developed in the clinic for therapy may not be the most appropriate for scientific research. This possibility becomes especially relevant if one realizes that there is good evidence that therapeutic efficacy is unrelated to the "truth" of the psychoanalytic explanation offered to the patient.[9] The positive aspect of this fact has long been admitted by analysts, namely, that the truth of the analytic explanation is not *sufficient* to effect a therapeutic improvement. But it is the possibility that truth is not even *necessary* for therapeutic efficacy which is more disturbing, and this point has only recently been admitted by some psychiatrists.[10]

It is interesting to recognize that the sort of contextual analysis which we have developed has definite ramifications as regards therapy. Specifically, it is quite possible that therapeutic efficacy, while not correlated with the truth or accuracy of the narrative, *is* related to its adequacy as we have defined this term. There seems to be a definite and very basic "rationalizing drive" in human experience, a need to see one's own behavior as forming a reasonable and coherent pattern. The adequate psychoanalytic narrative, by providing such a pattern, by giving reasons for "unreasonable" behavior, satisfies this need and thereby allays anxiety—a therapeutically valuable consequence. Moreover, if a person who performs a piece of neurotic, maladaptive behavior can be made to believe that his reason for this action traces back to an infantile developmental crisis, and is therefore quite unrealistic in present situations, he may be able to substitute new and better reasons for more adaptive behavior. The psychoanalytic explanation provides the patient with a handle, a lever by which behavioral change may be effected. Both these obvious therapeutic benefits—diminished

---

[9] A good review of this evidence is in Jerome Frank's *Persuasion and Healing* (1961, Ch. 1).

[10] The point has, of course, been made previously by many nonmedical men, for instance B. A. Farrell in the 1962 P. A. S. Symposium on psychoanalysis. Symptomatic improvement has always been acknowledged to be possible with various nonanalytic methods, or even through "spontaneous remission." What is meant here, however, is the permanent improvement effected through getting at the "unconscious causes." Only recently have some psychiatrists seriously considered the possibility that psychotherapy does not function by exposing the causes of disturbance and getting the patient to accept them intellectually and emotionally. The new discussions are in terms of persuasion techniques. See Frank's *Persuasion and Healing* (1961), Sargant's *Battle for the Mind* (1957), and Levy's *Psychological Interpretation* (1963).

anxiety and more realistic behavior—will result from a patient's acceptance of a psychoanalytic narrative, whether or not that narrative does in fact outline the true causes of the patient's neurotic behavior. Therapeutic efficacy, then, may be entirely unrelated to the truth of such narratives. It will depend solely upon the ability of the analyst to persuade the patient through a variety of subtle, often nonverbal techniques to accept his narrative as being true; if this occurs, then the therapeutic benefits outlined above will be achieved.

Obviously, a great deal more should be said on these points. However, this issue of the therapeutic function of psychoanalytic narratives lies outside the limits of this study and should not be allowed to distract us. One possible implication of these remarks, however, might be that psychoanalytic explanations function *only* therapeutically. In view of this, to ask the question whether a psychoanalytic explanation is true is senseless, because the question ignores what is the real purpose involved. This argument, like the contention that psychoanalysis deals with actions and reasons, is almost exclusively an outsider's, used by benevolent and enlightened laymen to "save" psychoanalysis from what they feel is the impossible task of competing with the physical sciences. It is obvious from the whole tenor of our argument that we must reject such a position. It is true that more than one psychoanalytic narrative may be equally adequate in a particular case, according to the criteria we have outlined. It is also possible that several different narratives may each be therapeutically efficacious. But this is only part of the story, for the close examination of an actual narrative makes clear that something more than either adequacy or therapeutic efficacy is at stake, namely, that some sort of truth claim is being made. Psychoanalysis has been considered from its beginnings to be a research tool and its findings to contribute toward a science of behavior—not simply an awe-inspiring and evocative mythology. Hence we come to the final problem, criteria of accuracy.

2. Criteria of Accuracy

Psychoanalytic explanations like the Lorenz narrative make definite empirical assertions about the individuals with whom they deal. Earlier in this chapter some of the assertions made in the Lorenz case were presented. Insofar as these assertions are confirmed by actual observation, then the explanation can be regarded as at least partially true or accurate. Certain of the assertions concern the actual case material at hand: the patient hates his father, loves Gisela, etc. Others take the form of predictions, including predictions about the patient's past, which are sometimes called retrodictions. Freud makes a number of such assertions, the most striking being his "construction" about a very early sexual misdemeanor for which the patient had been castigated by his father, a prediction described in Chapter 4, Section B,2.[11]

One criterion of accuracy, then, is this criterion of correspondence, that is, the correspondence of empirical assertions with what is actually found to be the case. In this respect psychoanalytic narratives are quite similar to explanations in the physical sciences. It is, of course, no contradiction of our contextual analysis that psychoanalytic narratives are capable of yielding testable predictions. We have argued that the process of explaining is not to be analyzed according to the hypothetical-deductive model and that prediction is not a correlative procedure to explanation. Nevertheless a narrative explanation of behavior can be used to make predictions about the past or future of the individual. Given that we have a narrative about the individual as a whole, we can use parts of that narrative to derive predictions about particular pieces of behavior; and because such predictions are possible, the criterion of correspondence can be applied to determine whether the predictions are falsified or confirmed by actual events in the patient's life history.

It is often objected at this point that although in theory a psychoanalytic narrative makes empirical statements about behavior and is therefore open to refutation, in fact many of its statements lack a precise experiential reference.[12] A good example of such a statement, taken from the Lorenz case, was given earlier in this chapter: Obsessional acts tend to approximate more and more "to infantile sexual acts of a masturbatory character." The problem that might arise with such an assertion is not that "masturbatory character" is a nonobservable, high level concept. We have come to recognize the fact that all sciences employ unobservables in their theoretical formulations. The problem is that these concepts may not be tied by various rules to direct observational language. Note that this criticism is related to, but different from, the one mentioned in the last section. It is not that the concept of "masurbatory character" is ambiguously or inconsistently defined, as, one could argue, is the case with "oedipus com-

---

[11] Other predictions also occur throughout the case record. Several interesting ones are made early in the clinical notes, and we actually see Freud rejecting them later on the basis of further observation (see, for instance, 1909b, p. 276, for an example of a prediction, and also a recantation).

[12] This criticism occurs in several papers of the *Psychoanalysis, Scientific Method, and Philosophy* symposium mentioned earlier (Hook, 1959). Many other statements of this point can be found, in various writings, including Karl Popper's "Philosophy of Science: A Personal Report" (1957) and Michael Martin's "The Scientific Status of Psychoanalytic Clinical Evidence" (1964a).

plex." It is rather that the concept, no matter how clearly defined in theory, may not be tied to direct observation, and hence assertions involving it are not open to empirical confirmation. Of course, it is quite possible, as some critics would claim, that particular psychoanalytic concepts suffer both these faults. It might be, for instance, that the concept "oedipus complex" is so vaguely defined that (1) we cannot be sure whether statements using it are mutually consistent or contradictory, and (2) even if we could be sure that our statement was logically consistent within our theory, we could not test it in clinical or experimental situations.

Perhaps the greatest problem of this kind results from the ambiguous use of the term "unconscious." It seems as if the psychoanalyst who asserts "X unconsciously hates his father" is making a definite empirical assertion about the individual in question. Yet often there appears to be no evidence, clinical or experimental, behavioral or neurological, which the analyst would admit as counting against his statement. But if he will hold to his view no matter what X does or says, and no matter what X might do or might say, then it is hard to see what empirical content there actually is in his assertion. If, for instance, I assert "X (really, unconsciously, beneath it all, . . .) believes the moon is made of green cheese" and hold to this assertion no matter what X says or does, and am prepared to hold to it no matter what else I can discover about him, then I am simply being deceptive and perverse; I am using an assertive grammatical form but not in fact making any empirical assertion at all. It could be argued that much the same thing occurs when a psychoanalyst insists that "Johnny unconsciously hates his father," in spite of all the ostensible, discoverable "evidence" against this assertion. Note that the objection is not that any *particular* piece of evidence is ruled out by the analyst as being irrelevant, but rather that it is never specified, and perhaps can never be specified, what observations *of any sort whatever* would be relevant, would count as evidence.

As we mentioned in Chapter 5, the problems involved in the psychoanalytic use of the concept "unconscious" lie outside the scope of this study, but it would be pointless to deny that the difficulty raised by the criticism outlined above is a very real one in psychoanalysis. Nevertheless, it is not a problem in principle, only in practice. There is no logical reason, however difficult it turns out to be in practice, why the concepts used in psychoanalytic narratives cannot be, first, formulated unambiguously, so that the criterion of self-consistency can be applied. And, second, there is no logical reason why these concepts cannot be used in conjunction with rules which tie them to observable phenomena so that the criterion of correspondence can also be applied.

It has been objected, however, that if one clarifies and reformulates psychoanalytic statements into testable hypotheses, the confirmation of these new statements does not directly confirm the original theory.

> . . . no one, as far as I know, has ever denied that psychoanalysis can be reformulated so that it is testable. . . . The question is, rather, whether psychoanalysis in its *original* form can be tested (Martin, 1964b, p. 87).[13]

This contention is very odd; one feels like protesting that this is precisely *not* the question at all, and that it certainly was not the question for Freud. It is of course true that if one reformulates, to that extent one diverges from the original; but this is a rather trivial point. The important question is whether in reformulating the theory we have, on the one hand, saved the insights and flexibility of the original, and on the other, rendered the theory more rigorous and capable of confirmation. And note that such "reformulation" means essentially nothing more than specifying what observations are to count for or against the theory's assertions. There is a good deal of historical evidence to suggest that Freud considered the facts and not his theory valuable, and that his various hypotheses were virtually always held open to revision or even rejection.[14] Indeed, as we have seen in Chapter 4, anyone who tries to stick to the single "original form" of psychoanalytic theory, even as it was expressed during a certain period, faces an almost impossible task.

Most psychoanalysts would, I think, agree, first, that their psychoanalytic explanations are intended to make truth claims that are potentially confirmable about the particular patients and, second, that their actual statements often turn out to be too loosely formulated to allow such confirmation. A real conflict with analysts does occur, however, over another typical criticism. It is often argued that for various reasons clinical experience within the therapeutic relationship is an unacceptable source of confirming or dis-confirming observations. This relates to the important issue of suggestibility, and as we mentioned in Chapter 4, as early as 1893 Freud had been aware of this criticism and had tried to answer it. Even today the issue is very much alive; most analysts, in direct opposition to their critics, claim that the psychoanalytic situation is *the most important* source of evidence for psychoanalytic theory.[15] We do not intend examining this problem. Our present purpose is simply to outline the various criteria that can

---

[13] Martin's italics.

[14] The history of the "trauma" theory of hysteria is perhaps the best known example of Freud's fundamental shifts of thought, but a number of others could be cited, for instance, his analysis of the cause of anxiety. On the other hand, while modification was possible, total abandonment of early concepts was a great deal harder for Freud, but that is part of another story.

[15] See, for instance, Heinz Hartmann's contribution to the *Psychoanalysis, Scientific Method, and Philosophy* symposium, edited by Professor Hook, which is reprinted in his *Essays on Ego Psychology* (1964).

be used in evaluating psychoanalytic narratives, and we have mentioned several typical criticisms of psychoanalysis only to indicate the different points to which each is directed.

The discussion of criteria of accuracy has so far focused on the fact that psychoanalytic narratives make assertions about the particular individual concerned. Ultimately, the accuracy of the narrative depends upon the accuracy of these assertions, leaving open the question of the sources of evidence, that is, whether clinical observation or something else is to be used. If, as we have argued, the narrative is independent of the general psychoanalytic theory of human behavior in the sense of not being dependent on the truth of it, then the particular individual himself must remain the final touchstone for determining the narrative's accuracy. Nevertheless, the Lorenz case clearly shows that Freud does use both his previous clinical experience and his beliefs about human nature in general as supporting evidence for his explanatory narrative. Both the general theory and past experience have, as we have argued, a directive role; and the truths gained from past experience or general theory together form a second criterion of accuracy for a psychoanalytic narrative. It is essential to see just how such evidence functions.

Freud uses his clinical experience in two different but related ways. First, we pointed out earlier in this chapter the appearance of a considerable number of generalizations about human behavior, some expressed in common language, others in terms of theoretical constructs such as "reaction-formation" and "rationalization." Second, there are some seven different references to five other patients, aspects of whose cases show similarities to the Lorenz case (see 1909b, pp. 189; 192, 197; 227, 243; 247; and 249). In using both sorts of material Freud is trying to show that the Lorenz narrative is consistent with either general truths about human behavior or with what was true in certain other particularly apposite cases. It must be repeated that the truth of the narrative does not depend upon the truth of these generalizations or similarities to other cases. Nevertheless, they are relevant to it in the following way.

Consider first the use of generalizations about human behavior. If in the Lorenz narrative Freud makes assertions about the patient which are contrary to general truths about human behavior, then if these assertions are true at all, they are true because of certain additional relevant features of this particular case. This follows from the nature of the "explanatory commitment," discussed earlier, which is involved in using generalizations for explanatory purposes. If X is generally sufficient to account for Y, then in any case where Y does not occur after X, there must be good reasons for this happening, namely, the presence of other additional relevant conditions. Thus, the more general truths a psychoanalytic narrative contravenes, the more additional peculiarities about its subject it must posit. Clearly, then, although we cannot immediately disprove Freud's narrative by showing certain parts of it to be contrary either to general experience or to his own theory, we raise doubts about it and put the burden of proof onto Freud to demonstrate why, for instance, although a certain mechanism is generally operative in human behavior, it was nevertheless absent in this particular case.

Alternatively, Freud may claim that certain observations made concerning Lorenz are in fact generally true. If, however, our own evidence suggests that such empirical generalizations do not hold up, then once again the burden falls back upon Freud to demonstrate that although not generally true, a particular explanation was indeed true in this particular case. The following generalizations are good examples where such an attack on the Lorenz narrative might begin:

> Indeed, all obsessional neurotics behave as though they shared this conviction [that they have the power to make their thoughts and wishes come true] (1909b, p. 233).

> [Obsessional patients'] thoughts are unceasingly occupied with other people's length of life and possibility of death . . . (1909b, p. 236).

> The histories of obsessional patients almost invariably reveal an early development and premature repression of the sexual instinct of looking and knowing . . . (1909b, p. 245).

It is just not true to say that psychoanalytic explanations offer no confirmable generalizations. These statements, and others referred to earlier, are straightforward empirical assertions about certain characteristics of obsessional neurotics. *Do* obsessional patients show this peculiar belief in the potency of their wishes? *Do* they show this interest in longevity and death? *Are* obsessional neurotics almost invariably sexually precocious as children? These assertions are obviously meant as unambiguous clinical observations. We may not categorically disprove Freud's narrative in the Lorenz case by showing these generalizations to be false, but we would certainly raise some justifiable doubts about it, and suggest that Freud is obliged to explain why the patient did show these characteristics, even though they are not generally true of obsessional patients.

The same arguments hold for the use of comparisons with other patients. Insofar as Lorenz is similar to some earlier patient, then Freud need only look for, be directed toward, those factors which explained that earlier case. If, however, Freud explains Lorenz's behavior in a different way from that of an apparently similar patient, then it is up to him to demonstrate the additional relevant features which distinguished Lorenz from that other patient. Thus, consistency with general truths of human nature and with truths about other similar individuals, while not a sufficient feature of a true narrative, is certainly one important criterion of accuracy.

The criteria of adequacy and accuracy discussed above are not the only ones that might be listed, nor have we formulated them as carefully as should be. But our purpose in this last section has been mainly programmatic. Our point has been to emphasize that the analysis of psychoanalytic explanations which we have tried to develop would definitely allow for experiential (that is, experimental and clinical) testing and evaluation. However, as we stated in Chapter 1, a full discussion of the very important methodological issues concerned with the actual testing of psychoanalytic hypotheses lies outside the scope of this study. By raising the various standard criticisms of psychoanalysis we have tried simply to indicate some of those methodological issues and to suggest how they might be dealt with.

Chapter 8/**POINTINGS**

This study has had but one main purpose, the examination of psycho-analytic explanations as they actually occur within individual case histories. One of the most important results has been the refutation of a variety of common errors, errors which could all be grouped under the rubric of the "monolithic fallacy." Defenders of psychoanalysis are guilty of it when they claim too quickly that the whole discipline is completely scientific, or testable, or, indeed, anything else. Philosophical critics likewise commit these errors when they apply any unitary analysis or model to all psycho-analytic statements, as do those who dismiss psychoanalysis in its entirety as a cult or a prescientific mythology. The fact is, to claim that psycho-analysis *as a whole* is anything at all is misleading, for it is much too complex a field. We have seen that psychoanalytic statements include high level theoretical principles, rule-of-thumb generalizations, empirical hypoth-eses, metaphorical utterances, and even utterances which may function only therapeutically to bring about changes in a patient's behavior. As varied as the types of statements employed, so, too, are the practical aims. In facing the individual case the analyst typically pursues several different goals: the therapeutic one of altered behavior, the diagnostic one of under-standing the etiology of the illness, and the scientific one of developing or testing some general theory of behavior. The fact that most analysts attempt these several tasks at once should not blind one to the realization that they remain logically independent, and that success in therapy, say, is independent of success in formulating a general theory of behavior, or even of success in understanding the particular patient.

If the first conclusion is that psychoanalytic explanations are extremely complex and difficult to analyze, the second conclusion is that they never-theless represent a type of scientific explanation. In Chapter 3 we argued the general point that there were no logical reasons why scientific explana-tions of human behavior should be impossible. In Chapter 4 we looked at one particular type of explanation that has been suggested, namely, psycho-analytic explanations, and we examined an actual case record in detail. In Chapter 5 the negative point was asserted that psychoanalytic explanations were not of a unique variety, existing in a special domain entirely separate from the causal language of the physical sciences. Finally, in the last two chapters the positive aspect of the argument has been stressed, that psychoanalytic explanations, properly understood, are in many essential respects scientific and amenable to rational, systematic evaluation.

Certainly, a number of interesting and important issues have not been explored; they occur in this study only as pointings, indications of further areas into which this analysis should be extended. In the last chapter we touched upon the problems concerning the evidential support for psychoanalytic theory, but our study would be of only academic interest if there were not at least some factual basis for this discipline. Inextricably connected to this issue of evidence is the second problem of "suggestibility," the possibility that psychoanalytic observations are systematically distorted by the effect of the theoretical commitments of the analyst, or worse, that these assumptions make the observations self-confirming. This problem is, of course, the more fundamental, since before one can examine the evidence one must be clear as to what sorts of evidence would be acceptable, what sorts systematically biased, and the extent to which that bias can be dealt with.

Another issue we have only broached concerns psychotherapy. We have considered the logic of the psychoanalytic explanation, but an entirely separate problem is its role in the therapeutic process. Indeed, even to formulate this issue and to accept the basic dichotomy which it implies is another vitally important result of our study. Just as the logic of psychoanalytic explanations, considered as the basic element in a science of human behavior, is considered eminently worthy of detailed investigation so, too, is the entirely different question of the role of psychoanalytic explanations in the therapeutic process. What precisely is the function of the psychoanalytic narrative or explanation in the actual treatment of the patient? The traditional view, common even today among laymen, is that the psychoanalyst understands the true causes of the patient's illness and gradually brings him to an intellectual and emotional acceptance of those causes. Modern studies have shown that this view is undoubtedly too simple, and that therapeutic efficacy may be completely independent of the truth of the proposed explanation. As we implied in the previous chapter, it is possible that an analysis in terms of a narrative could be extended to shed some light on this puzzling discovery.

We have, therefore, ignored two important aspects of the Lorenz case and, thereby, two further aspects of psychoanalysis: whether or not Freud's explanation is in fact true, and the problem of what is the relationship between his explanation and the therapeutic success that occurred. Still other issues, however, remain to be faced. It would be valuable, for instance, to compare Freud's account of Paul Lorenz with what some other analysts might have said about the same or similar cases. How would his explanation compare with that of a Jungian or a behaviorist? Even granting that our analysis of this case is fairly accurate, would it be at all applicable to those explanations from other theoretical schools? Indeed, it is possible that Freud's explanation in the Lorenz case is quite different from what he himself might have given at a later period in his development. Insofar as the Lorenz case is therefore unusual and unrepresentative, the utility of our analysis is diminished.

Finally, there is the problem of how far our analysis could be extended beyond psychoanalysis. For instance, since the concept of a narrative has been so essential a feature of the argument, one would want to know how it fits explanations in other disciplines, from history to the natural sciences. One interesting study would be to compare a historian's extended explanation of some event or great personage to Freud's explanation about Paul Lorenz.

There are, then, important problems which we have only touched upon, and others which have been specifically avoided. Yet it is encouraging that all these issues seem to raise straightforward questions of science or logic which are capable of being effectively studied. It is true that psychoanalysis has difficulties peculiar to itself alone, and that in certain respects it differs from other disciplines. Some of these differences have been pointed out in the course of our argument. Certainly, it would be as parochial to insist that psychoanalysis must use the sorts of evidence appropriate to physics as to insist that it use models of explanation appropriate to that discipline. But it is essential that psychoanalysis be able to specify *some* evidence to which it must hold its theories accountable. It is essential that psychoanalysis specify *some* model, *some* canon of procedure by which its explanations can be evaluated and rationally debated—if there is to remain any scientific claim at all. For the essence of science is not so much the existence of a body of facts as the existence of a method, a procedure by which "facts" can be systematically ascertained and progressively revised. Science depends upon communication and, ultimately, upon an orderly process of argument. For there to be any argumentative communication in a scientific sense, there must be rules for argument. We must be able to agree on what makes for a good argument and what is to count as a good explanation. If we cannot do this, we must forsake any claim to a scientific status and rest content in the solitude of our incontestable, because incommunicable, musings. Our assumption implicit throughout, however, is that psychoanalysis can indeed stand on its own as a scientific discipline, and it can at least be on speaking terms with the natural sciences. This study has been an attempt to facilitate that dialogue.

Appendix/HISTORICAL AND TEXTUAL PROBLEMS IN THE LORENZ CASE

When one examines Freud's published case histories as a group, a number of intriguing historical problems arise, for they form a peculiar, not to say extraordinary, assortment. There are in all six extended accounts of individual patients: Dora (1905a), Little Hans (1909a), Lorenz (1909b), Schreber (1911), Wolf Man (1914), and the female homosexual (1919a). The small number is itself surprising, and also the fact that they all date from the early years when Freud's theories were still undergoing profound change. The fact that these particular cases should have been chosen under any circumstances is even more interesting, since each has certain basic shortcomings, especially if one considers that Freud intended them, at least in part, to demonstrate the utility of psychoanalysis both as a therapeutic technique and as an instrument for studying behavior. The two cases of female patients are in fact only fragments of analyses, since both were terminated after only a very short time. In neither are we given a complete history or the chance to watch development and change under the impact of a continuing therapeutic process. With the Little Hans and Schreber cases the problem is different; these are not really examples of direct analysis at all, since Freud had no real firsthand contact with either patient. With Little Hans, Freud used the patient's father (himself a follower of Freud) as an intermediary, who would report his son's behavior to Freud and then go back to the child with the interpretations offered. Indeed, Freud saw the boy only once during the period of analysis, and then only for a short time. The Schreber case is not in any sense the record of an analysis at all, and therefore not a case history, but rather a historical reconstruction based entirely upon the individual's own published memoirs of his mental illness. The situation with the Wolf Man case is rather the opposite; there is not the problem of a fragmentary analysis, or of little contact with the patient, but of a seemingly interminable analysis stretching over many years and under different analysts. After studying this very long history, only the earlier portion of which Freud reports, there is, I think, good reason to doubt whether Freud ever satisfactorily understood his patient. This is said with all due respect for the patient's own opinions on this matter, which are recorded in his *own* published memoirs (Wolf Man, 1958).

Of all six cases only the Lorenz record is a complete analysis. It is in this respect unique; moreover, this analysis was followed by substantial and apparently permanent behavioral improvement, which might suggest, although it does not imply, that Freud had a fairly good understanding of the psychodynamics of this patient. Indeed, one receives this impression just from reading the case. This being so, it is all the more unfortunate that the editors of the Standard Edition chose not to publish all the remaining clinical notes that were found among Freud's papers after his death. It must be emphasized that these notes are absolutely unique; we have no other remaining record of the day-to-day progress of any of Freud's analyses, let alone of an analysis occurring during this important formative period. If only for this reason these notes ought to have been published in full. In the case of other of Freud's writings the editors have made an admirable decision to make the Standard Edition a sort of variorum edition, carefully noting all textual revisions, etc.; it seems unfortunate that this procedure was not followed in regard to the Lorenz notes.

The criticism, however, is not simply a pedantic quibble. There is a much more important reason than editorial completeness for publishing these notes; for they could provide essential source material to aid in the solution of one of the most difficult methodological issues to have arisen concerning psychoanalysis—the so-called problem of suggestion, the problem of evaluating the extent to which theoretical presuppositions affect the material elicited from the patient and the progress of the analysis itself. A related issue is the question of differential memory and selectivity and how these factors can affect reconstructions of cases. Some general points must be made concerning these problems.

It might be expected that the potential for an analyst's influence would be greatest in the very first sessions, the meetings with the patient in which the general themes and areas for eventual exploration are mapped out. Interestingly, it is precisely these notes, for the first seven sessions of Lorenz's analysis, which are omitted by the editors. It is illuminating to look at their reasons for this omission:

> Approximately the first third of the original record was reproduced by Freud almost *verbatim* in the published version. This covers the preliminary interview on October 1st, 1907, and the first seven sessions—that is, up to and including October 9th (to the end of Chapter I (D), p. 186). The alterations made by Freud were almost exclusively verbal or stylistic. In the published version Freud added a certain amount of commentary, but the principal change was that he made the story of the manoeuvres less confused than it

was as it emerged in the day-to-day record. On the whole, the differences between the two versions do not seem to be of sufficient importance to justify the publication of this first part of the record. It may be of interest, however, to give the original version of Freud's first interview with the patient, which will afford some idea of the nature of the changes, though they are greater here than elsewhere in the first sessions (1909b, p. 284).

There follows (pp. 254–255) the full text of Freud's notes concerning the preliminary interview; we can therefore take the editors' advice and compare this material with the published account (pp. 158–159) to see whether the changes are in fact "almost exclusively verbal or stylistic." Certainly, there are a number of changes that do fall into this category. There are, however, two other sorts of variations which must be considered. First, there are two additions—material appearing in the published record which does not occur in the original notes. These are (1) Freud's statement that "his potency was normal" (p. 158), and (2) Freud's whole reference to the fact that the reason the patient stressed his sexual life was that he had recently come across one of Freud's books, *The Psychopathology of Everyday Life* (1901). There are two obvious possible explanations for these additions. The first is that in May or June of 1909, when he was writing up the case for publication, Freud simply remembered some further remarks of the patient from that preliminary interview of October, 1907. I think, however, such a feat of memory is unlikely, and a more probable explanation is that Freud was here transposing, purposely or accidentally, material that emerged later on in the analysis into his reconstruction of that first interview. The patient's statement that his potency is very good does in fact occur in the notes for December 10, 1907 (1909b, p. 295), and the statement that he had seen one of Freud's books apparently occurred in the unpublished notes of the third session (1909b, p. 173).

The second sort of important variation that occurs between the notes for the preliminary interview and the published account of that interview are the omissions, of which there are three:

1. "His ideas only affected his professional work when it was concerned with criminal law."
2. "He also suffered from an impulse to do some injury to the lady whom he admired. This impulse was usually silent in her presence, but came to the fore when she was not there. Being away from her, however—she lives in Vienna—had always done him good."
3. "After I told him my terms, he said he must consult his mother."

These three quotations occur in the original notes (1909b, p. 255) but not in Freud's published account of this interview (1909b, pp. 158–159).

What conclusions can be drawn from this listing of the various addi-

tions and omissions? Perhaps none at all, or at least none of any consequence. Nevertheless, the additions demonstrate that transpositions of
material have almost certainly occurred, and this itself is an important discovery, for it has been held that one indication of an interpretation's truth
has been its "fruitfulness," its power to "engender" new memories or associations that have previously remained unconscious. Transposing of material, however, can bring together ideas that were not originally associated,
thereby giving an outside reader a distorted indication of fruitfulness. A
very good example occurs in the Lorenz case, concerning Freud's intriguing
construction which led to the uncovering of the "beating incident."

> Starting from these [previously described] indications and from other data
> of a similar kind, I ventured to put forward a construction to the effect
> that when he was a child of under six he had been guilty of some sexual
> misdemeanour connected with masturbation and had been soundly castigated
> for it by his father. . . . To my great astonishment the patient then in-
> formed me that his mother had repeatedly described to him an occurrence
> of this kind which dated from his earliest childhood and had evidently
> escaped being forgotten by her on account of its remarkable consequences.
> He himself, however, had no recollection of it whatever. The tale was as
> follows . . . (1909b, p. 205).

Here would seem to be a classic example of "fruitfulness," of an interpretation aiding the immediate recall of important new material. However, when
we consult the relevant notes (1909b, pp. 263–265) we find that the
patient said simply that Freud's construction brought a number of ideas
into his mind. It is only at the next session, two days later, that the patient
describes this incident as being one of those new ideas. We cannot be
certain whether this memory was immediately brought to mind by Freud's
construction, or only after two days of careful recollection. In the published
record, however, these possibilities are ignored, since the recollection of the
beating incident has been transposed, and the two-day gap has not been
mentioned. We need not speculate on the possible reasons for this trans-
position, but simply note that its occurrence makes the assessment of
"fruitfulness" all the more difficult, for just how much of a gap are we
prepared to allow between the interpretation or construction and the
emergence of new material? Unless we have the original notes, we cannot
begin to evaluate such problems.

Again, let us consider the difficulties raised by Freud's omissions. Each
of them, I think, is quite important. The first immediately suggests that the
patient's obsessive thoughts are connected with a sense of his own guilt;
hence, the fact that they affect only his work with criminal law. The second
omission, about the impulse to do his lady some injury, would have immediately conveyed to us the deep sense of ambivalence that affected this

relationship. Perhaps these statements were omitted because Freud knew they would be developed in detail as the case unfolded, in which case it is only the outside reader who is forced to remain in the dark for the moment. With the third omission there is another, more interesting possibility. One of the modern criticisms of the Lorenz case is the virtual absence of any exploration of the patient's relationship to his mother. The easiest answer to this charge is simply to assert that Freud dealt only with the material that did in fact emerge, and that the patient himself did not discuss this relationship. But now we can see that this answer will not do, for in the very first session we find this 29-year-old lawyer confessing that he must ask his mother whether to begin a course of medical treatment. And this peculiar piece of behavior is *not* explained, but made *more incongruous* when we learn that this consultation with his mother is necessitated by the fact that she controlled all the patient's finances. We can imagine another analyst, particularly some modern one, beginning at such a point to construct an alternative analysis:

A: Why must you consult your mother?

L: You see, she controls all my money. I must ask her to see whether she will allow me to pay your fees.

A: Your mother gives you an allowance, then?

L: Yes. I have an inheritance from my father, but I let my mother manage it. She always ran our family's budget, even when my father was alive.

A: You depend on your mother to handle your money, then?

L: Yes, she's very good, too. She prevents me from spending it on a lot of foolish things I might be tempted to buy if I had all that money myself. Of course, anything I really need, she lets me have— she's very good to me that way.

A: Your mother is very kind to you?

L: Oh yes. We're very close, especially since father died, but even before I think I was always the favorite. Yes, she certainly knows what's best for me. . . .

And so on, and so on. It is evident, I think, that a very different analysis might quickly emerge if the analyst's interests were different. Freud's own analysis of Lorenz proceeded on different lines with the main emphasis falling on the relationship of the patient with his father. This of course fits in with what we know of Freud's theoretical development at this time, namely, his concentration on the oedipal complex and its resolution. When some material about other relationships does emerge, it tends to be disregarded, omitted, even when Freud has the material in front of him, as he must have done when he wrote up the case. We could hardly find a better example of differential recollection and emphasis, presumably dependent upon the analyst's theoretical presuppositions and interests.

All of the above discussion must strike the reader as nit-picking on a monumental scale, and so, perhaps, it is; for we should need much better evidence than this to reach any firm conclusions. What we can say, however, is that the editors' contention that the alterations "were almost exclusively verbal or stylistic" is not supported by the very evidence that they themselves present. Indeed, we find both important additions and omissions. The problem is not simply one of textual accuracy; it goes much deeper. We have tried to suggest that these alterations reflect basic methodological difficulties of just the sort that are so often ignored by psychoanalysts, and it is disappointing to find these same blind spots recurring even in the editors of the Standard Edition. It is quite naive for editors of such a historic edition to state that "On the whole, the differences between the two versions do not seem to be of sufficient importance to justify the publication of this first part of the record." Everything Freud wrote is important to students of psychoanalysis, and the unique opportunity to study day-to-day clinical notes would be invaluable. Methodological studies must proceed through such material precisely in this dry and boring manner, by way of logical quibbling over minutiae; and although the method is tedious the results may be worthwhile. It is to be hoped that at some future time this and any other material, preserved but unpublished, will be made public. One can be confident that the corpus of Freud's work is of such great and lasting value that it will survive and perhaps even benefit from a great deal more logical nit-picking than has so far been done.

BIBLIOGRAPHY

This bibliography includes only those books and articles which have been actually quoted, or which have been generally influential on various issues. In the listing of Freud's writings, the dates given are those when the work was substantially written, not when published. The letters in parentheses, used where several papers are cited for the same year, are the author's, not those of the Standard Edition.

Adler, A. *Individual psychology.* (1929 edition). Paterson, N. J.: Littlefield, Adams, 1959.

Adler, G. *The living symbol.* London: Routledge & Kegan Paul, 1961.

Allport, G. W. *Personality.* London: Constable, 1937.

Anscombe, G. E. M. *Intention.* Oxford: Blackwell, 1957.

Ayer, A. J. *Man as a subject for science.* London: Athlone Press, 1964.

Benjamin, J. D. Methodological considerations in the validation and elaboration of psychoanalytical personality theory. *American Journal of Orthopsychiatry,* 1950, **20,** 139–156.

Benjamin, J. D. Prediction and psychopathological theory. In L. Jessner & E. Pavenstedt (Eds.), *Dynamic psychopathology in childhood.* New York: Grune & Stratton, 1959. Pp. 6–77.

Berg, C. *Deep analysis.* London: Allen & Unwin, 1947.

Braithwaite, R. B. *Scientific explanation.* New York: Harper, 1953.

Bridgman, P. *The logic of modern physics.* New York: Macmillan, 1927.

Brown, J. A. C. *Freud and the post-Freudians.* London: Penguin Books, 1961.

Brown, R. *Explanation in social science.* London: Routledge & Kegan Paul, 1963.

Cheshire, N. On the rationale of psychodynamic argumentation. *British Journal of Medical Psychology,* 1964, **37,** 217–230.

Colby, K. (1958). Causal correlations in clinical interpretation. Reprinted in L. Paul (Ed.), *Psychoanalytic clinical interpretation.* Glencoe, Ill.: Free Press, 1963. Pp. 189–199.

Davidson, D. Actions, reasons and causes. *Journal of Philosophy,* 1963, **60,** 685–700.

Davis, P. E. 'Action' and 'cause of action.' *Mind,* 1962, **71,** No. 281, 93–95.

Dicks, H. V. *Clinical studies in psychopathology.* London: Arnold, 1947.

Dodwell, P. C. Causes of behaviour and explanation in psychology. *Mind,* 1960, **69,** No. 173, 1–13.

Dray, W. *Laws and explanation in history.* London and New York: Oxford University Press, 1957.

Dyson, F. W., Eddington, A. S., & Davidson, C. A determination of the deflection of light by the sun's gravitational field. *Philosophical Transactions of the Royal Society of London,* 1920, **A220,** 291–333.

Eddington, A. S. *Report on the relativity theory of gravitation*. (2nd ed.) London: Physical Society of London, 1920.

Eddington, A. S. *The nature of the physical world*. London and New York: Cambridge University Press, 1928.

Eysenck, H. J. *Uses and abuses of psychology*. London: Penguin Books, 1953.

Farrell, B. A. Can psychoanalysis be refuted? *Inquiry*, 1961, **1**, 16–36. (a)

Farrell, B. A. On the character of psychodynamic discourse. *British Journal of Medical Psychology*, 1961, **34**, No. 7, 7–13. (b)

Farrell, B. A. The criteria for a psycho-analytic interpretation. *Proceedings of the Aristotelian Society*, 1962, Suppl. Vol. 36, pp. 77–100.

Farrell, B. A. Scientific approaches to psychology. In A. Crombie (Ed.), *Scientific change*. London: Heineman, 1963. Pp. 562–576. (a)

Farrell, B. A. Introduction to *Freud's Leonardo*. London: Penguin, 1963. (b)

Federn, P. Prof. Freud: The beginning of a case history. Reprinted in *Yearbook of Psychoanalysis*, 1948, **4**, 14–20.

Fenichel, O. *The psychoanalytic theory of neurosis*. London: Routledge & Kegan Paul, 1945.

Fine, R. *Freud. A critical re-evaluation of his theories*. London: Allen & Unwin, 1963.

Flew, A. (1949). Psycho-analytic explanation. Reprinted in M. Macdonald (Ed.), *Philosophy and analysis*. Oxford: Blackwell, 1954. Pp. 139–147.

Flew, A. Motives and the unconscious. In H. Feigl & M. Scriven (Eds.), *Minnesota studies in the philosophy of science*. Vol. I. Minneapolis: University of Minnesota Press, 1956. Pp. 155–173.

Flugel, J. C. *A hundred years of psychology*. London: University Paperbacks, 1964.

Ford, D. H., & Urban, H. B. *Systems of psychotherapy*. New York: Wiley, 1963.

Frank, J. *Persuasion and healing*. Baltimore: Johns Hopkins Press, 1961.

Freud, A. *The ego and the mechanisms of defence*. London: Hogarth Press, 1937.

Freud, S. *The Standard Edition of the Complete Psychological Works*, Vols. 1–23. London: Hogarth Press and Institute of Psychoanalysis, 1955–1964. (*Standard Edition* abbreviated as *S.E.* in listings below.)

Freud, S. *Studies on hysteria*, 1893, *S.E.* **2**.

Freud, S. The neuro-psychoses of defence. 1894, *S.E.* **3**, 45–61. (a)

Freud, S. Obsessions and phobias. 1894, *S.E.* **3**, 74–82. (b)

Freud, S. A reply to criticisms of my paper on anxiety neurosis. 1895, *S.E.* **3**, 123–139.

Freud, S. Heredity and the aetiology of the neuroses. 1896, *S.E.* **3**, 143–156. (a)

Freud, S. Further remarks on the neuro-psychoses of defence. 1896, *S.E.* **3**, 162–185. (b)

Freud, S. The aetiology of hysteria. 1896, *S.E.* **3**, 191–221. (c)

Freud, S. *The interpretation of dreams*. 1899, *S.E.* **4–5**.

Freud, S. *The psychopathology of everyday life*. 1901, *S.E.* **6**.

Freud, S. Fragment of an analysis of a case of hysteria. 1905, *S.E.* **7**, 7–122. (a)

Freud, S. *Three essays on the theory of sexuality*. 1905, *S.E.* **7**, 130–243. (b)

Freud, S. My views on the part played by sexuality in the aetiology of the neuroses. 1905, *S.E.* **7**, 271–279. (c)

Freud, S. *Jokes and their relation to the unconscious*. 1905, *S.E.* **8**. (d)

Freud, S. Obsessive actions and religious practices. 1907, *S.E.* **9**, 117–127.

Freud, S. Hysterical phantasies and their relation to bisexuality. 1908, *S.E.* **9**, 159–166. (a)

Freud, S. Character and anal erotism. 1908, *S.E.* 9, 169–175. (b)

Freud, S. 'Civilized' sexual morality and modern nervous illness. 1908, *S.E.* 9, 181–204. (c)

Freud, S. Analysis of a phobia in a five-year-old boy. 1909, *S.E.* 10, 5–149. (a)

Freud, S. Notes upon a case of obsessional neurosis. 1909, *S.E.* 10, 155–318. (b)

Freud, S. *Five lectures on psychoanalysis.* 1909, *S.E.* 11, 9–55. (c)

Freud, S. Leonardo da Vinci and a memory of his childhood. 1910, *S.E.* 11, 63–137. (a)

Freud, S. A special type of choice of object made by men. 1910, *S.E.* 11, 165–175. (b)

Freud, S. The psycho-analytic view of psychogenic disturbance of vision. 1910, *S.E.* 11, 211–218. (c)

Freud, S. Psycho-analytic notes on an autobiographical account of a case of paranoia. 1911, *S.E.* 12, 12–82.

Freud, S. Recommendations to physicians practising psychoanalysis. 1912, *S.E.* 12, 111–120.

Freud, S. The disposition to obsessional neurosis. 1913, *S.E.* 12, 317–326.

Freud, S. From the history of an infantile neurosis. 1914, *S.E.* 17, 7–122.

Freud, S. Instincts and their vicissitudes. 1915, *S.E.* 14, 117–140. (a)

Freud, S. Repression. 1915, *S.E.* 14, 146–158. (b)

Freud, S. The unconscious. 1915, *S.E.* 14, 166–215. (c)

Freud, S. 'A Child is being beaten': A contribution to the study of the origin of sexual perversions. 1919, *S.E.* 17, 179–204. (a)

Freud, S. The psychogenesis of a case of homosexuality in a woman. 1919, *S.E.* 18, 147–172. (b)

Freud, S. Psycho-analysis. 1922, *S.E.* 18, 235–254.

Freud, S. *Inhibitions, symptoms and anxiety.* 1925, *S.E.* 20, 87–172.

Freud, S. Constructions in analysis. 1937, *S.E.* 23, 257–269.

Freud, S., M. Bonaparte, A. Freud, and E. Kris (Eds.), *The origins of psychoanalysis* (Fliess correspondence) London: Imago, 1954.

Gallie, W. B. *Philosophy and the historical understanding.* London: Chatto & Windus, 1964.

Gardiner, P. *The nature of historical explanation.* London and New York: Oxford University Press, 1952.

Gibson, Q. *The logic of social enquiry.* London: Routledge & Kegan Paul, 1960.

Gill, M. The present state of psychoanalytic theory. *Journal of Abnormal and Social Psychology,* 1959, 58, 1–8.

Gill, M., & Brenman, M. Problems in clinical research. *American Journal of Orthopsychiatry,* 1947, 17,196–230.

Guntrip, H. *Personality structure and human interaction.* London: Hogarth Press, 1961.

Hall, C. S., & Lindzey, G. *Theories of personality.* New York: Wiley, 1957.

Hamlyn, D. Contribution to Causality and human behaviour. *Proceedings of the Aristotelian Society,* 1964, Suppl. Vol. 38, pp. 125–142.

Hanson, N. R. *Patterns of discovery.* London and New York: Cambridge University Press, 1958.

Hanson, N. R. On the symmetry between explanation and prediction. *Philosophical Review,* 1959, 68, No. 3.

Hardy, J. D., Wolff, H. G., & Goodell, H. *Pain sensations and reactions.* Baltimore: Williams & Wilkins, 1952.

Harre, R. Concepts and criteria. *Mind,* 1964, **73**, No. 291, 353–363.

Hart, H. L. A., & Honoré, A. M. *Causation in the law.* London and New York: Oxford University Press, 1959.

Hartmann, H. *Essays on ego psychology.* London: Hogarth Press, 1964.

Hempel, C. Deductive-nomological vs. statistical explanation. In H. Feigl & G. Maxwell (Eds.), *Minnesota studies in the philosophy of science.* Vol. III. Minneapolis: University of Minnesota Press, 1962. Pp. 98–169.

Hempel, C. *Aspects of scientific explanation.* Glencoe, Ill.: Free Press, 1965.

Hempel, C., & Oppenheim, P. The logic of explanation. Reprinted in H. Feigl and M. Brodbeck (Eds.), *Readings in the philosophy of science.* New York: Appleton, 1953. Pp. 319–352.

Hook, S. (Ed.) *Psychoanalysis, scientific method, and philosophy.* New York: N. Y. U. Press, 1959.

Horney, K. *New ways in psychoanalysis.* London: Routledge & Kegan Paul, 1939.

Hospers, J. (1946). What is explanation? Reprinted in A. Flew (Ed.), *Essays in Conceptual Analysis.* New York: Macmillan, 1960. Pp. 94–119.

Hospers, J. *An introduction to philosophical analysis.* Englewood Cliffs, N. J.: Prentice-Hall, 1953.

Hutten, E. H. On explanation in psychology and physics. *British Journal for the Philosophy of Science,* 1956, **7**, No. 25, 73–85.

Jones, E. Rationalisation in everyday life. *Journal of Abnormal Psychology,* 1908, **3**, 161–169. Reprinted in *Papers on psychoanalysis.* (1st ed.) London: Baillière, 1913.

Jones, E. (1912). Analytic study of a case of obsessional neurosis. Reprinted in *Papers on psychoanalysis.* (3rd ed.) London: Baillière, 1923.

Jones, E. (1913). Hate and anal erotism in the obsessional neurosis. Reprinted in *Papers on psychoanalysis.* (3rd ed.) London: Baillière, 1923.

Jones, E. *The life and work of Sigmund Freud.* Vol. I. New York: Basic Books, 1953.

Jones, E. *The life and work of Sigmund Freud.* Vol. II. New York: Basic Books, 1955.

Jones, E. *The life and work of Sigmund Freud. Vol. III.* New York: Basic Books, 1957.

Kolenda, K. Unconscious motives and human action. *Inquiry,* 1964, **7**, No. 1, 1–12.

Kubie, L. S. Problems and techniques of psychoanalytic validation and progress. In E. Pumpian-Mindlin (Ed.), *Psychoanalysis as science.* New York: Basic Books, 1952. Pp. 46–124.

Levy, L. *Psychological interpretation.* New York: Holt, 1963.

Mabbott, J. Freewill and punishment. In H. D. Lewis (Ed.), *Contemporary British philosophy.* 3rd Series. London: Allen & Unwin, 1956. Pp. 287–309.

MacIntyre, A. C. *The unconscious.* London: Routledge & Kegan Paul, 1958

MacIntyre, A. C. A mistake about causality in social science. In P. Laslett and W. Runciman (Eds.), *Philosophy, politics and society.* (Second Series) Oxford: Blackwell, 1962. Pp. 48–70.

Madison, P. *Freud's concept of repression and defense.* Minneapolis: University of Minnesota, 1961.

Mannison, D. My motive and its reasons. *Mind,* 1964, **73**, No. 291, 423–429.

Martin, M. The scientific status of psychoanalytic clinical evidence. *Inquiry,* 1964, **7**, No. 1, 13–36. (a)

Martin, M. Mr. Farrell and the refutability of psychoanalysis. *Inquiry,* 1964, **7**, No. 1, 80–98. (b)

McLaughlin, F. Some considerations for the further development of psychoanalysis. *International Journal of Psychoanalysis,* 1963, 44, 454–460.

Melden, A. I. *Free action.* London: Routledge & Kegan Paul, 1961.

Mischel, T. Concerning rational behaviour and psycho-analytic explanation. *Mind,* 1965, 74, No. 293, 71–78.

Moore, G. E. (1955). Wittgenstein's lectures in 1930–33. Reprinted in *Philosophical papers.* London: Allen & Unwin, 1959.

Munroe, R. L. *Schools of psychoanalytic thought.* New York: Holt, 1955.

Nordenskiöld, E. *The history of biology.* London: Kegan Paul, 1929. (Transl. from Swedish, 3 Vols. in original, 1920–1924.)

Nunberg, H., & Federn, E. (Eds.) *Minutes of the Vienna psychoanalytic society.* Vol. I. New York: International Universities Press, 1962.

Paul, L. (1963). The logic of psychoanalytic interpretation. In L. Paul (Ed.), *Psychoanalytic clinical interpretation.* Glencoe, Ill.: Free Press, 1963. Pp. 249–272.

Peters, R. S. (1950). Cause, cure and motive. Reprinted in M. Macdonald (Ed.), *Philosophy and analysis.* Oxford: Blackwell, 1954. Pp. 148–154.

Peters, R. S. *The concept of motivation.* London: Routledge & Kegan Paul, 1958.

Pickford, R. W. *The analysis of an obsessional.* London: Hogarth Press, 1954.

Popper, K. R. *The poverty of historicism.* London: Routledge & Kegan Paul, 1957. (a)

Popper, K. R. Philosophy of science: A personal report. In C. Mace (Ed.), *British philosophy in the mid-century.* London: Allen & Unwin, 1957. Pp. 155–191. (b)

Pumpian-Mindlin, E. (Ed.) *Psychoanalysis as science.* New York: Basic Books, 1952.

Putnam, H. The analytic and the synthetic. In H. Feigl and G. Maxwell (Eds.), *Minnesota studies in the philosophy of science.* Vol. III. Minneapolis: University of Minnesota Press, 1962. Pp. 358–397.

Quine, W. V. Two dogmas of empiricism. Reprinted in *From a logical point of view.* Cambridge, Mass.: Harvard University Press, 1961. Pp. 20–46.

Rapaport, D. Principles underlying projective techniques. *Character and Personality,* 1942, Vol. 2, No. 2, 213–219.

Rapaport, D. The structure of psychoanalytic theory. *Psychological Issues.* 1960. Vol. II, No. 2, 1–158.

Rogers, C. R. *Counseling and psychotherapy.* Boston: Houghton, 1942.

Rogers, C. R. *Client-centered therapy.* Boston: Houghton, 1951.

Ryle, G. *The concept of mind.* New York: Barnes & Noble, 1949.

Sargant, W. *Battle for the mind.* London: Pan Books, 1957.

Scriven, M. A possible distinction between traditional scientific disciplines and the study of human behavior. In H. Feigl and M. Scriven (Eds.), *Minnesota studies in the philosophy of science.* Vol. I. Pp. 330–339.

Scriven, M. Definitions, explanations and theories. In H. Feigl, M. Scriven, and G. V. Maxwell (Eds.), *Minnesota studies in the philosophy of science.* Vol. II. 1958. Pp. 99–195.

Scriven, M. Explanations, predictions and laws. In H. Feigl and G. Maxwell (Eds.), *Minnesota studies in the philosophy of science.* Vol. III. Minneapolis: University of Minnesota Press, 1962. Pp. 170–230.

Scriven, M. The frontiers of psychology: Psychoanalysis and parapsychology. In R. Colodny (Ed.), *Frontiers of science and philosophy.* London: Allen & Unwin, 1964. Pp. 79–129.

Sherwood, M. Bion's *Experiences in groups:* A critical evaluation. *Human Relations,* 1964, 17, No. 2, 113–130.

Smart, J. Contribution to 'Causality and human behaviour.' *Proceedings of the Aristotelian Society,* 1964, Suppl. Vol. 38, pp. 143–148.

Smith, F. V. *Explanation of human behaviour.* London: Constable, 1951.

Stein, M. I. (Ed.) *Contemporary psycho-therapies.* Glencoe, Ill.: Free Press, 1961.

Stevens, S. S. Mathematics, measurements and psychophysics. In S. S. Stevens (Ed.), *Handbook of experimental psychology.* New York: Wiley, 1951. Pp. 1–49.

Strachey, J. Personal communications, dated Nov. 30, 1964, Dec. 7, 1964, and Dec. 29, 1964, the latter signed by Mrs. Angela Harris, Mr. Strachey's research assistant.

Szasz, T. S. Psychoanalysis as method and as theory. *Psychoanalytic Quarterly,* 1958, **27**, 89–97.

Thompson, C. *Psychoanalysis: Evolution and development.* London: Allen & Unwin, 1952.

Thorndike, L. *A history of magic and experimental science.* Vol. V. New York: Columbia University Press, 1941.

Toulmin, S. (1948). 'The logical status of psycho-analysis' and 'Postscript.' Reprinted in M. Macdonald (Ed.), *Philosophy and analysis.* Oxford: Blackwell, 1954. Pp. 132–139.

Training Prospectus 1963–1964. London: British Psycho-Analytical Society and Institute of Psycho-Analysis, 1963.

White, A. R. *Explaining human behaviour.* Hull: University Press, 1962.

Wolberg, L. R. *The technique of psychotherapy.* New York: Grune & Stratton, 1967.

Wolf Man. How I came into analysis with Freud. *Journal of the American Psychoanalytic Association,* 1958, **6**, 348–352.

Wolpe, J., & Rachman, S. (1960). Psychoanalytic evidence: A critique based on Freud's case of little Hans. Reprinted in S. Rachman (Ed.), *Critical essays on psychoanalysis.* Oxford: Pergamon Press, 1963. Pp. 198–220.

SUBJECT INDEX

A

Actions versus movements, 127–146
Ambivalence
  concept of, 112
  in case history, 115–117
Anal erotism, in case history, 121
Analysis, scientific,
  concept of, 43–44
  in human behavior, 44–46
Analytic-synthetic distinction, 64–66

B

"Beating" incident, in case history, 78
Behavior, definition of term, 4
Behavioristic explanation, alternative in case history, 120
Bisexuality, 95, 103

C

Case histories
  criteria for selection, 72–73
  Freud's published cases, 261–262
  Lorenz case, 76–92
Causal explanation, 128–131
Causally relevant factor, 147–149
Causation, Freud's theory of, 172–174
Causes versus causally relevant factors, 149–153
Causes versus reasons, 146–171
Cell theory, history of, 41
Classes versus instances of actions, 133–134
Component instincts, 94–95
  coalescence with maturity, 100–101, 103
Condition sine qua non, 148
Context-dependence, 16–17

Covering law model, see Hypothetical-deductive model
Criteria
  for absence of generalizations from a system, 67
  for distinguishing movements and actions, 136–140
  for evaluating any explanation, 20–21
  for evaluating psychoanalytic explanations, 244–257
  for scientific investigation, 48–51
  for selection of case material, 72–73

D

Data recording, problems of, 70–71
Defense, Freud's concept of, 96
Description
  versus explanation, 14–16
  versus explanation in psychoanalysis, 185–188, 223–225
Directive function of general theory, 241–244
Displacement, Freud's concept of, 113
"Dissection" analogy, 44–45
"Doing" versus "suffering," 137–138

E

Effects versus manifestations of causal factors, 169–170
Ego-instincts, 95–96
Erotogenic zones, 94
Examples of explanation
  arm bruise, 156–158, 160–162
  arsenic poisoning, 151–152
  bacterial culture plates, 24–25
  bread stealing, 156–158, 160–162
  Lorenz's dieting, 199–200, 223–224
  Lorenz's miserliness, 225–228